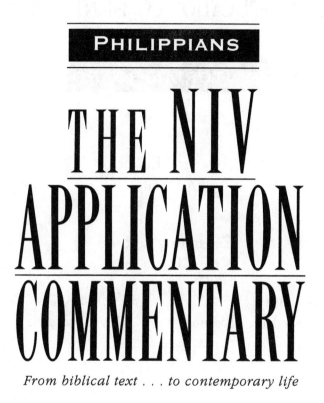

# PHILIPPIANS

# THE NIV APPLICATION COMMENTARY

*From biblical text . . . to contemporary life*

# THE NIV APPLICATION COMMENTARY SERIES

## EDITORIAL BOARD

### General Editor
*Terry Muck*

### Consulting Editors
### New Testament

*Eugene Peterson*

*Scot McKnight*

*Marianne Meye Thompson*

*Klyne Snodgrass*

### Zondervan Editorial Advisors

*Stanley N. Gundry*
Vice President and Editor-in-Chief

*Jack Kuhatschek*
Acquisitions Editor

*Verlyn Verbrugge*
Senior Editor

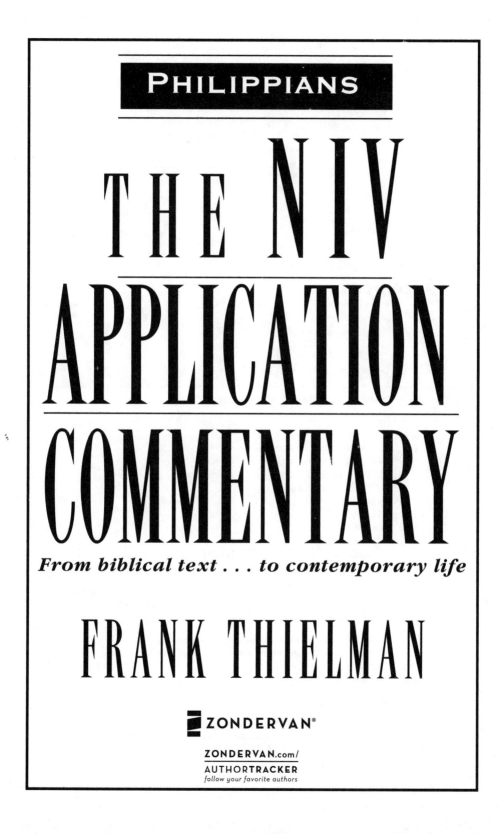

PHILIPPIANS

# THE NIV APPLICATION COMMENTARY

*From biblical text . . . to contemporary life*

FRANK THIELMAN

ZONDERVAN®

ZONDERVAN.com/
AUTHORTRACKER
*follow your favorite authors*

For my parents,

Calvin and Dorothy Thielman,

servants of Christ Jesus

 **ZONDERVAN**®

*The NIV Application Commentary: Philippians*
Copyright © 1995 by Frank Thielman

Requests for information should be addressed to:
Zondervan, *Grand Rapids, Michigan 49530*

**Library of Congress Cataloging-in-Publication Data**

Thielman, Frank.
     Philippians / Frank Thielman.
        p. cm. — (NIV application commentary)
     Includes bibliographical references and index.
     ISBN-10: 0-310-49300-5
     ISBN-13: 978-0-310-49300-6
     1. Bible. N.T. Philippians — Commentaries. I. Title. II. Series.
    BS2705.3.T47 1995
    227'.606—dc 20
                                           95 – 16836
                                              CIP

This edition is printed on acid-free paper.

*Edited by Verlyn D. Verbrugge*

*Printed in the United States of America*

10 11 12 13 14 • 32 31 30 29 28 27 26 25 24 23 22 21

# Table of Contents

# The NIV Application Commentary Series

When complete, the NIV Application Commentary
will include the following volumes:

To see which titles are available,
visit our web site at www.zondervan.com

# NIV Application Commentary
# Series Introduction

THE NIV APPLICATION COMMENTARY SERIES is unique. Most commentaries help us make the journey from the twentieth century back to the first century. They enable us to cross the barriers of time, culture, language, and geography that separate us from the biblical world. Yet they only offer a one-way ticket to the past and assume that we can somehow make the return journey on our own. Once they have explained the *original meaning* of a book or passage, these commentaries give us little or no help in exploring its *contemporary significance*. The information they offer is valuable, but the job is only half done.

Recently, a few commentaries have included some contemporary application as *one* of their goals. Yet that application is often sketchy or moralistic, and some volumes sound more like printed sermons than commentaries.

The primary goal of The NIV Application Commentary Series is to help you with the difficult but vital task of bringing an ancient message into a modern context. The series not only focuses on application as a finished product but also helps you think through the *process* of moving from the original meaning of a passage to its contemporary significance. These are commentaries, not popular expositions. They are works of reference, not devotional literature.

The format of the series is designed to achieve the goals of the series. Each passage is treated in three sections: *Original Meaning, Bridging Contexts,* and *Contemporary Significance.*

THIS SECTION HELPS you understand the meaning of the biblical text in its first-century context. All of the elements of traditional exegesis—in concise form—are discussed here. These include the historical, literary, and cultural context of the passage. The authors discuss matters related to grammar and syntax, and the meaning of biblical words. They also seek to explore the main ideas of the passage and how the biblical author develops those ideas.

After reading this section, you will understand the problems, questions, and concerns of the *original audience* and how the biblical author addressed those issues. This understanding is foundational to any legitimate application of the text today.

THIS SECTION BUILDS a bridge between the world of the Bible and the world of today, between the original context and the contemporary context, by focusing on both the timely and timeless aspects of the text.

God's Word is *timely*. The authors of Scripture spoke to specific situations, problems, and questions. Paul warned the Galatians about the consequences of circumcision and the dangers of trying to be justified by law (Gal. 5:2–5). The author of Hebrews tried to convince his readers that Christ is superior to Moses, the Aaronic priests, and the Old Testament sacrifices. John urged his readers to "test the spirits" of those who taught a form of incipient Gnosticism (1 John 4:1–6). In each of these cases, the timely nature of Scripture enables us to hear God's Word in situations that were *concrete* rather than abstract.

Yet the timely nature of Scripture also creates problems. Our situations, difficulties, and questions are not always directly related to those faced by the people in the Bible. Therefore, God's word to them does not always seem relevant to us. For example, when was the last time someone urged you to be circumcised, claiming that it was a necessary part of justification? How many people today care whether Christ is superior to the Aaronic priests? And how can a "test" designed to expose incipient Gnosticism be of any value in a modern culture?

Fortunately, Scripture is not only timely but *timeless*. Just as God spoke to the original audience, so he still speaks to us through the pages of Scripture. Because we share a common humanity with the people of the Bible, we discover a *universal dimension* in the problems they faced and the solutions God gave them. The timeless nature of Scripture enables it to speak with power in every time and in every culture.

Those who fail to recognize that Scripture is both timely and timeless run into a host of problems. For example, those who are intimidated by timely books such as Hebrews or Galatians might avoid reading them because they seem meaningless today. At the other extreme, those who are convinced of the timeless nature of Scripture, but who fail to discern its timely element, may "wax eloquent" about the Melchizedekian priesthood to a sleeping congregation.

The purpose of this section, therefore, is to help you discern what is timeless in the timely pages of the New Testament—and what is not. For example, if Paul's primary concern is not circumcision (as he tells us in Gal. 5:6), what *is* he concerned about? If discussions about the Aaronic priesthood or Melchizedek seem irrelevant today, what is of abiding value in these passages? If people try to "test the spirits" today with a test designed for a specific first-century heresy, what other biblical test might be more appropriate?

Yet this section does not merely uncover that which is timeless in a passage but also helps you to see *how* it is uncovered. The author of the commentary seeks to take what is implicit in the text and make it explicit, to take a process that normally is intuitive and explain it in a logical, orderly fashion. How do we know that circumcision is not Paul's primary concern? What clues in the text or its context help us realize that Paul's real concern is at a deeper level?

Of course, those passages in which the historical distance between us and the original readers is greatest require a longer treatment. Conversely, those passages in which the historical distance is smaller or seemingly nonexistent require less attention.

One final clarification. Because this section prepares the way for discussing the contemporary significance of the passage, there is not always a sharp distinction or a clear break between this section and the one that follows. Yet when both sections are read together, you should have a strong sense of moving from the world of the Bible to the world of today.

THIS SECTION ALLOWS the biblical message to speak with as much power today as it did when it was first written. How can you apply what you learned about Jerusalem, Ephesus, or Corinth to our present-day needs in Chicago, Los Angeles, or London? How can you take a message originally spoken in Greek and Aramaic and communicate it clearly in our own language? How can you take the eternal truths originally spoken in a different time and culture and apply them to the similar-yet-different needs of our culture?

In order to achieve these goals, this section gives you help in several key areas.

First, it helps you identify contemporary situations, problems, or questions that are truly comparable to those faced by the original audience. Because contemporary situations are seldom identical to those faced in the first century, you must seek situations that are analogous if your applications are to be relevant.

Second, this section explores a variety of contexts in which the passage might be applied today. You will look at personal applications, but you will also be encouraged to think beyond private concerns to the society and culture at large.

Third, this section will alert you to any problems or difficulties you might encounter in seeking to apply the passage. And if there are several legitimate ways to apply a passage (areas in which Christians disagree), the author will bring these to your attention and help you think through the issues involved.

In seeking to achieve these goals, the contributors to this series attempt to avoid two extremes. They avoid making such specific applications that the commentary might quickly become dated. They also avoid discussing the significance of the passage in such a general way that it fails to engage contemporary life and culture.

Above all, contributors to this series have made a diligent effort not to sound moralistic or preachy. The NIV Application Commentary Series does not seek to provide ready-made sermon materials but rather tools, ideas, and insights that will help you communicate God's Word with power. If we help you to achieve that goal, then we have fulfilled the purpose for this series.

— *The Editors*

# General Editor's Preface

As FRANK THIELMAN'S commentary shows, Paul's letter to the Philippians manages to take the everyday experiences of Christian living and make them seem as important as the peaks of spiritual euphoria and the valleys of despair. True, our life in Christ may be punctuated with the exclamation points of weddings and the question marks of funerals, but it is mostly made up of the words and sentences that describe what it means to be a child of God. It is on the smooth, satisfying hum of everyday language that this letter to the Christians in Philippi resides.

Paul refers here to some of the highs and lows, to be sure. Persecution, for example, gets representative treatment. But Philippians is mostly written to church people who are doing pretty well. It is not a letter from a parent to a prodigal, but a letter to that delightful child who has always obeyed and, although by no means perfect, is at least giving the straight and narrow path a try. Paul does not have to rail against heresy in the church (as he does in some other letters), and he does not try to write a mini-systematic theology. He is writing to people he likes, people who have been with him for the long haul. Thus, one of the lessons we can learn from Philippians is how to encourage people who are doing pretty well.

Actually, the first lesson is that one *should* write such a letter. It is the nature of things that the squeaking wheels get the grease. But the truth of pastoral work is that those of us slogging along in the spiritual trenches need attention too. From his prison cell, Paul practices what we might call ordinary pastoral care, affirming the faithful and encouraging the true-hearted.

The message of Philippians, therefore, is that maintenance of the healthy is as crucial as surgery on the ill. And as Paul demonstrates, preventive medicine has a character all its own. First, it shows gratitude ("I thank God every time I remember you," 1:3). Second, it rewards good work with encouragement. Third, it does not shirk its duty to be careful. Paul warns even his faithful children against the Judaizers and the perfectionists. Warnings against potential mistakes is a sign of love, if done in a loving way.

Like members of even good families, the Philippians did have their problems, Apparently they argued, and Paul warns against division. It is easy to come away from reading this letter and miss the deeper theological implications for today's church on Paul's teaching on unity in chapters 1 and 2. Fortunately, Frank Thielman doesn't let this happen. He shows how Paul's prescription for health—unity—applied to the original church at Philippi and how it applies to all the faithful, if slightly contentious churches today.

Neither does Professor Thielman let us miss any of the other implications of this rich, encouraging letter for the church today. The best guard against a faithful church becoming a problem church is to "rejoice in the Lord always" (4:4). That is a truth that has applied across the centuries.

—*Terry Muck*

# Author's Preface

WRITING THIS COMMENTARY has been a singularly edifying experience for me. Like most university professors of biblical studies, my past work has been devoted primarily to clarifying the historical circumstances in which the biblical books were composed and showing how those circumstances help the modern reader understand the meaning of the text to its first readers. That, it seems, is a full-time job, and the work of application is usually left to the systematic theologians. A little thought reveals, however, that this arrangement is not ideal. To say what the text meant but never to say what the text means is to tie up heavy loads and to put them on people's shoulders without lifting a finger to move them. It is to apply one's self wholly to the text without applying the text wholly to one's self.

By design, this commentary series prevents that from happening, and the result for me has been both exhilarating and sobering. The exhilaration has come from entering the world of the courageous early Christians who walk across the stage of Philippians. Who could fail to be inspired by Paul's selfless commitment to the gospel despite hardship so severe that it would crush the spirit of most people? Who could not admire the courage and faithfulness of Timothy, whose commitment to the gospel led him to share Paul's hardship? How could anyone not be moved by the constant and costly support that the Philippians showed for Paul despite poverty and persecution? The requirement to apply the text, however, has made me face the sobering reality of how far short I fall of its standard. I have had to ask at each step whether, having preached to others, I myself might be disqualified for the prize.

Perhaps readers of this commentary, having worked through Philippians with me, will have similar feelings of exhilaration and inadequacy. I have been encouraged, and others may be encouraged also, to discover that Paul himself had these concerns, and that they led him not to discouragement but to run the race more swiftly, to forget what is behind and strain forward toward what is ahead (Phil. 3:14).

Many friends have helped me clarify and apply Philippians. Students who have attended my courses at Beeson Divinity School, congregations who have heard my preaching, and Sunday school classes who have listened to my teaching have all imbibed much of the material in this commentary and helped me to sharpen my thinking, particularly on how to apply the letter to the modern church. Two dear friends and valued colleagues at Beeson Divinity School, Dean Timothy George and Professor Kenneth Mathews, supported this project from the first through personal encouragement and practical help. Editors Terry Muck, Klyne Snodgrass, and Jack Kuhatschek made many useful suggestions for improving my first draft and saved me from several embarrassments. Verlyn Verbrugge not only made my manuscript more lucid, but from his own expertise in Pauline studies, offered a number of suggestions and corrections for the book's improvement.

Beyond my own professional circles, two close friends, Steve and Tracy Whitner, prayed faithfully for this commentary from inception to completion, read portions of the initial draft, and made helpful suggestions for improving its readabililty. My wife Abby contributed in ways so numerous and profound that the book would simply have never materialized without her. Her unselfish devotion to me, to our children, and to the work of the Lord serves as a living illustration of what it means to look not only to one's own interests but also to the interests of others (Phil. 2:4).

I deeply appreciate the help of all these friends. Any success that this commentary has in clarifying the original meaning and the contemporary significance of Philippians is due in large measure to them.

The theological perspective that emerges from this commentary originated with the patient teaching of my father and mother, Calvin and Dorothy Thielman. My father was ordained to the ministry of Word and Sacrament in the Presbyterian Church (U.S.A.) forty years ago, and for thirty-three years he and my mother have labored faithfully in the Montreat Presbyterian Church, Montreat, North Carolina. Their congregation at home was always as important as their congregation at church, and so by word and deed they have shown me, my two brothers, and our families what it means to have the mind of Christ.

Philippians has been a favorite book of theirs over the years. My father preached his senior sermon at Columbia Theological Seminary on Philippians 3:10 and has made the book a special object of study through his forty years of ministry. Many of the commentaries cited in the notes to this volume came from his shelves. One of the first biblical passages I committed to memory was Philippians 4:4–8, at the encouragement of my mother. Without their persistent training, constant love, and unwavering support over the years, this commentary would have been impossible. In a profound sense, it belongs to them.

—*Frank Thielman*
*Eastertide, 1995*

# Introduction

TWENTY CENTURIES AGO an itinerant tentmaker was tossed into prison for creating a public disturbance. There he spent considerable time dictating a letter that might have taken up a dozen sheets of stiff, scratchy paper. Today few people would recognize the name of the Roman emperor at the time and, although Nero was a prolific author, nothing of his literary output remains. Paul's name, on the other hand, is instantly recognized by millions, and existing copies of his letter to the Philippians, in many languages, run easily into the millions. Indeed the time has come, as T. R. Glover observed, when people call their dogs Nero and their sons Paul.[1]

Paul would be a little uncomfortable with his success. He never harbored doubts that the gospel would progress unhindered until the final day when Christ himself would appear and every tongue confess him Lord. But the cross had stamped an indelible imprint on the gospel and had made it clear to Paul and, in his view, to all who understood the gospel aright, that God's power is made perfect through weakness. Were Paul to visit a church in a twentieth-century Western democracy, he might wonder how his letter, written from prison to a small, persecuted group of believers, could be understood by people so different from him and from the Philippians. How can people who worship in cathedrals named after Saint Paul, he might wonder, understand that God advanced the gospel through the apostle's imprisonment and the Philippians' persecution?

Although Paul cannot visit us with his question in the flesh, we can in some sense visit him and bring his perspective back with us. That is the purpose of this commentary—to enter Paul's world and the world of the Philippians and then with cautious steps to carry Paul's perspective on the issues that he and the Philippians faced into our own world. Before we attempt this feat, however, we first need to equip ourselves with some basic tools.

## Philippi and Its Church

IN THE MID-FIRST century, Philippi, although not large, was a strategically located city with a rich heritage and distinctive culture. It spilled down a mountainside and onto a fertile, well-watered plain about ten miles inland from the important port of Neapolis. The Egnatian Way, a critical artery of

---

1. See F. F. Bruce, *Paul: Apostle of the Heart Set Free* (Grand Rapids: Eerdmans, 1977), 7.

commerce linking the city of Rome with its eastern provinces, passed through the city center.[2]

Although located many miles east of Rome in a province whose common tongue was Greek, Philippi had been a Roman colony since Mark Anthony and Octavian had defeated the forces of Brutus and Cassius, the assassins of Julius Caesar, at the site in 42 B.C.[3] Large numbers of Philippians were descended from the soldiers who settled in the city after the battle or from those who came to the city slightly less than a decade later in the wake of Octavian's victory over Mark Anthony.[4] As a result Latin was the common language in Philippi, and the city proudly maintained a Roman character.[5] Its architecture and administration, for example, appear to have been modeled on Rome's, and worship of the emperor was an important element in the religious life of the city.[6]

No mystery, then, shrouds Paul's reasoning for choosing Philippi as the base for his first evangelistic effort in Macedonia. He chose one of the most important cities in the region for his efforts.[7]

That he went to Macedonia at all, however, was not a matter of his own choice. As so often in his labors, his own plans were overruled by God's clear direction.[8] In this case, despite his intention to take the gospel to Bithynia,

---

2. See the ancient descriptions of Philippi in Appian (b. ca. A.D. 90), *Bella Civilia*, 4.105, and Dio Cassius (fl. A.D. 194–229), 47.35; see also the extensive photographs in Paul Collart, *Philippes: ville de Macédoine, depuis ses origines jusqu'à la fin de l'époque romaine* (Paris: École Française d'Athènes, 1937).

3. The battle is described in Appian, *Bella Civilia*, 4.105–131, and Dio Cassius, 47.35–49.

4. See the useful article on Philippi by G. L. Borchert in *The International Standard Bible Encyclopedia*, rev. ed., ed. Geoffrey W. Bromiley, Everett F. Harrison, Roland K. Harrison, and William Sanford LaSor, 4 vols. (Grand Rapids: Eerdmans, 1979–88), 3:834–36.

5. This pride is clearly visible in the slave owners' accusation against Paul and Silas in Acts 16:21. Although the slave owners themselves were more interested in having their seedy means of income restored than in anything else, they played upon the patriotism of the magistrates and the assembled crowd when they said that Paul and Silas were advocating customs unlawful for "us Romans" to practice.

6. See O'Brien, *Philippians*, 4; Bruce, *Paul: Apostle of the Heart Set Free*, 220; Pheme Perkins, "Philippians: Theology for the Heavenly Politeuma," *Pauline Theology. Volume I: Thessalonians, Philippians, Galatians, Philemon*, ed. Jouette M. Bassler (Minneapolis, Minn.: Fortress, 1991), 89–104, esp. p. 93; Collart, *Philippes: ville de Macédoine*, 412.

7. Acts 16:12, in the NIV, says that Philippi was "the leading city of that district of Macedonia." Macedonia had been divided into four districts after the Romans conquered it in 167 B.C. and Philippi was in the first district. The leading city of that district was Amphipolis rather than Philippi, making it more probable that some Latin texts of the New Testament preserve the correct reading of Acts 16:12: "a city of the first district of Macedonia." See Ernst Haenchen, *The Acts of the Apostles: A Commentary* (Philadelphia: Westminster, 1971), 494. Philippi was, nevertheless, an important city in the district.

8. See Rom. 1:13; 15:20–22; 2 Cor. 1:12–2:4.

a region in north central Asia Minor, the Spirit of Jesus led him and his companions away from there to Troas on Asia Minor's northwestern coast (Acts 16:7–8). There Paul experienced a nighttime vision in which a Macedonian appeared to him, saying, "Come over to Macedonia and help us" (Acts 16:9). So Paul and his companions, Silas, Timothy, and Luke, set sail for Macedonia.[9] Their ship landed at Neapolis, and from there they followed the Via Egnatia to Philippi.

Their stay, although only several days, was eventful. On Paul's first missionary journey he had made a habit of going first to the synagogue in the towns to which he traveled (Acts 14:1), but in Philippi he found only a place outside the city gate and by a river where some women who worshiped the God of Abraham, Isaac, and Jacob gathered each Sabbath for prayer (Acts 16:13). Presumably, not enough Jewish men lived in Philippi to form a synagogue, and the women may have sought out the site because Jewish worship was not welcome in this deeply Roman city.[10]

Jews had an uneven relationship with the Romans, and whereas anti-Semitism was not universal among Romans, it was also not unusual.[11] It comes through clearly in the charges that the owners of a slave, from whom Paul had cast a fortune-telling demon, brought against Paul and Silas before the city magistrates. "These men are Jews," they said, "and are throwing our city into an uproar by advocating customs unlawful for us Romans to accept or practice" (Acts 16:20–21). The persecution that resulted and continued after Paul left the city appears, in other words, to have been motivated as much by the young church's connection with Judaism as by anything else (Acts 16:22–24; Phil. 1:30; 1 Thess. 2:2).

When Paul, Timothy, and Silas left Philippi at the request of the city magistrates, they left behind a diverse group of believers. The wealthy merchant Lydia and her household believed (Acts 16:15), as did a jailer and his family (Acts 16:16–18), and perhaps a slave girl (Acts 16:28). Apparently by the time Paul and Silas left, the group was meeting in Lydia's house (Acts 16:40), no doubt the largest residence among them. This was certainly not a homogeneous social unit, but God had called each believer from her or his sphere to be part of his people and, although they lived in a highly stratified society, they had no choice but to work at unity. If Paul's letter to them is a measure of their success, then they found the task difficult (Phil. 2:14; 4:2).

---

9. The "we" in Acts 16:10 shows that Luke had joined Paul, Silas, and Timothy for the trip to Macedonia.

10. The place of prayer may have been by the river, however, to facilitate the ritual washings required by Jewish custom. See E. P. Sanders, *Jewish Law From Jesus to the Mishnah: Five Studies* (London/Philadelphia: SCM Press/Trinity Press International, 1990), 259.

11. See, for example, the description of the Jews in Tacitus (b. ca. 56), *Historiae*, 5.

Despite such struggles, the Philippian church appears to have been Paul's favorite church. The Philippians were willing to support Paul's missionary efforts in other towns from the beginning (4:15a) and gave him help even during times when other churches were either unable or unwilling to assist him (4:15b). Even in nearby Thessalonica Paul's missionary efforts received financial assistance from the Philippians more than once (4:16), and the Philippians joined other Macedonian churches in supporting Paul's stormy ministry in Corinth (2 Cor. 11:8–9). In addition, the Philippians gave so generously to Paul's collection for the famine-stricken churches of Jerusalem that Paul could use them and the other Macedonian churches as examples to the Corinthians of people who had "the grace of giving" (2 Cor. 8:1–7). All of this generosity, moreover, came not from any abundance of resources, but from poverty (2 Cor 8:1–2).[12] During a time of often difficult relationships with his other churches, Paul must have valued this tangible and sacrificial support of his efforts to proclaim the Gospel as a token of genuine friendship.[13]

## The Reasons for Philippians

WHEN PAUL WROTE Philippians, he was in prison awaiting a trial whose outcome could result in his execution (Phil. 1:7, 13–14, 17, 20, 30; 2:17). Exactly where he was in prison is a matter of dispute. Much ancient evidence places him in Rome, and many modern scholars argue for this position as well.[14] Paul does say, after all, that because of his imprisonment the gospel

---

12. Lydia appears to have been the only person in the Philippian church of any means. On the question of Paul's monetary relationships with his churches, especially as they touch Paul's collection for the Christians in Jerusalem, see Verlyn D. Verbrugge, *Paul's Style of Church Leadership Illustrated by His Instructions to the Corinthians on the Collection* (San Francisco: Mellen Research University Press, 1992), 118–27.

13. Some scholars believe that Philippians belongs to a class of letters known in ancient rhetorical handbooks as the "friendly type" (*philikos typos*). Such letters frequently mentioned the author's longing to be with his or her friends (cf. 1:7, 8; 4:1), emphasized the unity and reciprocity necessary for friendship (cf. 1:5, 7; 2:17–18; 4:14–15), stressed that friends are of one mind (cf. 1:27; 2:2), and recognized that friends often have common ememies (cf. 1:29–30). See Stanley K. Stowers, "Friends and Enemies in the Politics of Heaven: Reading Theology in Philippians," *Pauline Theology. Volume I: Thessalonians, Philippians, Galatians, Philemon*, ed. Jouette M. Bassler (Minneapolis, Minn.: Fortress, 1991), 105–21, esp. 107–14.

14. This position was current as early as the second century as its preservation in the Marcionite prologue to Philippians indicates: "The Philippians are Macedonians. Having received the word of truth they persevered in the faith, and did not accept false apostles. The apostle commends them, writing to them from prison in Rome." See F. F. Bruce, *The Canon of Scripture* (Downers Grove, Ill.: InterVarsity Press, 1988), 142. It is also the position of, for example, Bruce, *Philippians*, 23–26; Silva (with reservations), *Philippians*, 8; and O'Brien, *Philippians*, 25.

has spread throughout the whole praetorian guard (1:13), and the largest contingent of the praetorian guard lived near the emperor's residence in Rome.[15] Moreover, Paul sends greetings to the Philippians from believers among Caesar's household (4:22), and what better place to find Caesar's staff than in Rome?

More recently, some scholars have rejected the claim that Paul was in Rome when he wrote the letter, primarily because of the distance between Rome and Philippi and the difficulty, as a result, of accounting for the number of journeys that Paul's letter presupposes between the apostle and the Philippians. Thus, according to these scholars, the letter implies that the Philippians had heard from someone that Paul was in prison, had sent Epaphroditus to Paul, had heard that Epaphroditus was ill, and had sent word of their concern about Epaphroditus (2:26; 4:18). In addition, Paul plans to send Epaphroditus back to Philippi, to send Timothy shortly thereafter, and to follow himself, Lord willing, at a later time (2:19–23, 24–25, 28).[16] It is unlikely, these scholars claim, that this many journeys from Rome to Philippi could be undertaken during the period of Paul's Roman imprisonment.

In light of this problem, a variety of other options have been proposed. Corinth once gained some support, and Caesarea has been more popular, but most who dissent from the traditional view believe that Paul wrote from Ephesus.[17] Paul spent nearly three years there (Acts 19:8, 10; 20:31), and since Ephesus was closer to Philippi than to Rome, the number of trips that the letter presupposes between Paul and the Philippians is plausible.

The Ephesian theory is not without its own problems, however. Acts tells us that Paul was in prison in Rome for two years (Acts 28:16, 30) but mentions nothing of an Ephesian imprisonment. During his Ephesian ministry, Paul was consumed with interest in his collection for the saints in Jerusalem, but that subject never arises in Philippians. And Paul's reference to the praetorian guard fits Rome better than Ephesus, because the largest contingent was stationed in Rome. Moreover, the difficulty of travel between Rome and Philippi has been exaggerated: Roads were better and means of transportation were actually more efficient in ancient times than many have assumed.[18]

---

15. The "praetorians" were bodyguards to the emperor and his family. For a brief summary of their history, see Henry Michael Denne Parker and George Ronald Watson, "Praetorians," *The Oxford Classical Dictionary*, 2d ed., ed. N. G. L. Hammond and H. H. Scullard (Oxford: Oxford University Press, 1970), 873–74.

16. See Bruce, *Philippians*, xxv; O'Brien, *Philippians*, 25.

17. See, for example, Michael, *Philippians*, xii–xxi; Bonnard, *Philippiens*, 10; Collange, *Philippians*, 15–19.

18. See Silva, *Philippians*, 6–7; for the ease and frequency with which travel could be undertaken in Roman times, see Lionel Casson, *Travel in the Ancient World* (Baltimore: Johns

These problems with the Ephesian theory are significant, but their importance should not be exaggerated. Luke was under no obligation to describe
every imprisonment of Paul, and Paul's own account of his sufferings in
2 Corinthians 11:23–33 (cf. 6:5) shows that he had suffered many more flog-
gings, shipwrecks, and near escapes than appear in Acts. In addition,
1 Corinthians, which was written from Ephesus, speaks of great opposition
to Paul (1 Cor. 16:9), and 2 Corinthians, written shortly after Paul left Ephesus for Macedonia, reflects on hardships in Asia so severe that Paul "felt the
sentence of death" in his heart (2 Cor. 1:9; cf. 1 Cor. 15:32). The difficulty
of travel in ancient times has indeed loomed larger than it should in objec-
tions to locating Paul in Rome, but even under the best circumstances, journeys between Rome and Philippi were long and fraught with danger. And
members of the praetorian guard may have been stationed in the large and
important city of Ephesus.

The most convincing evidence in favor of an Ephesian origin for the letter, however, comes from the central portion of the letter itself, where a dating of Philippians during Paul's Ephesian ministry solves two thorny
problems. In 3:1–11 Paul attempts to persuade the Philippians not to follow
the teaching of Jewish Christian missionaries who are especially adamant that
Gentile Christians become circumcised (3:2–3), and in 3:12–4:1 he advises
the Philippians to shun certain "enemies of the cross of Christ" (3:18) who
have deified their stomachs and who glory in what they should consider
shameful. Attempts to understand these passages as descriptions of a single
group have not been successful, since the Jewish Christians whom Paul
describes in the first passage are ill suited for the charges of gluttony and what
looks like sexual immorality in the second.

In addition, attempts to claim that false teachers were on the scene at
Philippi advocating the notions that Paul attacks in chapter 3 are also uncon-
vincing. Paul stands on good terms with the Philippians. When he remembers the Philippians in prayer, he is thankful and joyful (1:3). They are his
partners in the grace that God has given to him (1:5, 7; 4:14–16), his joy and
his crown (4:1).[19] This is not the language Paul typically uses when his con-

---

Hopkins University Press, 1974), 115–329. Advocates of a Roman imprisonment have also
pointed out that the number of journeys actually required by Paul's statements in Philippians can be reduced if we assume that Epaphroditus became ill on his way to Paul (cf. 2:30),
sent word of his illness back to the Philippians, and simply assumed that when they heard
it they would be worried about him.

19. Paul sounds one slightly negative note about the Philippians' doctrinal leanings in
3:15, but it probably means only that some slight deviation in the direction of an over-
spiritualized gospel was present at Philippi.

gregations have compromised their loyalty to him by adopting another understanding of the gospel.[20]

Chapter 3 makes sense, however, if we read it against the background of Paul's ministry in Ephesus. On the most widely accepted dating of Galatians, Paul was in Ephesus when he wrote that letter, and he was certainly in Ephesus when he penned 1 Corinthians. Galatians is an urgent appeal to Paul's predominantly Gentile congregations in southern Asia Minor not to continue to succumb to the false teaching of Jewish Christian missionaries. The primary concern of these missionaries was that the Galatians should accept circumcision as a requirement for entry into the people of God (Gal. 6:12), and by the time Paul wrote the letter, they had experienced some success at alienating the Galatians both from Paul and from his gospel of justification by faith alone (Gal. 1:6; 3:3–5; 4:17).

First Corinthians is also an urgent letter to a belligerent congregation ready to throw off the yoke of Paul's authority in order to pursue their own highly spiritualized form of the gospel (1 Cor. 4:18; 9:3). Knowledge and the Spirit were the critical elements in their form of the gospel, and those who did not show proof of them by means of flashy outward signs of power stood on a lower spiritual plane (1 Cor. 4:6–13; 8:1–13; 14:12). Some of those who did possess them, moreover, felt themselves free from the normal requirements of society, including some requirements that coincided with the morality advocated in the gospel (1 Cor. 5:1–13; 6:12–20; 8:1–11:1).[21] In both letters Paul is worried that these congregations, won to the gospel at the cost of the apostle's best efforts, will leave him and the truth of the gospel behind.

If Philippians was written shortly after Galatians and 1 Corinthians but before Paul's retrospective glance at his troubles in Asia in 2 Corinthians 1:8–11, then Philippians 3:1–4:1 is probably a warning to his favorite congregation not to succumb to the errors of these other churches. With sweat still on his brow from wrestling with Judaizers in Galatia and enthusiasts in Corinth, he is unwilling to let even a group as loyal as the Philippians go without a stern warning not to deviate from the gospel. So if Philippians was written from an Ephesian imprisonment, Paul's warnings in 3:1–4:1 make sense.

Philippians was not only written to deflect theological error, however, but also to thank the Philippians and commend their messenger Epaphroditus.

---

20. Contrast Paul's language, for example, in Gal. 1:6–9; 3:1; 4:11, 15–16; 5:7; 6:17; 1 Cor. 3:1–4; 4:8, 18; 6:5a; 11:17; 2 Cor. 11:19–20; 12:1, 20–21; 13:1–10.

21. For a similar attempt to connect the spirituality of the Corinthians with this section of Philippians, see Robert Jewett, "Conflicting Movements in the Early Church As Reflected in Philippians," *Novum Testamentum* 12 (1970): 362–90.

When the Philippians heard that Paul was in prison, true to their generous nature, they commissioned Epaphroditus both to carry monetary gifts to Paul (2:25; 4:14–18) and to help the apostle in his imprisonment (2:30). But either on his way to Paul or after his arrival, Epaphroditus became so ill that he nearly died (2:27a, 30b). Somehow the Philippians heard of this illness, and Epaphroditus, knowing that they would be concerned about his condition, in turn began to worry about them (2:26). Paul felt it best to send Epaphroditus back with his commission only half fulfilled: He had brought the gifts to Paul, but the apostle was still in prison (2:28). Paul's letter, then, served both as a thank-you note to the Philippians for their generous gifts (4:14, 18) and as a word of commendation for Epaphroditus: Although Epaphroditus had not been able to stay as long as the Philippians intended, Paul explained, he nonetheless deserved a hero's welcome when he arrived home (2:29).

It is not likely that Epaphroditus left, however, before delivering to Paul a thorough report on the Philippians' progress in the faith. Paul's generally positive tone in the letter (1:3–8; 4:1, 18) probably means that the report was basically good, though one point of concern is difficult to miss: The Philippians were not unified. A quarrel between Euodia and Syntyche had apparently infected the entire church (4:2), with the result that arguing and complaining had begun to plague the group and tarnish its witness before the wider, unbelieving society (2:14–16). Without unity, the Philippians would not only hinder their witness to the gospel, but they would find it difficult to withstand the trials of persecution that they continued to experience at the hands of their unbelieving neighbors (1:27).

The reasons for Philippians, then, are manifold. Paul took the opportunity of Epaphroditus' necessary trip home to warn the Philippians against the errors of his other churches, to commend the Philippians' messenger for a job well done, and to urge the Philippians, amid the challenge of pagan opposition, to "stand firm in one Spirit, contending as one man for the faith of the gospel" (1:27).

## Meeting the Interpretive Challenge of Philippians

AS WE ATTEMPT to bring these ancient purposes into the modern church, we should keep in mind two basic rules of interpretation. First, we must respect the literary genre of Philippians. Philippians is a real letter. Unlike the letters of the Roman statesman and Stoic philosopher Seneca, it is not a showpiece, ostensibly written to friends but actually intended from the first for the widest possible publication. Like any piece of real correspondence, it refers to people we know virtually nothing about and to circumstances we cannot fully understand.

The epistolary character of Philippians presents us with two temptations, both of which we must avoid if we want to bring its message undistorted into the twenty-first century. First, since some of the letter is obscure, it is tempting to clarify the obscurities from the resources of our own imagination. Suddenly the "loyal yokefellow" in 4:3 becomes Paul's wife and is even identified with Lydia (despite the masculine form of the Greek word!), Paul's opponents in 1:17 become Corinthian enthusiasts who are ashamed of Paul's suffering, and the advancement of the gospel through the praetorian guard in 1:13 happens one guard at a time as different Roman soldiers take turns watching Paul. Although we must admit with embarrassing frequency that we simply do not know what a particular reference means, it is better to do so than to base our interpretation of an obscure passage on an imaginative reconstruction. Our inability to understand every detail of the letter is simply the consequence of God's choice to reveal his word within the time-bound and culture-bound form of a personal letter.[22]

On the other hand, we must not read out of the letter less than is there. At first, passages like 1:1–2 in which Paul greets the church, 2:19–30 where he describes his travel plans for Timothy, for himself, and for Epaphroditus, and 4:3 where he asks an unnamed "loyal yokefellow" to arbitrate between Euodia and Syntyche look like they are casualties of the time-bound nature of Paul's correspondence. Yet often such texts assume theological principles that can be brought to the surface and applied in a way that the text itself cannot. In a letter admonishing its readers to follow Paul's example and the examples of others who understand the gospel (3:17; 4:9) and also to defer humbly to others (2:3, 8), we are surely not remiss in following the principle behind Paul's humble refusal to take apostolic honors for himself in the letter's greeting while dignifying the Philippian leaders with their titles of honor (1:1). Nor in a letter that values the advancement of the gospel even at the expense of personal desires (1:12, 25) would we be wrong to take Paul, Timothy, and Epaphroditus as examples of people who give the gospel's progress greater importance than the success of their own personal agenda (1:12–26; 2:20, 29–30). Nor in a letter that values unity would be wrong to learn from Paul's example of appointing a mediator between two disputants (4:2–3). In such cases, more theology is packed into the passage than at first meets the eye, and in order to glean its full value for the modern church we must think deeply about the theological presuppositions lying beneath it.

In addition to respecting the letter character of Philippians, we must also respect the historical and literary contexts of the passages we interpret.

---

22. See Gordon D. Fee, *Gospel and Spirit: Issues in New Testament Hermeneutics* (Peabody, Mass.: Hendrickson, 1991), 24–36.

## Introduction

Philippians contains more memorable sentences than most of Paul's letters, and as a result we often know it in bits and pieces:

- "For to me, to live is Christ and to die is gain."
- "Your attitude should be the same as that of Christ Jesus."
- "Rejoice in the Lord always. I will say it again: Rejoice!"
- "And the peace of God, which transcends all understanding, will guard your hearts and your minds in Christ Jesus."
- "I can do everything through him who gives me strength."
- "And my God will meet all your needs according to his glorious riches in Christ Jesus."

When we know sentences such as these well, they tend to take on a life of their own apart from the historical context that gave them birth and the literary context that gives them Paul's meaning. Yet each of the phrases is closely tied to some aspect of the historical situation that produced the Philippian letter, a situation in which unity with one another and commitment to the gospel was vital for the survival of the church amid intense persecution. Without this context, rejoicing in the Lord can become a superficial happiness, and the promise that God will supply every need can become the proof text for a selfish gospel of material prosperity.

The historical and literary contexts of the passages that we study act as safeguards against making the text a mirror of what we already believe rather than a challenge to our sinfulness and an encouragement to our faithfulness. We dare not neglect these contexts, for nothing less than Scripture's ability to speak prophetically to the modern church is at stake.[23]

### The Challenge of Philippians to the Modern Church

WHAT DOES PHILIPPIANS have to say to the modern church? Four theological themes seem to form the foundation on which Philippians was built. Each of these four themes presents a significant challenge to Western Christians at the turn of the twenty-first century.

(1) First, and most important, Philippians is about Christian unity. The importance of unity to the church is apparent from two passages, 1:27–30 and 2:12–18, in which Paul says that Christian unity is necessary for withstanding the onslaught of forces hostile to the gospel (1:27–28; 2:16), for presenting a credible witness to the unbelieving world (2:15), and, above all, for being found blameless and pure on the day of Christ (2:12–13, 16).

Philippians also shows, however, that this unity is not to be purchased at

---

23. See Gordon D. Fee and Douglas Stuart, *How to Read the Bible for All Its Worth*, 2d ed. (Grand Rapids: Zondervan, 1993), 45–77.

the price of changing the gospel's essence. Thus in 3:1–11 Paul has only harsh words for people who claim to follow Christ but do not believe that the righteousness God supplies through Christ is sufficient for salvation. He uses equally straightforward language in 3:18–19 for those who claim to be believers but who take offense at the cross and who, refusing to await God's timing, believe that they have already achieved spiritual perfection. Christian unity is absolutely crucial to being a Christian, but that unity is only *Christian* if it is founded on the apostolic gospel of Christ and him crucified. "We belong to one another only through and in Jesus Christ."[24]

Paul does not simply emphasize the importance and boundaries of Christian unity, he also shows us the path toward achieving it. He does this both through the usual means of specific commands and through offering examples of unifying conduct for his readers to follow. Thus we not only read, "Do nothing out of selfish ambition or vain conceit" (2:3a), and "Do everything without complaining and arguing" (2:14), but we also find Paul exemplifying a gentle approach toward Christian brothers with whom he disagrees (1:17–18a; 3:15–16) and a willingness to put the interests of others first (1:1, 24–25; 2:25–26). We discover that Christ's willingness to humble himself provides a model for us to follow (2:5–11), and that both Timothy's willingness to put the Philippians ahead of his own interests (2:20–21) and Epaphroditus' willingness to risk his life to help Paul (2:30) provide illustrations of Christian unity in action.

In this country, one third of the present population are "babyboomers"—people born between 1946 and 1964. Today this group is the single most influential social group in society and has a distinctive, frequently studied, set of traits.[25] Among these are a deeply seated commitment to self-fulfillment and to the notion that each person should be free to choose what he or she wants to believe. The result of this perspective for this generation's religious commitments has been an attempt for each person to borrow elements from a variety of religious traditions in order to meet his or her special spiritual longings. Thus people can refer to themselves today, and be readily understood, as "primarily Catholic." In the same breath, they can name as heroes people with religious traditions as diverse as Mother Teresa, Martin Luther King, Jr., and Mikhail Gorbachev; when asked why these three stand out, they answer that if they all got together they would respect each other. According to recent studies, 80 percent of this country's population believe that "an individual should arrive at his or her own religious

---

24. Dietrich Bonhoeffer, *Life Together* (New York: Harper & Row, 1954), 21.
25. See Wade Clark Roof, *A Generation of Seekers: The Spiritual Journeys of the Baby Boom Generation* (San Francisco: HarperSanFrancisco, 1993), 1–8.

beliefs independent of any churches or synagogues," and among the baby-boom generation, that figure can only be higher.[26]

In such a climate, the mandate of Philippians to subordinate self-interest to the interests of Jesus Christ and to draw bold, unyielding boundaries around the essence of the gospel needs to be heard. If it is not, the church stands in danger of following the culture away from the truth of the gospel and into a syncretistic morass of "answers" to the search for self-fulfillment.

(2) Philippians has much to say to the church about the problem of suffering. It offers no clear solution to the age-old question of how God can be good and all powerful and yet have created a world in which suffering is often so intense, but it does describe the Christian perspective on the experience of suffering. Paul was suffering when he wrote Philippians. Although he had done nothing worthy of blame, he was in prison awaiting a trial that could result in his condemnation and execution as a criminal (1:13–14, 17, 20). To make matters worse, some Christian brothers in the city of his imprisonment, instead of helping him, were adding to his troubles in order to advance their own cause (1:17). The Philippians were also suffering at the hands of hostile unbelievers in the society around them (1:28a).

Despite all of this, indeed because of it, Paul is filled with joy and expects the Philippians to be joyful also (1:4, 18, 25; 2:2, 17–18, 28–29; 3:1; 4:1, 4, 10). The reason for this joy is not that Paul believes suffering to be good, or that people ought to force themselves to laugh at pain. Paul acknowledges the pain in his own situation and is grieved by it (2:28). Nevertheless, he knows that God is, through the death and resurrection of Jesus Christ, accomplishing the good purpose of reconciling the world to himself. Thus Paul's imprisonment enables the gospel to advance (1:12), and the Philippians' persecution affords an opportunity to shine like stars in a crooked and perverse generation (2:15).

The Christian bookstore around the corner from my home has racks and racks of books by advocates of the "health and wealth gospel," and, according to the proprietor, they sell very well. Philippians 4:19 figures prominently in this literature and, plucked from its historical and literary context, is taken to mean that God will not simply meet the material needs of believers, but that, if they can muster the faith to believe it, he will make them rich, "according to his glorious riches in Christ Jesus." He will also, it is said, make them free from sickness, for sickness is evil and therefore cannot be God's will.[27]

---

26. Ibid., 245–46, 256.

27. These notions are endlessly recycled in the mass of pamphlets produced by Kenneth Copeland and Kenneth E. Hagin. See, for example, Copeland's *Laws of Prosperity* (Fort Worth, Tex.: KCP Publications, 1974), and Hagin's *Redeemed From Poverty, Sickness, and Spiritual Death*, 2d ed. (Tulsa, Okla.: RHEMA Bible Church, 1983).

Philippians tells us that biblical Christianity cannot tolerate such simplistic answers to the evils of poverty and disease. As Paul plainly says in 3:12–14 and 20–21, Christians have not already attained all that God has in store for them. Instead, they eagerly await the time when their "lowly bodies" will be transformed to resemble Christ's "glorious body." In the meantime, God often works through weakness and suffering to accomplish his goals, and any form of the gospel that does not carry the stamp of the cross represents a deviation from the apostolic faith.

(3) The relationship between God's grace and human works is frequently an issue in Philippians. Salvation is not a present possession in the letter, but lies in the future at "the day of Christ" (1:6, 10; 2:16). Those who will experience salvation on that day, Paul says, are those who are presently working out their salvation "with fear and trembling" (2:12). God responded to Christ's obedience, moreover, by exalting him to the highest place (2:9–11), and he will respond to the Philippians' generous spirit by supplying all of their needs (4:19). Does this mean that in Philippians salvation comes by works?[28]

As paradoxical as it may seem, Paul affirms in Philippians that although God expects believers to make concrete efforts at obedience, at the final day we will not be acquitted on the basis of our obedience but on the basis of the righteousness that God gives to us (3:9). Even the task of working out our salvation does not belong to us, since God began it, works through us, and will complete it (1:6; 2:13). That Philippians begins (1:2) and ends (4:23) with references to God's grace, therefore, is more than a perfunctory nod in the direction of a pious concept.

As with Paul's perspective on suffering in the letter, he makes no attempt to explain philosophically how the two sides of the grace-works antithesis can be held together. He simply affirms that believers must obey, but that in obeying they are only doing what God himself enables them to do, not buying acquittal on the final day.

In the modern church, as in the church of all ages, striking the balance between an emphasis on grace and an emphasis on works is difficult. Many people who believe in God and in a day of judgment think that God will ultimately decide for or against them on the basis of their works. Whether it is faithful church attendance, regular tithing, doing the occasional "good deed," or merely avoiding theft, murder, and adultery, people often imagine that what they do will earn them eternal life. Many others believe that simply because at some point in the past they have made a public profession of faith or been baptized, they are "safe."

---

28. As Robert T. Fortna argues in "Philippians: Paul's Most Egocentric Letter," *The Conversation Continues: Studies in Paul and John in Honor of J. Louis Martyn*, ed. Robert T. Fortna and Beverly R. Gaventa (Nashville, Tenn.: Abingdon, 1990), 220–34.

Philippians provides a powerful antidote to both notions. Acquittal on the day of Christ is a free gift of God to those who believe (3:9), but those who believe will inevitably experience the work of God within their lives to produce purity, blamelessness, and obedience (1:10; 2:12).

(4) Perhaps less obviously, Philippians says much about the church's relationship to the fallen world around it. The societal structures of the day were not friendly to either Paul or the Philippian church, but Paul resisted the notion that the believer should retreat from the world. Thus he engaged the unbelieving world around him with the gospel, as his joy over the spread of the gospel among the praetorian guard demonstrates (1:12–13; cf. 4:22), and he expected the Philippians, likewise, to shine like stars within the hostile society of which they were a part (2:15). He also encouraged the Philippians to look for the good around them, wherever it might be, and take it to heart (4:8). There is no naive optimism here—Paul recognizes that the unbelieving world is a "crooked and depraved generation" (2:15)—but he is convinced that the world belongs to God, that although it is fallen, some good remains within it, and that in Christ God was reconciling the world to himself (2 Cor. 5:19).

Christians today often feel that society is hostile to them. Parodied in the entertainment world, neglected or misrepresented in the news media, and shut out of the public education system, the world at times seems to lie under a veil of impenetrable darkness. As Christianity moves from being the dominant religious perspective in Western society to being only one perspective that competes equally with many others, such feelings of exclusion and misrepresentation are inevitable. Nor are they always unhealthy. The biblical view of the world affirms its fallenness and its need for the redeeming work of God's grace. As the veneer of outward Christian piety drops from the larger society, it is perhaps a spiritual advantage that Christians see clearly what the larger society has actually been all along.

Philippians shows us what to do with the reality we find beneath the veneer. If we follow Paul's example and his advice to the Philippians, we should not allow our feelings of exclusion either to lead us on a conquest of society's structures so that we can restore the Protestant veneer of the 1950s, or to push us into retreat behind walls designed to keep the world away. Our goal, like Paul's, should be to advance the gospel by engaging the culture, remembering all the while that the world belongs to God and that he loved it so much that he sought to reconcile it to himself through the death of his Son.

In the pages that follow we will observe these principles in action in Paul's world of twenty centuries past; but just as Epaphroditus carried them to the

church at Philippi, we will try to convey them safely from Philippi into our
own communities and lives.

## Outline

---

29. This outline, and the commentary generally, assume the unity of the letter. As the
bibliography reveals, some scholars believe that our canonical Philippians is a composite
document made up of two or more fragments of letters that Paul sent to Philippi. For a thorough examination of these theories and a cogent case for the unity of the letter, see David
E. Garland, "The Composition and Unity of Philippians: Some Neglected Literary Factors,"
*Novum Testamentum* 27 (1985): 141–73.

# Annotated Bibliography

## Commentaries on Philippians

Barth, Karl. *The Epistle to the Philippians*. Richmond, Va.: John Knox Press, 1962. The most effective attempt in modern times to unleash the theological power of Philippians on the modern church.

Beare, F. W. *A Commentary on the Epistle to the Philippians*. Harper's New Testament Commentaries. New York: Harper & Row, 1959. A brief, lucid, and theologically sensitive exposition of the letter, which nevertheless defends an eccentric position on the letter's unity. Beare believes that an early editor of Paul's letters fashioned our Philippians out of three Pauline letters (4:10–20; 1:1–3:1 + 4:2–9 + 4:21–23; 3:2–4:1), one of which (3:2–4:1) may not have even been written to Philippi.

Bonnard, Pierre. *L'Épître de Saint Paul aux Philippiens*. Commentaire du Nouveau Testament. Neuchatel/Paris: Delachaux & Niestlé, 1950. A short, sound exegesis of the letter from a Reformed European perspective. Intelligible to anyone with high-school level French.

Bruce, F. F. *Philippians*. Good News Commentary. New York: Harper & Row, 1983. A brief, clear exegesis of the letter from the greatest evangelical biblical scholar of this century.

Caird, G. B. *Paul's Letters From Prison (Ephesians, Philippians, Colossians, Philemon) in the Revised Standard Version*. Oxford: Oxford University Press, 1976. A brilliant exposition of Philippians within only a few pages, from one of Oxford's greatest New Testament scholars.

Collange, Jean-François. *The Epistle of Saint Paul to the Philippians*. London: Epworth Press, 1979. The 1973 replacement for Bonnard in the Commentaire du Nouveau Testament. Whereas Bonnard assumes the unity of Philippians, Collange argues that the canonical document is a composite of three letters (4:10–20; 1:1–3:1a + 4:2–7 + 4:21–23; and 3:1b–4:1 + 4:8–9).

Hawthorne, Gerald F. *Philippians*. Word Biblical Commentary. Waco, Tex.: Word Books, 1983. An insightful exposition of the Greek text by a revered and erudite professor of the Greek language.

Lightfoot, J. B. *Saint Paul's Epistle to the Philippians*. London: Macmillan, 1896. An exegesis of the Greek text by a brilliant historian of early Christianity, Cambridge professor, and devout Anglican bishop. Valuable as much for its appendices as for the commentary itself.

Martin, Ralph P. *Philippians*. New Century Bible Commentary. Grand Rapids/London: Eerdmans/Marshall, Morgan & Scott, 1976. A short, clear, and exegetically sane exposition, based on the Revised Standard Version. Not to be confused with Martin's less technical exposition of Philippians in the Tyndale New Testament Commentary series.

Meyer, Heinrich August Wilhelm. *Critical and Exegetical Handbook to the Epistles to the Philippians and Colossians, and to Philemon*. New York: Funk & Wagnalls, 1885. A detailed analysis of the grammar of the Greek text.

Michael, J. Hugh. Moffatt New Testament Commentary. *The Epistle of Paul to the Philippians*. London: Hodder and Stoughton, 1928. A clear, concise reading of the letter, which nevertheless labors to argue several exegetically unsound positions, including the notion that 3:1b–19, although from Paul's pen, is an interpolation.

O'Brien, Peter T. *The Epistle to the Philippians: A Commentary on the Greek Text*. New International Greek Testament Commentary. Grand Rapids: Eerdmans, 1991. The most detailed exposition of the Greek text in over a century and a reliable guide to virtually every exegetical problem in the epistle.

Silva, Moisés. *Philippians*. Baker Exegetical Commentary on the New Testament. Grand Rapids: Baker, 1992. An exegetically sound and theologically sensitive work written from a Reformed perspective.

Vincent, Marvin R. *A Critical and Exegetical Commentary on the Epistles to the Philippians and to Philemon*. International Critical Commentary. Edinburgh, Scotland: T. & T. Clark, 1897. A brief and uneven exposition of the Greek text.

Witherington, Ben. *Friendship and Finances in Philippi: The Letter of Paul to the Philippians*. Valley Forge, Pa.: Trinity Press International, 1994. A clearly written exposition of the letter in light of ancient rhetorical and cultural conventions.

## Popular Expositions of Philippians

Barclay, William. *The Letters to the Philippians, Colossians, and Thessalonians*. Daily Study Bible. Revised Edition. Louisville, Ky.: Westminster, 1975. A helpful attempt to bridge the ancient context of the letter and the devotional needs of the modern Christian.

Boice, James Montgomery. *Philippians: An Expositional Commentary*. Ministry Resources Library. Grand Rapids: Zondervan, 1971. A series of exegetically responsible and theologically sensitive sermons.

Briscoe, Stuart. *Philippians: Happiness Beyond Our Happenings*. Revised edition. Wheaton, Ill.: Harold Shaw Publishers, 1993. A widely used guide to the letter's significance for the modern believer.

Lloyd-Jones, D. Martyn. *The Life of Joy: An Exposition of Philippians 1 and 2.* Grand Rapids: Baker, 1989. This and the next volume constitute a collection of exegetically responsible and theologically insightful sermons originally preached in 1947 and 1948 by one of Britain's great Congregationalist preachers.

_____. *The Life of Peace: An Exposition of Philippians 3 and 4.* Grand Rapids: Baker, 1990.

Wiersbe, Warren W. *Be Joyful.* Wheaton, Ill.: Victor Books, 1974. A widely used and straightforward attempt to apply Philippians to contemporary Christian living.

## Theological Studies Relevant to Philippians

Bonhoeffer, Dietrich. *Life Together.* New York: Harper & Row, 1954. A classic study of Christian unity by a theologian who, like Paul, paid for his theology with his life.

Carson, D. A. *How Long, O Lord? Reflections on Suffering and Evil.* Grand Rapids: Baker, 1990. A cogent and sensitive approach to one of the most difficult of all theological problems.

Dieter, Melvin E., Anthony A. Hoekma, Stanley M. Horton, J. Robertson McQuilkin, and John F. Walvoord. *Five Views on Sanctification.* Grand Rapids: Zondervan, 1987. An informative and civil literary debate by spokesmen for five major trends in thinking about holy living.

Ellul, Jacques. *Money and Power.* Downers Grove, Ill.: InterVarsity Press, 1979. A provocative essay on the challenge that money presents to the church.

Erickson, Millard J. *The Word Became Flesh.* Grand Rapids: Baker, 1991. A thorough account of the incarnation by a thoughtful evangelical theologian.

# Philippians 1:1–11

PAUL AND TIMOTHY, servants of Christ Jesus,
    To all the saints in Christ Jesus at Philippi, together
    with the overseers and deacons:
²Grace and peace to you from God our Father and the
Lord Jesus Christ.

³I thank my God every time I remember you. ⁴In all my
prayers for all of you, I always pray with joy ⁵because of your
partnership in the gospel from the first day until now, ⁶being
confident of this, that he who began a good work in you will
carry it on to completion until the day of Christ Jesus.

⁷It is right for me to feel this way about all of you, since I
have you in my heart; for whether I am in chains or defending
and confirming the gospel, all of you share in God's grace with
me. ⁸God can testify how I long for all of you with the affection of Christ Jesus.

⁹And this is my prayer: that your love may abound more
and more in knowledge and depth of insight, ¹⁰so that you
may be able to discern what is best and may be pure and
blameless until the day of Christ, ¹¹filled with the fruit of
righteousness that comes through Jesus Christ—to the glory
and praise of God.

Original
Meaning

IN PAUL'S TIME letters typically began with the
name of the sender, the name of the recipient,
and a brief salutation. Occasionally these initial
phrases were followed by mention of the
sender's thanks to the gods and of continual prayers for the recipient's well-
being. Paul's letters follow the outline of these customs, but he radically modifies the customs themselves so that they become tools for bringing the grand
themes of his theology to bear on the concrete problems of the churches to
which he writes. So skillful is Paul at adapting the letter-writing customs of
his day in this way that the careful reader can often discover the primary
concerns of his letters by examining the opening paragraphs. This means
that in a Pauline letter the opening paragraphs are not meaningless pleasantries, like "Dear John" and "Sincerely yours," but powerful expressions of
the gospel and critical guides to the proper understanding of the letter as a

whole. Philippians 1:1–11 is one of the best examples in the Pauline corpus of this principle in operation.

The passage can be divided into three paragraphs, a greeting (1:1–2), a prayer of thanks (1:3–8), and a prayer of intercession (1:9–11). In the first paragraph Paul modifies the standard letter form for greetings to provide a model of the kind of humility he will urge upon the Philippians in later sections. In the second and third paragraphs he reshapes the typical form of the prayer section to describe the Philippians' concern for the advancement of the gospel and his own concern for their progress in the faith. As the letter progresses beyond these initial paragraphs, it becomes clear that these themes are Paul's primary interest.

**Humility, Unity, Sanctity, and Hello (1:1–2).** The opening words of first-century letters followed almost unfailingly the pattern "[Name] to [Name]: Greetings (*charein*)." For example, the Jewish leaders of the Jerusalem church began their letter to Gentile Christians with: "The apostles and elders, your brothers, To the Gentile believers in Antioch, Syria and Cilicia: Greetings" (Acts 15:23). The military commander in Jerusalem who was in charge of Paul likewise began his letter to the governor of Judea with: "Claudius Lysias, To His Excellency, Governor Felix: Greetings" (Acts 23:26). And in A.D. 40 the Egyptian Ammonios began each of four surviving letters to his friend and business associate Aphrodisios with the phrase, "Ammonios to his dearest Aphrodisios: Greetings."[1] Paul follows this pattern in verses 1–2 but, in a way completely uncharacteristic of other letters from his time, expands it to make the normally simple words of greeting theologically significant. Three changes to the standard formula are particularly important.

First, in verse 1 Paul does not simply mention his and Timothy's names but includes a descriptive phrase: They are "servants of Christ Jesus." Paul's word for "servants" (*douloi*) does not refer to hired household help but is the term commonly used in ancient times for "slaves." Although in the Old Testament the term "slave" sometimes appears as a title of honor to indicate the special relationship of great heroes like Moses, Joshua, and David to God (Josh. 14:7; 24:29; Ps. 89:3), in the Greco-Roman context of Paul and his Philippian readers, it would have had unmistakable overtones of humility and submission.[2] Paul's readers would probably have understood the term as Paul

---

1. The text of these letters appears in John L. White, *Light From Ancient Letters* (Philadelphia: Fortress, 1986), 121–24.

2. See Dale B. Martin, *Slavery as Salvation: The Metaphor of Slavery in Pauline Christianity* (New Haven: Yale University Press, 1990), xvi–xviii; Witherington, *Friendship and Finances in Philippi*, 30–31. A helpful and readable description of slavery in the Roman Empire can be

used it here to refer to people conscripted into the service of Christ instead of into service to sin (cf. Rom. 6:16–23; Gal. 4:1–9; 5:1).

That Paul intended to emphasize this aspect of the term becomes even clearer when we compare the opening words of Philippians to the salutations in Romans 1:1 and Titus 1:1. These are the only other letters in which Paul begins by referring to himself as a slave, and in both he follows the designation immediately with a reference to his apostolic office. "Paul, a servant of Christ Jesus, called to be an apostle and set apart for the gospel of God," he says in Romans 1:1, and in Titus 1:1, "Paul, a servant of God and an apostle of Jesus Christ." Here in Philippians, however, the only position that Paul claims for himself and Timothy is the office of slave of Christ Jesus. The honored title "apostle" is missing.

Second, Paul modifies the standard letter opening by referring not merely to "the believers in Philippi" (cf. Acts 15:23) but to "all the saints in Christ Jesus at Philippi, together with the overseers and deacons." He wants the Philippians to know that the letter is addressed to them *all*, although he also wants to recognize the leaders of the church in a special way.[3] Among Paul's thirteen canonical letters, only three others—Romans, 1 Corinthians, and 2 Corinthians—use the term "all" in the greeting, and only Philippians refers to the leaders of the church by their official titles in the opening section of the letter.[4]

Paul also follows his usual custom of calling his readers "saints" (*hagioi*). This term refers to the status of these believers as the people whom God has called out from among others and set apart, a position that carries with it the ethical responsibilities of the new covenant, just as in former times it carried the ethical responsibilities of the old covenant (Ex. 19:5–6; Lev. 11:45; Eph. 4:1; 5:3).

---

found in Paul Veyne's essay on "The Roman Empire," *A History of Private Life From Pagan Rome to Byzantium*, ed. Paul Veyne (Cambridge, Mass.: Harvard University Press, 1987), 51–70.

3. The terms "overseers" (*episkopoi*) and "deacons" (*diakonoi*) probably refer to two distinct offices of leadership within the Philippian church (cf. 1 Tim. 3:3–13), although precisely how they were distinguished from one another in Philippi is not clear. Since the "overseer" is elsewhere described as someone "able to teach" (1 Tim. 3:2; cf. 5:17; Titus 1:9; cf. Acts 20:28–31), a quality not required of the deacon (1 Tim. 3:8–10), and since the word "deacon" in its unofficial sense referred to one who waited on tables, it is possible that overseers were charged with teaching and guarding Christian doctrine whereas deacons were responsible for administrative matters. See Hermann Wolfgang Beyer, "διακονέω, κτλ." and "ἐπισκόπτομαι, κτλ.," *Theological Dictionary of the New Testament*, ed. Gerhard Kittel, 10 vols. (Grand Rapids: Eerdmans, 1964–76), 2:81–93, 599–622.

4. It is probably not insignificant that the Roman and Corinthian communities were, like the Philippian church, having trouble with divisiveness. See, for example, 1 Cor. 1:12–13; 3:4; 6:1; 8:10–12; 11:17–19; 12:12–26; and Rom. 14:1–15:13.

What can account for this combination of features in Paul's opening description of the Philippian church, particularly for Paul's unique reference to the church's "overseers and deacons"? An answer lies close at hand if we couple Paul's description of the Philippian church in the salutation with his own description of himself and Timothy. Paul provides a model of the humility and concern for the interests of others that he will soon urge on the Philippians (2:1–11). Although Paul is God's apostle, set apart and called by him to his task (Rom. 1:2; Gal. 1:1, 15), and although Timothy is an approved coworker with Paul in this important service (Phil. 2:22; cf. 1 Cor. 4:17), Paul refuses to mention these high qualifications in the letter's opening. He prefers instead to emphasize his and Timothy's common role as slaves of Christ Jesus. He is careful, on the other hand, to give the leaders of the Philippian church their appropriate titles of dignity. By constructing his greeting in this manner he has, in a small way, showed concern not for his own interests but for the interests of others (cf. 2:4).

As the rest of the letter shows, Paul hopes that when the Philippians adopt this attitude of humble service to others, their "complaining [and] arguing" (2:14) will cease and individual church members at odds with each other, like Euodia and Syntyche, will "agree … in the Lord" (4:2). Paul's statement that he writes the letter to "all the saints" in Philippi adds additional punch to this subtle but powerful message. Although he singles out the leaders of the church for special recognition, he does not write only to them; and although either Euodia or Syntyche may have been delighted to have Paul on her side, Paul refuses to play favorites. The letter is addressed instead to the entire church. Moreover, the term *saints* reminds the Philippians that they are united with one another not by their own decision but by God's having chosen them out of all the peoples of the earth to be his treasured possession (cf. Ex. 19:5–6).

Third, as in all but two of his other letters, Paul expands the typical greeting by transforming the term "Greetings!" (*charein*) into the term "grace" (*charis*) and by adding the Jewish salutation, "peace" (v. 2).[5] Paul's change of *charein* into *charis* shows that he does not intend for either of his two words of greeting to function as a simple salutation but to carry a deeper significance. By "grace" Paul means "the grace of our Lord Jesus Christ," who "though he was rich, yet for your sakes he became poor, so that you through his poverty might become rich" (2 Cor. 8:9). This is the "grace" in which believers now stand, since through the sacrifice of Christ on the cross, God has atoned for their sin and brought the hostility that sin engendered

---

5. In 1 Tim. 1:2 and 2 Tim. 1:2, Paul varies his custom slightly by inserting the term "mercy" between "grace" and "peace."

between God and his creation to an end (Rom. 3:24–25; 5:2). Similarly, the "peace" Paul commends to the Philippians is the blessing of reconciliation that has resulted from God's gracious work on their behalf (Rom. 5:1).

In the first two verses of this letter, then, and in a part of the letter that might have been left formal and theologically bland, Paul has compressed the elements of a profound message that he will unpack as the letter progresses. He has provided a model of what it means to put the interests of others and of the gospel ahead of one's own (cf. 2:3–4, 21–22), he has reminded the Philippians that their status as "saints" implies their unity as the people whom God has called to be his treasured possession (cf. 1:27; 2:14–16; 3:20; 4:2), and he has recalled the essence of the gospel for which he is in prison, whose progress the Philippians have supported, and for which he wants the Philippians to contend (1:5, 7; 2:27; 4:3, 15). This work of foreshadowing the primary themes of the letter continues in a more obvious way within the prayers of thanksgiving and intercession that follow.

**Thanksgiving for the Philippians' Partnership (1:3–8).** In the year 168 B.C., an Egyptian woman named Isias wrote to her husband, Hephaistion, to ask him to return home from a period of religious seclusion at a temple in Memphis. After greeting her husband in the customary way, Isias wrote,

> If you are well and your other affairs turn out in a like fashion, it would be as I have been continually praying to the gods; I myself am also well and the child and all in the household are continually thinking of you.[6]

Mention of prayer to the gods for the recipient of a letter was common in the private correspondence of Paul's time. As with his initial greeting, Paul follows the conventional pattern (vv. 3–11), but once again transforms it with the gospel. In the first part of this section (vv. 3–8) he reports to the Philippians his continual thanks to God for them and gives the reasons for his thankfulness. In the second part he tells the church that he intercedes for them with God and describes the content of that intercession (vv. 9–11). As with the greeting, Paul's prayer report foreshadows the letter's most important themes.[7]

---

6. White, *Light From Ancient Letters*, 65. On the functions of the opening thanksgiving prayers in Paul's letters, see Paul Schubert, *Form and Function of the Pauline Thanksgivings* (Berlin: Töpelmann, 1939); Peter Thomas O'Brien, *Introductory Thanksgivings in the Letters of Paul* (Leiden: Brill, 1977).

7. Schubert, *Form and Function*, 161–64, 180, points out that thanksgiving prayers in ancient letters outside the New Testament often introduce the subject of the letters in which they occur. But it is fair to say that Paul's thanksgiving prayers anticipate the themes of his letters in far greater detail than do the thanksgiving prayers in most private letters from his time.

Paul begins the description of his prayers of thanksgiving in verses 3–4 with the comment that he prays for the Philippians "with joy." His primary intention for this description is simply to affirm his affection for the Philippians; but it also announces a theme that runs throughout the letter: The believer should be joyful (1:18; 25; 2:17–18, 29; 3:1; 4:4; cf. 2:2; 4:1). Here we find Paul once again modeling for the Philippians a quality that he will later admonish them to cultivate among themselves (3:1; 4:4). For Paul, joy is not the result of finding himself in comfortable circumstances but of seeing the gospel make progress through his circumstances and through the circumstances of the Philippians, whatever they might be (1:18; 2:17). Thus, Paul, is joyful when he remembers the Philippians in prayer because God is at work in their midst for the advancement of the gospel. The two reasons he gives for his joyful thanks show this clearly.

Paul's first reason is that the Philippians have entered into "partnership" with him in the work of the gospel from the time that he first preached it among them to the present (v. 5). The term "partnership" (*koinonia*) means more than "fellowship" (KJV) or even "sharing" (NRSV). It refers to the Philippians' practical support of Paul's efforts to proclaim the gospel and meet the needs of other believers. Thus Paul uses the verbal form of this noun later in the letter to commend the Philippians for entering into partnership with him (*synkoinoneo*) in his troubles by means of their gifts to him during his imprisonment (4:14). He also uses it to recall their willingness to participate (*koinoneo*) "in the matter of giving and receiving" during his ministry at Thessalonica and elsewhere (4:15; cf. 2 Cor. 8:2). The "partnership" of the Philippians for which Paul thanks God in verse 5, therefore, is their practical assistance of his efforts to proclaim the gospel.[8] The apostle is particularly thankful, moreover, for the consistency of this support. The Philippians have given it "from the first day until now," even when no other church did so (4:15) and even though the church itself was not wealthy (2 Cor. 8:2–3).

Paul's second reason for joyful thankfulness to God is his confidence that God will complete the good work he has begun in the Philippians (v. 6). This work, which must be identified with the Philippians' salvation, will reach its consummation only at "the day of Christ Jesus." It is a work that God alone accomplishes, but the notion that it is not yet complete shows that it involves a progressive transformation of the lives of believers. The "good work" of salvation, then, includes God's gift to believers both of the will and of the ability to do good works. The presence of these good works in turn

---

8. See J. Hainz, "κοινωνός," *Exegetical Dictionary of the New Testament,* ed. Horst Balz and Gerhard Schneider, 3 vols. (Grand Rapids: Eerdmans, 1990–93), 2:303–5; Witherington, *Friendship and Finances in Philippi,* 37–38.

provides evidence of real belief—evidence that God has begun and will complete the work of salvation in the person who displays them. Thus Paul says in 1:28 that the Philippians' steadfastness in the midst of persecution serves as a sign of their future salvation, and in 2:12–13 that whereas the Philippians should "work out" their "salvation with fear and trembling," God is the effective power behind this work. This thought also lies behind Paul's confession in 3:12, that he presses on "to take hold of that for which Christ Jesus took hold of me." It is only because God in his grace has taken hold of believers and works within them to produce a life consistent with the gospel that they can in any sense "take hold" of salvation on "the day of Christ Jesus." In other words, those who will be saved in the future live holy lives in the present, but the holiness that characterizes their lives is God's work from beginning to end.[9]

If this represents a correct understanding of verse 6, then Paul's first two reasons for joyful thanks to God are probably bound to one another by a profound theological truth. Paul thanks God for the Philippians' partnership in the gospel not only because of the practical assistance it provided for the advancement of the gospel but also because it stands as a confirmation that God is at work in the lives of the Philippians (cf. 4:17). Paul knows, moreover, that if God has begun a work of grace in the Philippians, he will complete it, for he has the power "to bring everything under his control" (3:21); he is thus confident that God will conduct the Philippians safely into the realm of salvation on the day of Christ Jesus. This, he feels, is reason enough to rejoice.[10]

But there is another, more personal reason for thanks as well. In verses 7–8 Paul affirms that his joyful thanks to God is justified by his own deeply felt affection for the Philippians. He has them in his heart (v. 7a) and longs for them "with the affection of Christ Jesus" (v. 8). He feels this way about them because of their consistent partnership in his ministry through thick and thin (v. 7b). Paul describes this faithful commitment in terms that reflect his present position as a prisoner for the gospel. Whether he is in chains, he says, or "defending" and "confirming" the gospel, the Philippians have stood

---

9. The comments of Silva, *Philippians*, 50–52, on this aspect of v. 6 are especially helpful.

10. See 2 Cor. 9:6–15, which provides an illuminating parallel to this passage. Here Paul urges the churches in Achaia to give to his collection for the needy believers in Jerusalem by reminding them that God in his grace will give them both the resources and the desire to "abound in every good work" (v. 8). The result, Paul says, will not only be the meeting of the needs of God's people but "many expressions of thanks to God" (v. 12; cf. v. 11). This kind of obedience, which lies in the future for the Achaeans, lies in the past for the Philippians and has already resulted, according to Phil. 1:3–8, in Paul's frequent prayers of thanksgiving.

with him. The terms Paul uses for "defending" (*apologia*) and "confirming" (*bebaiosis*) are technical legal terms for providing a speech of defense before an official (Acts 22:1; 2 Tim. 4:16) and giving a guarantee that something is true (Heb. 6:16). Paul's imprisonment and impending trial (1:13, 17, 19–26) may have suggested these terms to Paul, as many commentators believe; but the Philippians' support of the apostle is not limited to his legal battles (cf. 4:15–16), and so his meaning here cannot be confined to that context. Whether he is in chains or persuading hearers of the truth of the gospel outside prison walls, Paul says the Philippians have stood with him.

They have been, literally, "fellow participants [*synkoinonoi*] with me of the grace." The NIV, along with most other translations, takes this to mean that the Philippians have shared with Paul in the benefits of God's grace, presumably his saving grace. But since Paul has just spoken of the Philippians' gifts to him as their "participation" (*koinonia*) with him in his ministry of preaching the gospel (v. 5), and since he often uses the word "grace" about himself to refer to his calling to preach the gospel to the Gentiles (Rom. 1:5; 12:3; 15:15–16; 1 Cor. 3:10; Gal. 2:7–9; Eph. 3:2), he is probably referring in verse 7 once again to the Philippians' practical support of his ministry.[11] Because of this practical support in a variety of situations, the Philippians hold a special place, perhaps unique among Paul's churches, in Paul's heart.

**Intercession for the Philippians' Spiritual Growth (1:9–11).** Paul next describes for the Philippians the content of his intercessory prayers on their behalf—that they might grow spiritually, with the ultimate result that God will receive glory and praise. Paul first expresses his basic request for the Philippians and then mentions the results that he hopes God will produce in them in answer to his prayers.

His basic request is that the Philippians' love will steadily increase "in knowledge and depth of insight." The term "love" is not further limited or defined, although if it bears the meaning here that it has in the rest of the letter (1:16; 2:1–2), it refers to the love believers should have for one another. Since this meaning fits well with the theme of unity pervading the letter and already introduced in subtle ways in verses 1–2, it is probably the correct meaning. Paul prays that their love for one another will increase first in "knowledge" (*epignosis*), a term that always refers elsewhere in his letters to religious knowledge, whether knowledge of God (Rom. 1:28; Eph. 1:17; Col. 1:10; cf. 3:10), of God's righteousness (Rom. 10:2), of his Son (Eph. 4:13; cf.

---

11. The KJV takes the phrase "with me" as the possessive pronoun "my" and translates, "ye all are partakers of my grace." Although this is probably not the best rendering of the Greek ("grace" should go with "partakers," as the NIV has it), it nevertheless correctly captures Paul's meaning.

Col. 2:2), of his will (Col. 1:9), of sin (Rom. 3:20), of the truth (1 Tim. 2:4; 2 Tim. 2:25; 3:7; Titus 1:1), or of everything good (Philem. 6). Since Paul does not specify the content of that knowledge here, he probably intends for it to cover spiritual knowledge generally. If so, the point of his petition is that the Philippians might understand how to obey God's command that believers love one another. Paul's term for "depth of insight" (*aisthesis*) appears only here in the New Testament, but in other ancient Greek literature it often refers to "moral perception," that is, to the ability to know the right action in a given situation. Paul's basic request for the Philippians, in other words, is that they might express their love in ways that show both a knowledge of how to obey God's will generally, and, more specifically, of how to make moral decisions based on God's will in the give-and-take of everyday living.

Paul's next phrase describes the result of possessing these qualities; he uses two clauses, the second one grammatically dependent on the first (vv. 10–11). If the above-mentioned characteristics mark the Philippians, they will "be able to discern what is best" and will "be pure and blameless until the day of Christ, filled with the fruit of righteousness that comes through Jesus Christ." The phrase "discern what is best" refers to the ability to distinguish "the things that really matter" from a variety of competing possibilities.[12] Paul probably has in mind here the false teaching to which he refers in 3:1–4:1, where he warns the Philippians of problems that have plagued his other churches, whether the Judaizing tendencies that tripped up the Galatians when they were running well (Gal. 5:7; cf. Phil. 3:1–11) or the misunderstanding of the relationship between the spiritual and the physical that plagued the Corinthians (1 Cor. 5:1–13; 6:12–20; 15:1–58; cf. Phil. 3:12–21). Paul's prayer is that the Philippians will avoid both traps by having the spiritual knowledge and moral insight necessary for choosing what is best, for continuing, in other words, to consider all things as loss in comparison with "the surpassing greatness of knowing Christ Jesus" (3:8). His hope is that they, his best-loved congregation, will not be led astray by soundings into the treacherous waters that have nearly shipwrecked the faith of others.

Such devotion to the gospel will keep the Philippians "pure and blameless" until the final day when they are called to stand before Christ (v. 10) and will ensure that they bear "the fruit of righteousness that comes through Jesus Christ" (v. 11). The phrase "fruit of righteousness" may refer either to the ethical conduct of those who have been declared righteous or simply to

---

12. See Walter Bauer, *A Greek-English Lexicon of the New Testament and Other Early Christian Literature*, 2d ed., trans., adapt. and rev. William F. Arndt, F. Wilbur Gingrich, and Frederick W. Danker (Chicago: University of Chicago Press, 1979), 190.

conduct that is righteous; a vigorous debate rages among scholars over which of the two options is best. The arguments are fairly evenly balanced, but in either case Paul's emphasis is on the ethical "fruit" that God's people should bear (cf. Isa. 5:1–7; Matt. 7:16–20; Luke 13:6–9). This fruit, he prays, will be evident in the Philippians' lives on the final day, and the result will be "the glory and praise of God."

In this introductory section, then, Paul has given theological depth to the conventional customs for opening a letter and has sketched out the major themes of the argument to come. He has reminded the Philippians of their unity as saints and of the gracious nature of the gospel. He has provided a model of the unselfish regard for others that will preserve the unity of their congregation. He has commended them on their participation in his ministry, provided encouragement that their efforts are evidence of God's work within them, and assured them of his prayers for their continued progress toward a successful verdict before God's tribunal on the final day. He has therefore prepared the way for the work of encouragement and persuasion that follows in this letter.

IN OUR ATTEMPT to bring the modern church into contact with the theology of this ancient text, we must pay particular attention to two fundamental tasks. First, we must understand how the passage functions in its original setting, and second, we must avoid several common misunderstandings of important terms within the passage.

**Form and Function as Guides to Meaning.** This passage performed two functions in its original context, both of which provide important clues to its meaning for the modern church. The passage functions first as the fulfillment of conventional expectations for the way a personal letter should begin. By using these conventions Paul signaled to his readers that in the paragraphs that follow they should expect neither a historical narrative nor a philosophical tractate but a personal letter, whose power to effect changes in the Philippians was based on his friendship with them. Paul's use of these conventions help the modern interpreter to understand that Philippians is not a theological treatise on, for example, joy but a personal letter written to a church for specific pastoral reasons. The letter has much to say about joy, and we can learn much from it about how the believer should obey Paul's commands to "rejoice in the Lord" (3:1; 4:4). But his comments on the subject will be selective, designed to meet the pastoral needs of the Philippians at the time the letter was written. The apostle's conventional epistolary opening, then, alerts us to a crucial interpretive principle for understanding the entire letter: His coverage of theological issues will be selective and driven by a pastoral concern for the Philippians, not systematically and directly addressed to us. To appropriate what he says to us in Philippians, we must first understand what he said to them and why he said it.[13]

Second, Paul uses the customs of his day for opening a letter in unprecedented ways. Some variation in the standard letter opening occurs among the ancient letters preserved to us, and many Christians imitated Paul in later years; but no extant letters prior to Paul's approach the radical and thoughtful transformation of epistolary conventions that he accomplished.[14] This startling way of using common conventions aids the modern interpreter in discovering the aspects of the initial passages in Paul's letters that he intended to emphasize. Where he deviates from convention—especially when these deviations anticipate themes that become important later in the letter—he reveals his primary concerns in the passage. By paying attention to these deviations from custom in our examination of the "original meaning" of Philippians 1:1–11, we uncovered three primary concerns: the unity of the Philippian church, their faithful partnership with Paul in the work of the gospel, and their growth in knowledgeable, perceptive love.

First, Paul stressed through his own example of humility and through his designation of the letter's recipients as "all the saints in Christ Jesus at Philippi" both the importance of Christian unity and one critical means of achieving that unity—placing the interests of others ahead of one's own. When we apply this theme to the contemporary church, it will be important to emphasize both aspects of the passage.

Paul's designation of the Philippians as "saints" recalls the Old Testament imagery of Israel as a people who had been set apart by God and who were to demonstrate their special status by their conduct. "I am the LORD your God, who has set you apart from the nations," says Leviticus. "You must therefore make a distinction between clean and unclean animals. . . . You are to be holy to me because I, the LORD, am holy, and I have set you apart from the nations to be my own" (Lev. 20:24–26). The most critical threat to the sanctity of the Philippians is their disunity (2:14–16; 4:2), and Paul demonstrates the seriousness of the problem by addressing it subtly in the first

---

13. See the valuable discussion on interpreting the New Testament letters in Gordon D. Fee and Douglas Stuart, *How to Read the Bible for All Its Worth*, 2d ed. (Grand Rapids: Zondervan, 1993), 61–77.

14. See the comments of William G. Doty, *Letters in Primitive Christianity* (Philadelphia: Fortress, 1973), 21–22, and compare Paul's letter openings with the predictable letter openings in White, *Light From Ancient Letters*. For the influence of Paul's innovation on later Christian letter writers, see, for example, 1 Peter 1:1–2; 2 Peter 1:1–2; and the salutations in the letters of Ignatius.

sentence of the letter and in a section that, in typical letters, carried little of significance to the primary message. Paul would be the last to say that the unity of the church should be preserved at the cost of its sanctity (1 Cor. 5:1–13; 2 Cor. 6:14–7:1), but in Philippians Paul affirms that unity is important and that when it is broken over issues that are not vital, the sanctity of the Christian community is itself threatened. The church in modern times, however, does not typically view unity as an element of sanctification. Sadly and ironically, the critical principle of Christian unity is often violated over matters of lesser or no importance in the name of the church's purity. Where this attitude is present in the church, Paul's link between unity and sanctity in this passage provides a prophetic rebuke.

Paul's manner of communicating this admonition is also important. He does so by example. The most effective way to achieve unity is not to demand that everyone agree with us but to look out for the interests of others and to refuse to claim for ourselves the privileges that rightfully belong to us. This is the path Paul follows in the first two verses of Philippians, and his example provides an appropriate springboard for challenging the modern church to seek unity through a genuine concern for the interests of others.

Second, Paul provides encouragement for the Philippians in the description of his thanksgiving prayers by telling them that their "partnership" with him in the work of the gospel (vv. 5, 7) is evidence both that God is at work in them now and that he will continue to work in them until the final day (v. 6). Several critical theological principles, all of which surface later in the letter, stand behind this statement, and they are principles that the modern church needs to hear. The clearest of these principles is that salvation is a process that God effects from beginning to end (v. 6). It does not depend on human effort either to get it started or to keep it going, for "it is God who works in you to will and to act according to his good purpose" (2:13). This principle in turn implies another: Practical demonstrations of obedience produce confidence that God is at work in us and in others (v. 6). The Philippians' monetary and personal support of Paul (2:25–30; 4:18) provided evidence of God's work in them and assured him that their good work was a result of God's "good work" of salvation in them.

Equal in importance with these other principles, although more subtly expressed, is the notion that God values the faithful support of his servants through both good times and bad. This principle emerges from Paul's expression of gratitude for the constancy of the Philippians' support. In verse 7 he says that they participated with him in carrying out his divine commission (his "grace"), whether he was "in chains or defending and confirming the gospel." If our interpretation of this phrase is correct, then Paul is concerned with more in this statement than his present imprisonment and impending arraignment—he is expressing thanks for the Philippians' willingness to stand with him not only when he was busy debating in the synagogue and public forum but also when he was imprisoned and unable to proclaim the gospel openly. By implication, then, the Philippians stood with Paul through thick and thin, both when he had the outward appearance of a powerful teacher and when he did not. This was not true of all of Paul's churches (2 Cor. 5:12; 10:7a, 10; 13:3–4), nor was it true of all believers in the city where Paul was imprisoned (Phil. 1:17; cf. 2:21), and it is perhaps against this background that he finds particular joy in the constancy of the Philippians' devotion to him and to his work.

Behind this affirmation of their constant support stands Paul's conviction that God works through what the world considers weakness. Paul says elsewhere that he delights "in weaknesses, in insults, in hardships, in persecutions, in difficulties," because when God works through these problems, it is clear to all that his power alone has been at work (2 Cor. 12:9–10; cf. 4:7). Perhaps because the Philippians had experienced this principle in their own lives (Phil. 1:29–30), they apparently understood it well and were willing to support Paul as faithfully when he was enduring hardship and lacked the signs of worldly success as when, from the world's perspective, all was going well.

The Philippians' faithfulness and Paul's commendation of them for it stand as an authoritative challenge to the modern church. Faithfulness to the church and its divinely called leadership should not be tied to such worldly definitions of success as physical facilities, numerical growth, a comfortable lifestyle, and impressive credentials. This passage challenges modern Christians to look beyond what is seen and focus on the heart (cf. 2 Cor. 5:12), and to remain faithful to the church, its leadership, and its missionaries even when, in the world's view, they look like failures.

Third, Paul reveals in the description of his intercessory prayer for the Philippians his concern for the growth of their ability to understand how best to express their love for one another. The reason for this concern, Paul says, is that the Philippians might discern "what is best" and therefore arrive at the final day pure and blameless. In 3:8, 11–14 Paul describes the most excellent among the things that are best when he says that he has suffered the loss of all things and runs straight toward a single goal, the goal of knowing Christ.[15] The love and unity the apostle wants to encourage among the Philippians, then, provides a safeguard against deviation from this most excellent goal. In bringing this passage out of the Philippians' situation and into our own, we should explain that love within the Christian community is not a sentimental feeling or a willingness to let our brothers and sisters go

---

15. O'Brien, *Philippians*, 78.

their own way. Because it is based on what Paul calls elsewhere "the truth of the gospel" (Gal. 2:5, 14), it must sometimes do everything within its power to keep fellow believers from stumbling off the path marked out by that truth (cf. Gal. 6:1–2).

In bringing Philippians 1:1–11 out of its ancient setting and into the modern church, then, we should use Paul's creative departures from convention and the important themes of the letter's subsequent paragraphs as guides to his chief concerns. The unity, faithfulness, and perceptive love of the church emerge from this exercise as his primary themes, and these should be our concerns as we turn to the work of application.

In addition to focusing on these theological principles, we should not miss a less direct, but equally important, message in the passage. Paul's method of transforming conventional customs of letter writing into vehicles for his theological concerns demonstrates the comprehensive nature of Christ's lordship. Paul is so consumed with his desire to see the gospel advanced that even mundane and perfunctory conventions of communication can be altered into means for the advancement of the gospel. We would perhaps be remiss in making much of this if it were not a standard feature of Paul's theological method. For Paul, God often used conventional means to advance his goals. Stoic ideals are transformed into useful moral guidelines for Christians (2 Cor. 9:8; Phil. 4:8, 11). The Old Testament preaches the gospel (Rom. 10:6–13). Customary roles for slaves and women become evangelistic tools (1 Tim. 6:1; Titus 2:3–5, 9–10). Similarly, in the letter-writing conventions of his day, Paul saw an opportunity to advance the gospel, and he took it. Although the text itself offers no explicit imperative to use social customs and inherited traditions to promote the gospel, the consistency of the theme in his correspondence shows that it is not inappropriate to find an expression of it here and to examine its implications for the modern church.

**Potentially Confusing Terminology.** The spadework necessary for a complete and accurate application of this passage to the modern church is not complete until several potentially confusing terms are carefully defined. Four terms in the passage have traditionally posed a problem for modern readers, and the meaning of each deserves consideration before the work of application can begin. The first two occur in the letter's greeting and the second two in Paul's description of his thanksgiving prayer.

First, for most modern readers the term *slaves*, which Paul uses to describe his and Timothy's relationship to Christ in 1:1, conjures up pictures of the degrading institution that held together the economy of the American South prior to the Civil War. The ancient institution was often more humane than its more recent counterpart, but in both the defining characteristic was the total ownership of one person by another. Masters could do as they wished with their slaves without fear of impunity, and for this reason the relationship between master and slave was often marked by distrust and cruelty.[16] Why, many modern readers of Philippians may ask, would Paul have described his relationship to Christ Jesus as one of slavery?

It is important to know that Paul understood the ancient institution of slavery well and had something to say about it in his letters. He recognized that the institution itself was an unalterable fact of life for some believers, but he also provided meaningful ways for Christian slaves to think about their plight. He transformed the common cultural obligations of slaves to masters into responsibilities that slaves should fulfill not because they were slaves but because they were Christians (Eph. 6:5–8; Col. 3:22–25; Philem. 11) and because they should be concerned about attracting others to the gospel (Titus 2:10; cf. 1 Tim. 6:1). He advised slaves who could do so to obtain their freedom so that their devotion might belong single-mindedly to Christ (1 Cor. 7:21–23), and he implied that the equality of believers before God undermined the foundation of social inequity on which the institution was built (1 Cor. 7:21–23; Eph. 6:9; Col. 4:1; Philem. 15–16).

When Paul used the term *slave* to describe his relationship to Christ, then, he did not reveal a faulty or calloused understanding of the institution. He knew many Christian slaves and understood their situation. Perhaps this is why, when he uses the slave metaphor in Romans 6:16–22, he indicates to his readers that he understands its limitations: "I speak in a human way," he says, "because of your human weakness" (Rom. 6:19, pers. trans.).[17]

Paul recognized, however, that no other metaphor conveys quite so clearly the total claim of God on the believer's life. Paul is a slave of Christ Jesus not because he is, to use Aristotle's definition, a "living tool" of his master (*Ethica Nicomachea* 1161[b]); he is Christ's slave because Christ's goals are his goals and God's call is his mission, and because it is his responsibility to fulfill the command of his master even when doing so is personally inconvenient (cf. 1:17–18).

Second, the term *saints* in 1:1 is likewise subject to misunderstanding. Since the second century, many within the church have venerated certain especially courageous, sacrificial, and insightful Christians as "saints." Large segments of the church still believe that Christians should pray to the

---

16. See Seneca's *Epistulae XLVII* for a revealing description of the inhumanity with which slaves were sometimes treated and a commentary on the resulting mutual fear that often characterized the slave-master relationship.

17. See the comments of C. E. B. Cranfield, *A Critical and Exegetical Commentary on the Epistle to the Romans*, 2 vols. (ICC; Edinburgh: T. & T. Clark, 1975–79), 1:325–26.

departed spirits of these people so that they might, through their extraordinary piety, secure the favor of God on their behalf. All of this means that when some people read the word *saints* (*hagioi*) in Paul's letters, they imagine that Paul is addressing people of exemplary piety. The greeting of 1 Corinthians alone provides enough evidence to refute this notion. Paul refers to the Corinthians as those who "have been sanctified [*hegiasmenois*] in Christ Jesus, called to be holy [*hagiois*]" (1 Cor. 1:2, pers. trans.). But despite their sanctity Paul later scolds them for sins so offensive that even the pagans, he says, find them scandalous (5:1). To be a "saint," therefore, is to be set apart as a believer, and sometimes "saints" live in ways that are displeasing to God. Every believer is a saint as a result of experiencing God's gracious work of redemption, not as a result of some prior act of courage, sacrifice, or theological brilliance.

In an effort to show the error behind the popular notion that Christians must do something special in order to become "saints," however, it is easy to go to another extreme. Karl Barth's comments on this term illustrate the problem:

> "Holy" people are unholy people who nevertheless as such have been singled out, claimed and requisitioned by God for his control, for his use, for himself who is holy. Their holiness is and remains in Christ Jesus. It is in him that they are holy, it is from this point of view that they are to be addressed as such, in no other respect.[18]

Barth makes the laudable point that in Paul's thinking, no one does anything to become a "holy" person or a "saint" (the same Greek word is used for both adjective and noun). But his implication that believers are holy only insofar as Christ's holy status is given to them ignores the ethical connotations that the terms *holy* and *saints* carry in Paul's letters. Paul's purpose in describing the Corinthians as "saints" and "sanctified" is in part to urge them to live in a way consistent with this status (1 Cor. 6:9–11; cf. 1 Thess. 4:3–5, 7). Just as in the Old Testament God separated Israel from the nations but then required his people to act in a way that showed their distinctiveness (Lev. 11:45; 20:22–26; 22:32), so Paul believes that the initiative in sanctification lies with God (1 Cor. 1:2; 6:11; Eph. 5:26; 1 Thess. 5:23) but that believers should live in a way that "is fitting for the saints" (Eph. 5:3, pers. trans.). "Holy people" are certainly "unholy people" when they are called by God (Rom. 3:9–26; 4:5; 5:6; cf. 9:11–12, 30; 11:6; 2 Cor. 5:21), but Paul urges those who have been set apart by God to match God's prior action for them with sanctified lives.

---

18. Karl Barth, *Philippians*, 10.

Third, in Philippians 1:4 we meet for the first time in the letter the noun *joy*, a word that, together with its verbal form *rejoice*, Paul will use fourteen times in this letter, more often than in any other letter. The terms are popularly used today to describe a feeling of pleasure derived from agreeable circumstances. If understood in this light, the reference to joy in this passage might be misunderstood to mean that Paul is happy because the Philippians have alleviated his personal suffering and made him more comfortable by their participation with him in the gospel. It is important in applying this passage to understand that joy was not linked for Paul to his personal comfort but *to the progress of the gospel*. Thus despite the impure motives and personal animosity of some who preached the gospel, Paul could rejoice that it was being preached at all (1:18). Paul could speak of the Philippians' progress and joy in the faith in a single breath (1:25). The Philippians' practical demonstration of that progress by their efforts to live in unity with one another made Paul's joy complete (2:2; cf. 1:4; 4:10). Paul's suffering and the Philippians' steadfastness combined to form an offering to God and therefore were reasons for rejoicing (2:17–18). And he expected the Philippians to rejoice when they saw Epaphroditus again *"because* he almost died for the work of Christ"* (2:30). So in 1:4, Paul's joy is unrelated to his own comfort but is instead the contentment that results from seeing the goals of the gospel advanced, whatever that might mean in terms of personal inconvenience.

Fourth, the terms *partnership* (v. 4) and *share* (v. 7), which are closely related to one another in Greek (*koinonia* and *synkoinonoi*), are central to a correct understanding of the reason why Paul gives thanks for the Philippians, yet they are easily misunderstood. It is easy to think of "partnership" and "sharing" in terms of an attitude alone—if we agree with someone, we "share" their beliefs and are "partners" with them at the level of ideas. This element is certainly present in these terms, as Paul's frequent references throughout Philippians to the attitudes that Christians should have toward one another show (2:2, 5; 4:2, 10; cf. 1:7–8). Yet these two terms within this context do not refer primarily to an attitude but to actions that the Philippians have performed, actions demonstrating that they are making common cause with Paul and the gospel he proclaims. The Philippians are partners with Paul and participants in the work of his calling because they have contributed money and personal encouragement to his missionary enterprise out of their poverty and personal sacrifice (2:29–30; 4:18; cf. 2 Cor. 8:2), not simply because they "share" his convictions.

In bringing this concept out of Paul's situation and into our own, therefore, we should remember that Paul's commendation is directed less toward an abstract attitude of the Philippians than toward a costly expression of their commitment to the gospel. Paul is not talking about the Christian "fellowship" that takes place at church suppers, coffee hours, Bible studies, and Sunday schools, nor is he talking primarily about the "kinship" Christians feel for one another even when they do not know one another well. These are good and edifying, but they are not his concern here. Rather, Paul is referring to a costly cooperation with the one who proclaims the gospel, a cooperation that in this instance meant that none of the Philippians but Epaphroditus would have "fellowship" with Paul in the sense of seeing him face to face, but that all would be his partners in their common goal of advancing the gospel.

In summary, we should be careful when applying Philippians 1:1-11 to the modern church to find situations within the church that need the restorative powers of Paul's concern with unity, deference to others, a love which watches out for others, and God's ability to transform social tradition into a means of communicating the gospel to others. As we make these applications, we must be careful to define terms such as *slave, saint, joy,* and *participation* as Paul intended them to be understood rather than as they are sometimes popularly understood in modern culture. With these interpretive tools in hand, the application of the passage to the modern church can begin.

MOST CHRISTIAN GROUPS today understand that being a Christian involves more than simply giving intellectual assent to biblical doctrine. They understand that an increasing awareness of God's will and a desire to do it should be the fruit of a life committed to Christ. In classic theological terms, the process of becoming more and more obedient to God's will after being set apart by the redeeming work of Christ is called *sanctification*. It is, in the words of the Westminster Shorter Catechism, "the work of God's free grace, whereby we are renewed in the whole man after the image of God, and are enabled more and more to die unto sin, and live unto righteousness" (A. 35). When sanctification becomes a topic of discussion in the modern church, however, it often has a narrow focus on avoiding sexual immorality, resisting impure thoughts, and remaining untainted by worldliness in general. Saintliness is seldom associated with Christian unity. Sadly, twisted notions about what constitutes sanctity sometimes destroy unity, so that everything from a nineteenth-century agrarian way of life (for the Old Order Amish) to a ban on viewing movies (for some fundamentalists) has been identified with living a "sanctified" life and has kept believers apart. Paul in this passage and elsewhere claims that the unity of believers is an important demonstration of the church's status as "saints," an important element, in other words, in the believer's sanctification.

How can we work for Christian unity? First we must identify the barriers that divide people who claim to be Christians and ask whether they are legitimate barriers. Some barriers, as Paul would quickly affirm, are necessary. Theologian Thomas Oden, for example, reports that he once quietly withdrew from a chapel service at the divinity school where he teaches when communion was offered in the name of the goddess Sophia. The weight of biblical and ecclesiastical tradition tells us that he made a wise choice.[19] Some barriers, however, are illegitimate, as when believers are barred from the communion table only because they have not been baptized within a particular church or denomination. It is difficult to imagine that the Lord of the feast, who himself prayed that all who believed the apostles' message would be one (John 17:21), would approve of such policies. Worse yet, some Christian congregations, usually only in subtle ways, continue to exclude believers on the basis of race—a practice Scripture expressly forbids (Gal. 2:11–21; Eph. 2:11–22). If we are to be faithful to the spirit of Philippians 1:1–2, such barriers to Christian unity are intolerable.

After identifying the barriers dividing us, we must be willing to follow the example of Paul's unselfishness in tearing them down. Just as Paul was willing not to claim his status as an apostle but was careful to give to the Philippians and their leaders titles of honor ("saints," "overseers," and "deacons"), so contemporary Christians, especially leaders, should be willing to preserve the unity of the church by forgoing their own rights and ensuring the rights of others. In Birmingham, Alabama, for example, enormous strides have been made in overcoming the specter of racism that haunted the city's institutions throughout the civil-rights struggles of the 1960s, and part of that progress is attributable to evangelical Christians within the city. Since 1986, and with little public notice or acclaim, a group of evangelicals has worked in inner-city Birmingham to bring both African-American and white believers together in an effort to aid some of the city's poorest citizens. The Center for Urban Mission and its New City Church have recruited white families and African-American families, poor and affluent, to worship together on Sundays and to work together throughout the week to help Birmingham's poor gain economic independence through tutoring and job-training programs. The founding of the organization was not without cost, at least in worldly terms, for its two leaders—one who by sheer determination had worked his way out of the projects himself, the other a graduate of

---

19. Oden first recounted the incident in "Encountering the Goddess at Church," *Christianity Today* (August 16, 1993), 18. A more complete account and a theological explanation of his withdrawal appears in his *Requiem: A Lament in Three Movements* (Nashville, Tenn.: Abingdon, 1995), 27–32, 140–51.

an exclusive college and top-ranking law school. Both eventually gave up their secure and lucrative careers to work with the mission and the church full time. They now depend for their income, much as Paul did, on the partnership of other believers who believe that what the Center for Urban Mission does is vital. This kind of sacrifice baffles unbelievers, but it is the quality of effort that should not be rare among a people who understand that striving for Christian unity is part of what it means to belong to "all the saints in Christ Jesus."[20]

Another aspect of sanctification that emerges from this passage and challenges the modern church is the principle of supporting other believers who are using their gifts for the advancement of the gospel. The modern church, like the Philippians in ancient times, should cultivate a type of support for other believers that is both sacrificial and consistent. As we saw in our study of verse 7, Paul joyfully thanks God that the Philippians have unselfishly supported the gift of apostleship given to him by God. They understood that Paul had received a special calling to proclaim the gospel among the Gentiles. In response, they had unselfishly supported his apostolic work in Macedonia with gifts "again and again" (4:15–16) and had generously given to his offering for the needy Jerusalem believers "out of the most severe trial" and "extreme poverty" (2 Cor. 8:2).[21]

This kind of partnership identifies those to whom God has given particular gifts for the proclamation of the gospel and the edification of the church and makes it possible for them to do the work to which God has called them. Such an approach to the advancement of the gospel demands the humility necessary to recognize that God has given to others gifts that he has not given to us, and a sacrificial attitude necessary for providing practical help to those gifted in such ways. The church that gives a pastor especially skilled in the exposition of God's word the extra time needed to prepare excellent sermons, parents who sacrifice financially to make it possible for a child to fulfill God's call to work among the poor, and the church that cancels plans for a new Christian education wing in order to send a missionary to the field are all demonstrating this kind of humble and sacrificial partnership.

Paul not only values the sacrificial nature of the Philippians' support; he is also grateful for its consistency. The Philippians supported him both when

---

20. A similar effort with many of the same goals is the partnership of Rock Church and Circle Urban Ministries in Chicago. For the compelling story of these two institutions, see Raleigh Washington and Glen Kehrein, *Breaking Down Walls: A Model for Reconciliation in an Age of Racial Strife* (Chicago: Moody Press, 1993).

21. See also 2 Cor. 11:9, where Paul mentions that while he was in Corinth (in the province of Achaia), "brothers who came from Macedonia" supported his ministry. These brothers probably included Philippians.

he was in chains and when he was defending and confirming the gospel in a wide variety of settings. They sent gifts to Paul when he was in Thessalonica. They supported his collection of money for the needy believers in Jerusalem. And they sent Epaphroditus to Paul when they heard that he was in prison. Our support of those to whom God has given special gifts for ministry should, likewise, be consistent. This means, for example, supporting missionaries not only when their work is producing visible results, but when it seems to languish or deteriorate as well.

Above all, we should remember that in choosing whom to support, God often works not through those whom the world identifies as gifted but through those who are without "eloquence or superior wisdom" and who do not speak "with wise and persuasive words" (1 Cor. 2:1, 4). Those who respond to the message, moreover, are often not people "of noble birth" but the "foolish," "weak," "lowly," and "despised" (1:26–28). The church errs when it targets the powerful people in the community and nation on the theory that if they can be persuaded of the gospel's truth, they will somehow advance God's goals more effectively than others. It is sad to see churches originally located in city centers in order to be near the halls of power now following the powerful out to the suburbs. Paul would have had little patience with such a strategy, for he reached the ears of the powerful only by meeting them in law courts.

The church also needs to hear Paul's concern that the Philippians' love grow "more and more in knowledge and depth of insight" that they might "be able to discern what is best and [might] be pure and blameless until the day of Christ" (vv. 9–10). Paul links the Philippians' perceptiveness about how to show love toward one another ("knowledge and depth of insight") with their ability to pick out from a variety of competing options what is consistent with knowing Christ ("what is best"). Love for one another, in other words, should include a determination to stand as sentinels over the commitment of one's fellow believers to the gospel, helping them not to be distracted from it by heresy and sin but to pursue single-mindedly "the prize for which God has called" believers heavenward (3:14).

This loving concern for the spiritual health of other believers can show itself in several ways, two of which are particularly important. First, the spiritually mature members of the church should instruct those who are younger in the faith. This is probably why Paul insists that the leader in the church "not be a recent convert" (1 Tim. 3:6), why he says that the leader must be able to "encourage others by sound doctrine and refute those who oppose it" (Titus 1:9), and why he urges "older women" in the church to "train the younger women to love their husbands and children, to be self-controlled and pure, to be busy at home, to be kind, and to be subject to their husbands. . . ."

(Titus 2:3–5). God can, and sometimes does, instill the spiritual discernment necessary for making right moral and theological decisions by direct intervention in the hearts of believers, but his normal way of doing this is apparently through teaching done by mature believers, whose commitment to the faith has been proven over the years. In our own churches, then, structures need to be in place through which the spiritually mature instruct those who have more recently come into the faith.

Second, some means of lovingly correcting those who stray into morally or theologically dangerous waters needs to be in place in our churches. At times those who have strayed know that they have done so and have experienced the terrible isolation of secret sin. They have perhaps confessed their sin to God, but they need a concrete expression of his forgiveness. They need to feel his acceptance through the acceptance of their brothers and sisters in the Lord. In such instances the ancient Christian practice of confession meets the need. In his book *Life Together*, Dietrich Bonhoeffer observes that sin, because it is often harbored secretly out of shame, tears fellowship apart and drives the sinner into isolation. In confession, however, sin loses its power to break Christian fellowship. Now the sinner

> is not alone with his evil any more, but in confession has laid his evil aside and handed it over to God. It has been removed from him. Now he stands in the fellowship of sinners who live by the grace of God in the cross of Jesus Christ. . . . Hidden sin isolated him from the community and made all outward fellowship false. Confessed sin helped him to true fellowship with the brethren in Jesus Christ.[22]

No biblical warrant exists for designating a single person to hear confession, for limiting those who hear confession to the "ordained" members of the congregation, or for confessing before the congregation itself. Nevertheless, if the church regards some form of confession of sin to others as a normal expression of Christian community, people who might otherwise be driven from the fellowship of the church by their feelings of guilt or hypocrisy will have an avenue for restoration.

Sometimes, however, those who have strayed either do not know that they have done so or are unwilling to acknowledge their sin. In such cases the church needs to exercise discipline over its members through censure or, in extreme cases, excommunication. Discipline can, of course, be abused and needs to be handled with the "knowledge and spiritual insight" that Paul

---

22. Dietrich Bonhoeffer, *Dietrich Bonhoeffer Werke*, vol. 5, *Gemeinsames Leben, Das Gebetbuch der Bible*, ed. Gerhard Ludwig Müller and Albrecht Schönherr (Munich: Chr. Kaiser Verlag, 1987), 95. Cf. *Life Together*, 113.

desires for believers in this passage, but neglecting it altogether from fear of its misuse is not a loving response. It is occasionally needed as a last effort to bring those who have strayed to their theological senses and to save them "by snatching them out of the flames" (Jude 23, pers. trans.). To use Bonhoeffer's words again:

> Where Christ, for love's sake, commands me to maintain community, I will maintain it. But where truth and love bid me to dissolve community, there I will dissolve it, despite all the protests of my emotional love.[23]

Finally, this passage challenges the church to be as creative as Paul was in using the inherited traditions of his day in the service of the gospel. Paul transformed the virtually unvarying way of opening a letter in ancient times into a startling means of conveying the message of the letter and the gospel itself in a nutshell. In seeking ways to be equally creative in our use of various communications media, we should beware of a danger: We should not think that we are imitating Paul when we pack the gospel into media that simply cannot hold it. Front bumper plates with "Jesus" on them and yard signs inscribed with "PREPARE TO MEET GOD," although well-intentioned, probably generate little meaningful discussion about the gospel.

In our efforts to communicate the gospel creatively with the cultural tools available to us, it seems sensible to use tools that can convey the gospel message with as much power and fullness as possible. Paul used the letter because in his time it was such an important means of communication: Governing officials used it to make their decrees public, philosophers used it to convey their philosophies, and politicians used it to gain a hearing for their parties.[24] The letter does not function in that way today; thus, a slavish imitation of Paul's transformation of the letter form will not work. In a society increasingly interested in the visual and performing arts both for entertainment and in a search for meaning, perhaps the church needs to be busy producing paintings, plays, television programs, movies, and operas deeply indebted to the gospel, which will prove both edifying to the church and attractive to outsiders.[25]

---

23. Bonhoeffer, *Gemeinsames Leben*, 30; cf. *Life Together*, 35.

24. See, for example, the letter of Publius Servillius Galba to the city of Miletus recorded in Josephus, *Antiquitates Judaicae* 14.244–46 (21), which demands that the city retract its anti-Jewish laws. See also Seneca the Younger's *Epistulae*, in which that author argues the case for Stoic philosophy. Cicero wrote some 931 extant letters, many of which he knew would be published and in which he often argued a political position.

25. For a discussion on the growing popularity of the visual and performing arts in North American culture and on the work of several Christians engaged in these endeavors, see

Probably the most valuable tool for conveying the gospel or preparing people to receive it, however, will always be the printed page. In fiction-writing, poetry, journalism, and historical narrative, perspective is crucial, and as long as the Christian perspective is presented in these media with skill and creativity, it will gain a hearing among people who appreciate good literature.[26] John Milton, Fyodor Dostoyevsky, and C. S. Lewis will probably continue to edify believers and challenge nonbelievers with the gospel for centuries because of their ability to use conventional means of communication in creative ways to advance the gospel. The church in every generation needs to ask who among its number will continue its legacy, and the legacy of Paul.

---

Russell Chandler, *Racing Toward* 2001: *The Forces Shaping America's Religious Future* (Grand Rapids: Zondervan, 1992), 114–25. In using such media to communicate the gospel, however, the church should heed the note of caution sounded in Jacques Ellul, *The Humiliation of the Word* (Grand Rapids: Eerdmans, 1985).

26. On the importance of perspective in the arts and of Christians expressing their perspective through the arts, see Leland Ryken, "The Creative Arts," *The Making of a Christian Mind*, ed. Arthur Holmes (Downers Grove, Ill.: InterVarsity Press, 1985), 105–31, esp. 127–28.

# Philippians 1:12–18a

I WANT YOU to know, brothers, that what has happened to me has really served to advance the gospel. ¹³As a result, it has become clear throughout the whole palace guard and to everyone else that I am in chains for Christ. ¹⁴Because of my chains, most of the brothers in the Lord have been encouraged to speak the word of God more courageously and fearlessly.

¹⁵It is true that some preach Christ out of envy and rivalry, but others out of goodwill. ¹⁶The latter do so in love, knowing that I am put here for the defense of the gospel. ¹⁷The former preach Christ out of selfish ambition, not sincerely, supposing that they can stir up trouble for me while I am in chains. ¹⁸But what does it matter? The important thing is that in every way, whether from false motives or true, Christ is preached. And because of this I rejoice.

**Original Meaning**

IN PAUL'S TIME when people wrote letters whose primary purpose was to inform a friend or family member of their circumstances, the transition from the initial greeting to the letter's crucial information was often made with the statement, "I want you to know that. . . ." The young soldier Theonas, writing to his mother from his military encampment, provides a good illustration of this kind of letter:

> Theonas to his mother and lady, Tetheus, very many greetings. *I want you to know that* the reason I have not sent you a letter for such a long time is because I am in camp and not on account of illness; so do not worry yourself (about me). I was very grieved when I learned that you had heard (about me), for I did not fall seriously ill. And I blame the one who told you. Do not trouble yourself to send me anything. I received the presents from Herakleides. My brother, Dionytas, brought the present to me and I received your letter.[1]

The papyrus sheet on which the letter was written is damaged, and as a result the letter breaks off at this point, but enough has been said to show that

---

1. John L. White, *Light From Ancient Letters* (Philadelphia: Fortress, 1986), 158.

Theonas was writing both to alleviate his mother's concern with news about himself and to thank her for a gift. Paul wrote Philippians, in part, for similar reasons, and he begins to address these matters in 1:12. Like Theonas, he opens this section of his letter with the customary phrase, "I want you to know that. . . ."

The Philippians were concerned about Paul's condition in prison, as their gift to him through Epaphroditus shows (2:25; 4:10, 14); thus an important reason for Paul's letter, which he sent back with Epaphroditus (2:24, 28–29), was to let them know his circumstances. He does this in 1:12–26. In the first part of this section (vv. 12–18a) he describes how his present circumstances have "served to advance (*eis prokopen*) the gospel" (v. 12), and in the second he reflects theologically on the two possibilities, death or release, that await him after his arraignment (vv. 18b–26). This second part of the section concludes with Paul's statement that he believes he will be released for the Philippians' "progress (*eis ten . . . prokopen*) and joy in the faith" (v. 25). The term *prokope* ("advancement, progress") appears in only one other passage in the New Testament (1 Tim. 4:15), and Paul's use of it at the beginning and end of this section probably has a deeper meaning than is readily apparent, especially in translation. He is showing his readers both the boundaries of the section itself and its primary concern—although at one level the purpose of the section is to inform the Philippians about Paul's circumstances, at a deeper level it shows how God is advancing "the gospel" and "the faith" through those circumstances.

The NIV appropriately divides the first part of this section, 1:12–18a, into two paragraphs: verses 12–14 and verses 15–18a. In the first of these Paul breaks the surprising news that the circumstances that surround him—his imprisonment and impending trial—have not hindered his mission of preaching the gospel among the Gentiles but actually advanced it (v. 12). He then describes two ways in which this has happened (vv. 13–14). In the second paragraph Paul adds a detail about his circumstances that the Philippians probably did not know—that some believers in the city where he is imprisoned are opposing him. Nevertheless, he contends, even in this circumstance the gospel is progressing.

**The Gospel Progresses Through Paul's Imprisonment (1:12–14).** Paul begins the body of his letter with the statement that "what has happened to me has really served to advance the gospel." The word "really" (*mallon*) can also be translated "rather" and shows that Paul felt that what he was writing would come as a surprise to the Philippians. They had heard he was in prison and were distressed by the news. Were the physical needs of their beloved apostle being met? Would he survive this encounter with the law? The journey of Epaphroditus to visit Paul and the gifts he brought were probably motivated by these concerns. The Philippians wanted to alleviate Paul's suffering and to learn how he was faring. Paul knows this, and so the first line of the letter's body breaks the surprising news that "what I have gone through has turned out to the furtherance of the gospel rather than otherwise" (Weymouth).

Such an unusual statement demands an explanation, and Paul provides it in verses 13–14. First, he says, the gospel has progressed through his circumstances because "it has become clear throughout the whole palace guard and to everyone else" that he is "in chains for Christ." The phrase "for Christ" is literally "in Christ" and probably not only carries the connotation of being in prison for Christ's sake but also of participating in Christ's suffering by being in prison. The purpose of Christ's suffering was the advancement of God's redemptive work, and so it was an evil through which God effected great good for humanity (Rom. 3:21–26; 5:12–21; 2 Cor. 5:21). Paul believes that his own suffering, since its origin lies in his efforts to fulfill the "ministry of reconciliation" to which God has called him (2 Cor. 5:18), has the same quality (Phil. 3:10; cf. 2 Cor. 1:5; 4:7–15; Col. 1:24–29). Thus his imprisonment is not simply a result of his Christian commitment but is the necessary means through which Paul fulfills his calling. It is not only "for Christ" but "in Christ" as well.[2]

The unusual character of his suffering, Paul says, "has become clear throughout the whole palace guard and to everyone else." The adjective "clear" (*phaneros*) probably means "known for what it really is" and expresses the notion that although Paul's imprisonment appeared at first glance to be truly miserable, on closer inspection its deeper significance came to light.[3] The gospel has been advanced because both among the palace guard and among others who live in the area, it has become widely known that Paul is no ordinary prisoner. These observers have considered the apostle's suffering, although on the surface as bitter as anyone else's, to be for the cause of Christ and therefore in the service of his ministry of reconciliation. Paul, it seems, has had the opportunity to explain to many around him the reasons for his imprisonment, and in explaining, to show them how "God was reconciling the world to himself in Christ, not counting men's sins against them" (2 Cor. 5:19). Paul may be in chains, but the gospel has gone forward unfettered.

---

2. See the comments of Silva, *Philippians*, 68; O'Brien, *Philippians*, 92.

3. The adjective "clear" (*phaneros*) appears in Matt. 12:16 and Mark 3:12 with this meaning. In both passages, Jesus gives instructions not "to make *known*" who he really is. See Walter Bauer, *A Greek-English Lexicon of the New Testament and Other Early Christian Literature*, 2d ed., trans., adapt., and rev. William F. Arndt, F. Wilbur Gingrich, Frederick W. Danker (Chicago: University of Chicago Press, 1979), 852.

Second, the gospel has been advanced rather than hindered by Paul's imprisonment because through it, according to verse 14, most of Paul's Christian brothers have taken courage to proclaim the word more boldly. The rendering of this verse in the NIV needs two refinements. (1) Paul normally uses the term "brothers" of fellow Christians (see especially Rom. 8:29), and so to speak of "brothers in the Lord" would be redundant. It is better to take "in the Lord" with the phrase "have been encouraged" and to translate the sentence, "most of the brothers have been encouraged in the Lord to speak the word more courageously and fearlessly."[4] (2) The words "of God" are not present in the earliest manuscript of Philippians, and since scribes tended to add words to their copies rather than omit them, Paul probably did not include "of God." This leaves the term "word" (*logos*) alone, but its meaning is no less clear. It refers here, as it often does in Paul's letters, to the gospel, "the *word* of life," as Paul will call it later (2:16; cf. 1 Cor. 1:18; 2:1; 14:36; 2 Cor. 4:2; 5:19).

If we put all this together, then Paul is saying that most of the Christians where he is have placed greater confidence in the Lord and have spoken the gospel more daringly and fearlessly than in the past because of his imprisonment. The reason why Paul's imprisonment has produced greater boldness in others is not that Paul, as one commentator has argued, is about to be released. The proclamation of the word by these brothers could hardly be described as fearless and daring were that the case.[5] Although we cannot know with certainty how Paul's imprisonment inspired his fellow believers to speak the word more boldly, it does not seem unlikely that they were challenged by his example to be as courageous as he was in communicating the gospel to others.

To summarize, Paul says in verses 12–14 that his imprisonment, surprisingly, has caused the gospel's progress. This progress can be measured by the way the gospel has swept through the ranks of those who live and work in the place of Paul's imprisonment and by the inspiration that Paul's circumstances have given to other believers to proclaim the gospel more boldly than ever before. The Philippians should not be concerned about Paul's circumstances, for they have proven to be a vehicle for his ministry of reconciliation.

---

4. See O'Brien, *Philippians*, 94–95; cf. Silva, *Philippians*, 68–69. On Paul's use of the term "brothers" (*adelphoi*), see J. Beutler, "ἀδελφός," *Exegetical Dictionary of the New Testament*, ed. Horst Balz and Gerhard Schneider, 3 vols. (Grand Rapids: Eerdmans, 1990–93), 1:30.

5. The view belongs to Collange, *Philippians*, 55. Against it, see the sage comments of O'Brien, *Philippians*, 95.

| Paul's Friends | Paul's Rivals |
|---|---|
| preach Christ | preach Christ |
| out of goodwill | out of envy and rivalry |
| in love | from selfishness, not sincerely |
| knowing | supposing |
| that I am put here for the defense of the gospel | that they can stir up trouble for me while I am in chains |
| in truth | in falsehood |

THE STRUCTURE OF 1:15–18a

**The Gospel Progresses Through the Preaching of Paul's Rivals (1:15–18a).** The troubled circumstances through which the gospel progresses, however, are not limited to Paul's imprisonment. In verses 15–18a Paul divides into two groups the Christians whose boldness to speak the gospel has been strengthened by his imprisonment. Paul's description of these groups is a carefully constructed piece of prose in which he balances the negative description of one group with a positive description of the other. One group is characterized by envy and rivalry, the other by goodwill. One group is motivated by love, knowing the truth about Paul's suffering; the other is motivated by selfish ambition, supposing they will make his suffering worse. The motives of one group are false, the other true. The carefully balanced structure of the paragraph prepares the reader for Paul's remarkable conclusion: Both preach Christ, and in this he rejoices. By balancing his description of the characteristics of the false group with that of the true, Paul rhetorically dismisses the effect of the false group on him. At the end of the day, after all their efforts to oppose Paul, they have only succeeded in doing the thing that matters most to him and the thing his friends also do: They have preached Christ.

Paul's focus is on this satisfying end result, not on the identity of either group. It is not surprising, then, that he gives only the most general information about the two groups and makes a positive identification of them impossible.[6] Those whose preaching is motivated "out of goodwill" and "love" for Paul understand the cruciform shape of Paul's ministry of reconciliation.

---

6. O'Brien, *Philippians*, 105.

They know that God has "put" Paul in prison "for the defense of the gospel" (v. 16), that, despite appearances, these circumstances are part of God's strategy for advancing the gospel just as, despite appearances, God used the supposedly foolish message of the cross to demonstrate his wisdom and power to save (1 Cor. 1:18–25).

Those whose preaching is motivated "out of envy and rivalry" are not, as some commentators have thought, Judaizing opponents similar to the troublemakers in Galatia.[7] Those opponents preached "a different gospel— which is really no gospel at all" (Gal. 1:6–7), a point of intense distress for Paul—but these "preach Christ," and Paul can therefore rejoice in their preaching (Phil. 1:15–16, 18a). Nor are these opponents, as others have thought, members of the group of "false apostles" who invaded Paul's Corinthian church (2 Cor. 11:13–14) and denigrated Paul for his powerless demeanor (10:10; 11:21, 30; 13:4).[8] It is difficult to see how this group could have been encouraged by Paul's imprisonment to preach the gospel more daringly and fearlessly (Phil. 1:14). These rivals to Paul instead seem to oppose the apostle for personal reasons and to have used Paul's imprisonment as an opportunity to advance their personal agendas.[9] Their preaching of the gospel, then, is motivated by "selfish ambition," and they imagine that as they freely seek to persuade people to join their party, Paul himself looks on with envy from his imprisonment (v. 17). Why any group would do this is impossible to determine from the distance of twenty centuries, but we know from early witnesses that Paul had a wide variety of detractors. Usually those groups preached a gospel that he considered heretical, but not always, and the rivals who stand behind this passage must belong to one of the more orthodox groups.[10]

To pay too much attention to the identity of the two groups whom Paul's imprisonment had emboldened to preach, however, is to miss the point of the passage. As the balanced rhetoric of the passage shows, Paul's concern is not with the groups themselves but with the advancement of the gospel. Ultimately the stance of either group toward Paul does not matter, for "the important thing is that in every way, whether from false motives or true, Christ is preached," and this gives Paul joy (v. 18a). Just as Paul's joy in verse 4 was connected with the participation of the Philippians in his own ministry

---

7. See, for example, Lightfoot, *Philippians*, 90.

8. See Robert Jewett, "Conflicting Movements in the Early Church as Reflected in Philippians," *Novum Testamentum* 12 (1970): 362–90.

9. O'Brien, *Philippians*, 104.

10. In addition to the references in Galatians and 2 Corinthians given above, see Acts 21:20–21 and Romans 3:8, as well as the comprehensive study by Gerd Luedemann, *Opposition to Paul in Jewish Christianity* (Minneapolis: Fortress, 1989).

so that the gospel might go forward, so here Paul rejoices that despite his imprisonment and the personal animosity of some fellow Christians, the gospel is being preached. Ultimately, for Paul, this is all that matters.

THE PRIMARY POINT. The theological principle lying at the foundation of this passage and supplying the motivation for virtually everything Paul says in it is that human circumstances lie in God's hands and that God uses them to advance the gospel. This principle emerges from the passage with special clarity in two ways. First, the Philippians would have expected this section of the letter to give them news about how Paul was doing personally. Epaphroditus had carried a gift intended to alleviate some of Paul's misery in prison (4:10–20), and when the Philippians saw a papyrus package in Epaphroditus' hand on his return, they would have expected it to contain Paul's own description of his condition. This expectation would only have been heightened when Paul passed from the greeting and prayer section of the letter to its body with the customary words, "Now I want you to know ... that. ... ."

What follows, however, supplies little information about Paul's personal condition. The Philippians would have to ask Epaphroditus whether Paul was sick or well, cold at night or comfortable, and alone or with other prisoners, and whether he was being treated with kindness by his guards. Instead of reporting how he was doing, Paul talks about how the gospel is doing. As Karl Barth says:

> He just would not be an apostle if he could speak objectively about his own situation in abstraction from the course of the Gospel, to which he has sacrificed his subjectivity and therewith also all objective interest in his person. To the question how it is with *him* the apostle *must* react with information as to how it is with the Gospel.[11]

Second, Paul's response to the fellow believers who have tried to "stir up trouble for [him]" shows vividly that he has placed his own circumstances under the authority of God and is convinced that God is using them to accomplish his purposes. Here he puts into practice the advice he had given to others. "Why not rather be wronged? Why not rather be cheated?" he had said to the Corinthian believers when he heard that some were taking others before pagan judges to try to force them to redress various injustices (1 Cor. 6:7). His point was that it was more important for the church to be

---

11. Barth, *Philippians*, 26.

the church than for its members to receive the personal satisfaction of winning lawsuits against fellow believers. Now Paul himself faces people who have wronged him, and, consistent with his advice to the Corinthians, his response is to subordinate his personal agenda to God's. Shrugging off their animosity, he rejoices that they preach Christ (cf. 1 Cor. 4:13a).

This is the primary theological freight that we should move from the original context of this passage into our own context. When difficult, even life-threatening, circumstances face us, we should take Paul as our example and look for how God might be working in such circumstances to advance the gospel either in our lives or in the lives of others. When fellow Christians tighten the shackles on our wrists rather than seek to alleviate our pain, and when they take advantage of our difficult circumstances to promote their own goals, we should remember Paul's perspective. What matters most is whether or not the gospel is going forward. If it is, then we should rejoice.

Much in the culture of modern technologically based societies makes this primary point more difficult for today's Christian to swallow than it was for the Philippians. In the ancient Hellenistic world in which Paul worked and wrote, atheism and materialism in the modern senses of those terms were virtually nonexistent. Everyone believed in the existence of the gods, and only an elite few held anything comparable to the modern notion that God, if he existed, was irrelevant to human affairs.[12] But that notion is widespread in technologically advanced cultures today. In contemporary cultures, life's goals are often articulated in strictly materialistic or, at best, humanistic terms. "The one who dies with the most toys wins" announces the bumper of a van parked outside a child-care center in my suburban neighborhood. Even those who would articulate their life's goals in the more noble terms of alleviating human suffering or creating a more just society often do so in strictly human terms with no reference to God.[13]

Paul, then, could assume that his Philippian readers were familiar with the notion of God's transcendence, but our culture pushes us to deny or forget this. What can we do to counteract its influence? A useful antidote is to remind ourselves frequently of evidence from the past that God has been at work in the church. Christians should be familiar with the outlines of church

---

12. Followers of the philosopher Epicurus believed that the movements of "atoms," the elemental building blocks of the universe, determined the course of all events. Although Epicureans believed in the gods, they thought that the gods were unable to influence the material world. On ancient religion generally during the period of Paul, see Helmut Koester, *Introduction to the New Testament*, vol. 1, *History, Culture, and Religion of the Hellenistic Age* (Philadelphia/Berlin: Fortress/Walter de Gruyter, 1982), 141–204.

13. See especially Stephen L. Carter, *The Culture of Disbelief: How American Law and Politics Trivialize Religious Devotion* (New York: Basic Books, 1993).

history from its beginnings to the present day and should make the accounts of God's mighty acts among his people in the Bible, the classic church historians, and well-documented modern testimonies frequent reading.[14] Thus when God's purposes seem far from our own suffering, we can remind ourselves through the example of others that he is nevertheless at work.

**Three Implications.** Three subsidiary points of this passage reverberate from this primary point. First, the passage demonstrates indirectly the value of finding believers who can serve as examples of how to grapple with suffering in the way a Christian should. Paul's imprisonment had given the believers around him greater confidence in the Lord, spurring them to proclaim the gospel more boldly than they had in the past. Although this passage contains no direct command to this effect, Paul elsewhere in the letter encourages the Philippians to compare their own hardship with his (1:30; cf. 2 Tim. 2:3) and tells them to imitate his example (Phil. 3:17; 4:9). It seems likely that part of his purpose in recording these words for the Philippians is to provide them with an example for how they should think about their own hardships (1:28–30). That kind of imitation has value: By seeing Paul's willingness to make the advancement of the gospel the most important aspect of his life, others have been challenged to preach the gospel with daring and fearlessness, and the Philippians hear a challenge to do the same.

To be sure, we too should accept the challenge of Paul's own courage. This passage shows the value in taking anyone as an example who has followed in Paul's footsteps (cf. 3:17). In bringing the passage out of Paul's time and into our own, then, it seems appropriate to find modern analogies to Paul's courageous devotion to the gospel under adversity and to his perspective on this adversity as a means for the advancement of the gospel.

Second, the passage demonstrates an important principle of Pauline theology, one often missed by modern Christians, particularly in the affluent West. God works not merely in spite of but *through* adverse circumstances. He chose the foolishness of the cross to accomplish his redemptive purposes (1 Cor. 1:18), he chose the foolish things of this world to redeem (1:27), and he chose an apostle whose physical and emotional condition could be compared with "jars of clay" to bear the message of redemption (2 Cor. 4:7–12; cf. 1 Cor. 4:8–13; 2 Cor. 11:21–33). God chose to work through these means in order to demonstrate that the advancement of the gospel was God's doing rather than a matter of human ingenuity (1 Cor. 1:29; 2 Cor. 4:7).

---

14. The most thorough attempts to banish God from society seem to occur in Communist countries. For a carefully documented account of God's work among believers despite such attempts, see Barbara von der Heydt, *Candles Behind the Wall: Heroes of the Peaceful Revolution That Shattered Communism* (Grand Rapids: Eerdmans, 1993).

Thus Paul is not surprised that God has turned his imprisonment and the jealousy of his rivals into means for the advancement of the gospel. This is God's typical way of working.

As we take Philippians 1:12–18a out of the Philippians' hands and put it in the modern church, we should be careful to preserve Paul's perspective on the way God works. We are not likely to find the greatest advances of the gospel within the circles of prestige, power, and wealth so pervasive in the West. We should expect instead that the gospel will make the greatest strides in places where no doubt exists that God is the agent of the work.

Third, this passage shows that when our joy is connected to the advancement of the gospel rather than to our physical condition or to the responses of other people to us, it remains firm, even when these circumstances stand against us. Paul could be joyful not only when those filled with goodwill and love toward him preached Christ, but also when the messengers of the gospel viewed themselves as his enemies and rivals. The fellowship of the modern church lies in tatters because of rivalry over turf, competition for money and influence, and petty theological disagreements. As we move from Paul's world into ours, then, we need to apply the healing salve of Paul's perspective to the divisions among Christians that touch our lives.

**A Few Red Herrings.** This passage is, as we have seen, rich in theological nourishment, but its message can be seriously contaminated by the temptation it presents to stray from the path it marks out. Some popular expositions of the passage, for example, fill in the historical gaps that the passage leaves with elaborate reconstructions of Paul's prison conditions. It is held to be certain that he is in Rome and often that this is his final imprisonment before death. Thus one expositor places him "at the end of a strenuous career, confined to prison, awaiting his probable execution, with only a faint hope of release."[15] Another builds on the thesis that Paul's imprisonment is the one recorded in Acts 28, the further thesis that Paul was able to spread the gospel throughout the praetorian guard by means of the soldiers who took turns guarding him.[16]

All such theories need to be drenched with a cold bucketful of exegetical reality. No one knows where Paul was imprisoned when he wrote Philippians, but even if it were certain that he was in Rome, it is unlikely that this imprisonment was his last.[17] Second Timothy also refers to a Roman impris-

---

15. Robert R. Wicks, "The Epistle to the Philippians," *The Interpreter's Bible*, ed. George A. Buttrick, 12 vols. (New York: Abingdon, 1952–57), 11:28.

16. Barclay, *The Letters to the Philippians, Colossians, and Thessalonians*, 22.

17. The NIV's phrase "palace guard" is better rendered simply "praetorian guard" (*to praitorio*) and refers to the Emperor's bodyguards wherever they might be quartered. See Lightfoot, *Philippians*, 88, 99–104.

onment, and, unless we think that that letter is a forgery, it seems unwise to assume that Philippians is Paul's final letter and the imprisonment to which he refers his final imprisonment. To claim that the soldiers who guarded Paul opened the door for the gospel's proclamation among the praetorian guard, moreover, simply goes beyond the evidence of anything in Scripture. Acts does say that Paul stayed by himself in Rome with a soldier guarding him (Acts 28:16), and we know that guards were usually manacled to prisoners under house arrest, but the text contains no hint that these guards were eager to hear the gospel.[18] Perhaps they were, and perhaps they told their comrades of it; but since this is only a guess, it forms a shaky foundation on which to construct an interpretation of the passage.

There is no need, in any case, to go beyond the text to make the point that Paul's circumstances were bleak but that God enabled Paul to use his ingenuity to communicate the gospel through these bleak circumstances. We have no reason to think that ancient imprisonment of any sort and in any location was comfortable and pleasant. Whatever the details of Paul's contact with the praetorian guard, it is simply remarkable that they all understood that Paul was in chains for proclaiming that God had turned the crucifixion of the Jewish Messiah into good news. God had transformed Paul's dismal circumstances into a means for the powerful advancement of the gospel. That is Paul's primary point, and in transporting this passage from Paul's world into our own, we should avoid chasing other fish.

A more serious detour from the theological path marked out by this passage would be to misunderstand Paul's comments in verses 15–18a to mean that the motives of the preacher of the gospel are unimportant, that as long as the gospel is preached, good is being accomplished, and that we should not worry much about who does the preaching or why they do it. That the motives and style of those who proclaim the gospel are not a matter of indifference to Paul is clear from his other letters. In 1 Thessalonians 2:1–12 Paul explains at length that his own motives in preaching to the Thessalonians were pure, not motivated by flattery or greed. In Thessalonica, Corinth, and probably Ephesus, Paul worked with his hands. Part of the reason for this was probably to provide himself with a forum for evangelism, but another reason was so that he might not be dependent for support upon gifts from those to whom he ministered, thereby opening the door to rumor and scandal about his motives for preaching the gospel (1 Cor. 9:12b; 2 Cor. 11:7–9;

---

18. On the custom of chaining prisoners who were under light custody to their guards, see Brian Rapske, *Paul in Roman Custody* (Grand Rapids/Carlisle, Eng.: Eerdmans/Paternoster, 1994), 31.

1 Thess. 1:5, 9).[19] Paul's quarrel with the "false apostles" of 2 Corinthians 10–13, moreover, focused not so much on the content of their gospel as on their personal demeanor and the way in which they proclaimed their message. They compared themselves to others (2 Cor. 10:12–18), especially to Paul, in a boastful spirit, claiming that they bested him in their speaking ability (11:6), their Jewish heritage (11:22), and their ability to work astonishing feats (12:12). And they used highhanded tactics to gain a following and keep it loyal (11:20). That motives in proclaiming the gospel were important to Paul, therefore, is clear.

What, then, could Paul mean when in Philippians he dismisses the preaching of his rivals with the comment, "But what does it matter? The important thing is that in every way, whether from false motives or true, Christ is preached" (1:18a)? The answer to this puzzle lies in the difference in the circumstances that Paul confronts in Philippians and in the other letters where he discusses the importance of motives in preaching. In the other letters Paul was speaking directly to the people who might be convinced that his motives were impure or who had fallen under the spell of those whose motives were impure. This letter, on the other hand, is addressed neither to Paul's rivals nor to people who have fallen under their influence.

Moreover, Paul is in prison and therefore powerless to stop the activity of his rivals or even to communicate with them about it. Laying out the case against his opponents' tactics would hardly do the Philippians any good and would put their focus back on Paul and his circumstances rather than on the gospel, where he wanted it. Thus Paul's focus remains on God's ability to make people with perverse motives serve his ends. The insincere preaching of these rivals stands parallel to Paul's imprisonment: Both are evil, but God is able to use them for his redemptive purposes. There is no lightheartedness here about the tactics of Paul's rivals, only joy that, as Paul says in another context, "where sin increased, grace increased all the more" (Rom. 5:20).

Perhaps the most harmful detour of all in interpreting this passage, however, would be to misconstrue Paul's approach in it to suffering. This passage contains no implicit claim that suffering is good, that God is its author, that the mysterious paradoxes that surround it have suddenly been solved, or that Christians should plaster smiles on their faces when they experience it and pretend that hardship is a joyful experience. When Paul says that his rivals have "raised up affliction for me in my imprisonment" (v. 17), he acknowl-

---

19. On the likelihood that Paul used the workplace to spread the gospel, see Abraham J. Malherbe, *Paul and the Thessalonians: The Philosophic Tradition of Pastoral Care* (Philadelphia: Fortress, 1987), 17–20.

edges that his imprisonment is an affliction and that his opponents have made it worse. His joy, moreover, is not because of the affliction or even in spite of it but because Christ is being preached. The suffering is real, and nothing Paul says implies that in itself it is good. Instead, in this passage God triumphs over suffering by using it as a tool to accomplish his goals.

There is no easy solution in this passage to the problem of suffering and no denial of its severity. The passage shows God at work in preventing pain from prevailing, however, and it offers hope that God will redeem the suffering that his people experience in order to bring eternal good out of it.[20]

THOSE OF US who constitute the church in Western democracies need to be reminded that the God of the Bible typically works not through the channels of economic and political power that are so accessible to us, but through the weakness and suffering that the world tells us to avoid at all costs. The oppression of the church under Marxist regimes during the past half century has provided a treasury of examples of how God's purpose triumphs despite all that human ingenuity can do to frustrate it and of how God even uses the suffering of the church to advance the gospel. Despite the imprisonment, torture, and execution of Christians in Eastern Europe during the era of the Cold War, and despite an all-out effort to teach the young that religion was the retreat of fools, by the 1980s most Marxist and Communist regimes recognized that their policies had failed. Church attendance had certainly declined during their years in power, but it had also declined in the West, and polls taken by these repressive governments consistently revealed that significant numbers of old and young alike continued to believe in God, to attend worship, to be married in the church, and to seek baptism for their children. Toward the end of their power, many of these governments simply gave up most of their repressive measures: The church had triumphed.[21]

Cuba provides an instructive case study. Five years after the collapse of the Berlin Wall, theologian Thomas Oden visited congregations in the Methodist Church of Cuba and discovered that despite thirty-five years of oppression and miserable economic conditions, the Methodists had grown

---

20. See the clear and biblically based study of this problem in Carson, *How Long, O Lord? Reflections on Suffering and Evil*, esp. 69–91.

21. See Owen Chadwick, *The Christian Church in the Cold War* (London: Allen Lane/Penguin, 1992), 73–108. Moving stories of courageous Christians whose faith led them to play a role in toppling their repressive governments appear in von der Heydt, *Candles Behind the Wall*.

from a low of 6,000 to over 50,000 members. Nothing short of a spiritual revolution reminiscent of Acts 2, said Oden, had taken place.[22] Much of this spiritual and numerical growth, moreover, could be attributed to people, both young and old, who had grown weary of the official atheist party line and turned to the church to find a more satisfying answer to the meaning of life. During the previous four decades, the best efforts of Fidel Castro's tyrannical regime had not succeeded in stamping out the church. Despite the personal cost of everything from a chance at a university education to long prison terms, Christians had remained faithful and the church had grown.

After reading Oden's report, it is hard not to wonder if the explosion of interest in the gospel after Fidel Castro relented and allowed the church a measure of freedom was in part due to the admiration that people felt for the church's constancy over many years. However that may be, there can be no doubt that the grim economic times that plagued Cuba after the collapse of the Soviet Union opened doors of opportunity for the gospel. One long-time Cuban believer made these observations:

> The search for meaning is just as crucial as the search for bread. While the economy around us is falling apart, Christians are living in a state of special grace. It is not difficult for Cubans to see the difference between the people of God and those who are desperately trying to live without faith. Ordinary Cubans are becoming aware of the church as a life-saving community of hope.[23]

God continues to advance the gospel through the weakness and suffering of his people today. This does not make that suffering good, of course, and we should work to alleviate the suffering of our Christian brothers and sisters everywhere, but it illustrates that beautifully appointed buildings, large parking lots, and programs designed to attract demanding church shoppers do not guarantee that God is at work. God typically works through means the world rejects.

The church at the turn of the twentieth century also needs to remember the encouragement that Christians who have shown courage amid difficult circumstances can provide to other believers. We do well to honor the recent heroes of the faith, not merely out of gratitude to God for their faithfulness, but in order to instruct others on how to be faithful during periods of personal and general crisis. The stories of heroic Christians who in the name of the gospel defied the twisted notions of genetic and racial purity of the Nazis during the 1930s and 1940s can inspire Christians to remain faithful to the

---

22. "The Church Castro Couldn't Kill," *Christianity Today* (April 25, 1994), 20.
23. Ibid., 21.

biblical perspective on the value of all human life today. Martin Niemöller was imprisoned, Karl Barth exiled, and Dietrich Bonhoeffer executed because of their resistance in the name of the gospel to Nazi-imposed policies.[24]

The church today needs to follow the example of these courageous Christians in its efforts to work for public policies that show mercy to the poor, encourage peace, and spare the lives of the unborn. Thankfully, because Christians in North America and most of the West live under democracies rather than under tyrannical governments, we can work effectively for these goals through vigorous public debate without having to go to prison. Nevertheless, the courage of these recent spiritual forebears should inspire the church to remain firm in its theological commitments, no matter how unpopular they become, and to be willing to sacrifice everything for what the gospel proclaims to be right.

The recent history of Christian missions also provides a treasury of examples of courage that inspire Christian commitment to labor sacrificially in the harvest fields of the world. The story of Jim, Elisabeth, and Valerie Elliot and their labor among the Quichua and Auca ethnic groups of Ecuador has become a monumental example of faithfulness among evangelical Christians to the gospel's missionary mandate.[25] And rightfully so. After Jim and four other missionaries lost their lives trying to establish contact with the Aucas, Elisabeth herself established contact with the tribe and went with her young daughter, Valerie, to live among them so that she might learn their language, reduce it to writing, and explain the gospel to them. Despite the emotional and physical hardship of life in the jungle among people whose language and culture neither she nor any other outsider understood, Elisabeth pressed forward in obedience and accomplished the work that God had given her to do. In her commitment to communicate the gospel in the face of loss and hardship, Elisabeth Elliot acted in the spirit of the imprisoned Paul.

Modern believers in the relative comfort of established churches in the West can profit spiritually from a study of such people as they attempt to apply the theological principles of Philippians 1:14 to themselves. Whatever our own "chains" might be, we can look for ways in which the gospel might be advanced through them. Ridicule for our commitment to the gospel from family members or coworkers, a feeling of alienation from the wider society because of its thoroughly secular orientation, or even lack of understanding from a church that has itself become too thoroughly accommo-

---

24. Among the many studies of these events, see especially Victoria Barnett, *For the Soul of the People: Protestant Protest Against Hitler* (New York: Oxford University Press, 1992).

25. See Elisabeth Elliot, *Through Gates of Splendor* (Old Tappan, N. J.: Fleming H. Revell, 1956); idem, *Shadow of the Almighty* (Grand Rapids: Zondervan, 1958); and idem, *The Savage My Kinsman* (New York/London: Harper & Brothers/Hodder & Stoughton, 1961).

dated to its culture are all ways in which forces beyond the believer's control can shackle the believer. In such situations our response, like Paul's and so many courageous Christians after him, should not be a gloomy focus on the pain of the circumstances themselves, but a joyful attempt to discover ways of communicating the gospel in the midst of difficulty.

This passage, finally, teaches the modern church something about the nature of joy. It is not the self-satisfied delight that everything is going our way, but the settled peace that arises from making the gospel the focus of life and from understanding that God is able to advance the gospel under the most difficult circumstances. Paul was at peace with his circumstances despite his unjust imprisonment and the presence of fellow believers who took advantage of his suffering to advance their own selfish ambitions. The reason for this remarkable attitude was that the advancement of the gospel was his primary goal in life. As a result, if his own adversity was the occasion through which the gospel could gain a wider hearing, then Paul could face that adversity with equanimity. If, in our own circumstances, we lack this kind of joy, then perhaps we should search our souls to be sure that our happiness is not more firmly connected to our physical and emotional comfort than to the goals of the gospel.

Specifically, this passage urges the modern church to recognize that God can sometimes use people whose Christian commitment is self-serving and insincere to advance the cause of the gospel. This does not mean approving of their motives or their methods, but it does mean not despairing that the insincere proclamation of the gospel will hopelessly confuse those who hear, damage the work of legitimate Christian ministers beyond repair, or somehow taint the faith of people who sincerely believe as the result of an unworthy witness. The clear teaching of Paul's statement in Philippians 1:18a is that God is able to prosper the preaching even of the insincere and to use it to advance the gospel.

The Donatist controversy in the fourth- and fifth-century church is instructive on this point. In the terrible persecutions under the Roman Emperor Diocletian (A.D. 245–313), the emperor's soldiers invaded many churches and demanded that the priests hand over any copies of the Scriptures so that they could be burned. Many refused to do so and paid with their lives, but some relented out of fear and stood by while the Scriptures were consigned to the flames. After the persecution subsided, any priest who had spared his life in this way was labeled a *traditor* and was forced out of the ranks of the clergy. The Donatists believed that any clergyman ordained by a *traditor* between the time of his unfaithfulness and the canceling of his ordination was somehow affected by that unfaithfulness and could not be considered a duly consecrated priest. The majority believed, however, that God himself made the sacraments valid, not the priest who officiated over them, and that no human unfaithfulness could thwart God's designs for good.

Philippians 1:18a shows that the majority were right. God can use unscrupulous televangelists, money-grubbing radio preachers, and sophisticated but unbelieving clergy to communicate his truth. The work is God's, and when we find ourselves surrounded by unfaithful people of the church who do not respond to our pleas that they mend their ways, our joy will remain intact if we remember that God is in control and that wherever Christ is preached, God can advance the gospel.

# Philippians 1:18b–26

I WILL CONTINUE to rejoice, [19]for I know that through your prayers and the help given by the Spirit of Jesus Christ, what has happened to me will turn out for my deliverance. [20]I eagerly expect and hope that I will in no way be ashamed, but will have sufficient courage so that now as always Christ will be exalted in my body, whether by life or by death. [21]For to me, to live is Christ and to die is gain. [22]If I am to go on living in the body, this will mean fruitful labor for me. Yet what shall I choose? I do not know! [23]I am torn between the two: I desire to depart and be with Christ, which is better by far; [24]but it is more necessary for you that I remain in the body. [25]Convinced of this, I know that I will remain, and I will continue with all of you for your progress and joy in the faith, [26]so that through my being with you again your joy in Christ Jesus will overflow on account of me.

PAUL'S REPORT ON his own circumstances continues in verses 18b–26 by turning to the future. He not only rejoices to see God at work in his present circumstances to advance the gospel, but he "will continue to rejoice" as God's faithfulness perseveres into whatever circumstances await him. The ultimate outcome of Paul's imprisonment is at one level not wholly certain. Paul's twofold "I know" in verses 19 and 25 does not reveal that he is certain about his future. It is spoken in faith and describes what he thinks will happen, but verses 20b–24 show that he is not certain about the outcome of his impending trial.[1]

At another level, however, his future circumstances are entirely certain, since he knows that "whether by life or by death" (v. 20) Christ will be exalted. This long paragraph eloquently states Paul's confidence in that reality and, at its conclusion, skillfully reintroduces the topic of the advancement of the gospel (v. 25), though this time focusing on the Philippians rather than on Paul. This serves as a transition from the first major segment of the letter's body, in which Paul's circumstances have been the chief topic, to the second, which focuses on the Philippians.

---

1. See the comments of Bruce, *Philippians*, 28.

Although the paragraph is a tight unit, analysis of it will be less cumbersome if we divide it into two parts. In the first part (vv. 18b–20) Paul states his conviction that whatever the future holds for him, he will not be deprived of his joy, because Christ will be exalted in him; in the second (vv. 21–26) Paul provides the reason for this unusual perspective and states what he believes the outcome of his circumstances will be. His opinion about the outcome of his trial brings him to the progress of the faith among the Philippians, and that subject will occupy most of the rest of the letter.

**Christ Exalted Through Life or Death (1:18b–20).** Paul concluded his discussion of his present circumstances in verses 12–18a with the comment that although he had undergone the hardship of opposition from Christian brothers, at least these rival preachers were proclaiming Christ, "and because of this I rejoice." He introduces the future emphasis of this new section by projecting his joy into the future with the statement, "Yes, and I will continue to rejoice." He then gives the reason for his certainty that his joy will continue: All that has happened to him, he says, will result in his "deliverance" (*soteria*).

The word *soteria* is commonly used in the New Testament, and especially in Paul's letters, to mean "salvation" in the ultimate sense of rescue from God's wrath on the final day. This is clearly its meaning only a few sentences later in 1:28, where Paul contrasts the Philippians' future salvation with the destruction that awaits their persecutors. It is probably also the meaning Paul intends here, since he equates the "deliverance" of verse 20 with Christ's being exalted in his body and says that this exaltation can happen either "by life or by death."[2] Even Paul's death, in other words, can result in his "deliverance," because the deliverance of which he speaks is unrelated to his physical release from the chains that bind him. It is instead his eschatological "salvation."[3]

In what follows, Paul qualifies this statement in two ways. First, he claims that the events described in 1:12–18a "will turn out" for his salvation through the Philippians' prayers and through the supply of the Spirit of Jesus Christ. Just as Paul has prayed that the Philippians would steadily mature in their

---

2. See the thorough discussion of the meaning of *soteria* in this verse by Silva, *Philippians*, 76–79.

3. Paul's words "this will turn out for my deliverance" echo exactly the Greek rendering of Job 13:16. There Job claims that despite the accusations of his detractors, he is innocent and therefore certain that when he stands before God's tribunal, he will be acquitted. Paul's focus too is not on acquittal before his earthly accusers, but before God on the final day. See the insightful discussion of Paul's use of this passage in Gordon D. Fee, *God's Empowering Presence: The Holy Spirit in the Letters of Paul* (Peabody, Mass.: Hendrickson, 1994), 737–38.

faith so that they might be able to discern what is best and arrive at the final day pure and blameless (1:9–11), so Paul believes that God will use the Philippians' prayers for him while he is in captivity to help him persevere with "sufficient courage" and ultimately to stand before God as one of his redeemed people.

The "Spirit of Jesus Christ" is the divine means through which this help will come. The word "help" (*epichoregia*) in the NIV rendering of verse 19 can also mean "supply" and is closely related to a Greek verb that means to "furnish, provide, give, grant," and, less frequently, "support."[4] Paul used this verb in Galatians 3:5 to speak of God as the one who has "given" his Spirit to the Galatians. It seems likely, then, that here in Philippians 1:19 the word does not mean the help that the Spirit gives to Paul but the Spirit himself, whom God supplies to Paul. This supply of the Spirit, moreover, is more closely tied to the prayers of the Philippians than the NIV implies. In the Greek text, one definite article stands in front of both "prayers" and "supply" so that the phrase runs, literally, "through the prayer [the term is singular in Greek] of you and supply of the Spirit of Jesus Christ." Paul is suggesting that the presence of the Spirit will be supplied to Paul through the prayers of the Philippians. In some mysterious way, those prayers are linked with God's furnishing of the Spirit to him, and together they provide the help he needs to face the Roman tribunal with courage.[5]

Second, Paul qualifies his statement of confidence that he will ultimately experience salvation by saying that his salvation will occur according to his expectation that he will endure successfully the trials that lie ahead of him (v. 20). The way in which Paul phrases this second qualification has created intense debate among commentators. (1) The word the NIV translates "eagerly expect" (*apokaradokia*) appears only here and in Romans 8:19 in the whole extant corpus of Greek literature prior to Paul, and many scholars believe that Paul coined it. What then does it mean? (2) The rest of the verse ("and [I] hope that I will in no way be ashamed, but will have sufficient courage") has sometimes been understood to mean that Paul hoped he would not be ashamed of his behavior during his future appearance before a Roman court of justice. Is this Paul's concern?

---

4. See Walter Bauer, *A Greek-English Lexicon of the New Testament and Other Early Christian Literature*, 2d ed., trans., adapt., and rev. William F. Arndt, F. Wilbur Gingrich, Frederick W. Danker (Chicago: University of Chicago Press, 1979), 305.

5. For the understanding of the passage presented here, which runs counter to that of most commentators, see Fee, *God's Empowering Presence*, 740–743, and Henry Barclay Swete, *The Holy Spirit in the New Testament* (London: Macmillan, 1909), 227–28. Cf. Witherington, *Friendship and Finances in Philippi*, 46.

The answers to these two questions are related to each other. The noun "eager expectation" (*apokaradokia*) is unusually strong, as Paul's use of it in Romans 8:19 shows. There it describes creation's "eager expectation" for ultimate salvation that it will one day be "liberated from its bondage to decay and brought into the glorious freedom of the children of God" (Rom. 8:21). The use of the verbal form of the word (*apokaradokeo*) in ancient Greek confirms the intensity of this meaning. Josephus, the Jewish historian and younger contemporary of Paul (b. A.D. 37/38), for example, uses the verb to describe how in the moments before the Roman armies attacked the Galilean city of Jotapata, which he was assigned to defend, he "breathlessly awaited (*akpekaradokei*) the hail of arrows."[6] The word, then, refers to the intense expectation of something that is sure to happen. It seems unlikely, therefore, that Paul would use this word to refer merely to the hope that he will conduct himself properly during his impending court appearance. Instead, he sees the upcoming test in court as a divinely appointed opportunity to defend the gospel (Phil. 1:16) on his way to the final salvation he eagerly awaits.

In the contest that awaits him before that final vindication, he says, he will not "be ashamed" (*aischyno*), but Christ will "be exalted" (*megalyno*) in his body. Here Paul uses the language of the Greek rendering of the Psalms. They affirm that "no one whose hope is in [the Lord] will ever be put to shame [*kataischyno*], but they will be put to shame [*aischyno*] who are treacherous without excuse" (Ps. 25:3). The Psalms often also speak of exalting (*megalyno*) the Lord (Pss. 34:3; 35:27; 39:16; 57:11; 69:30; 70:4; 92:5; 104:1, 24; 126:2–3). Paul's intention, then, is not to deny that he or anyone else will be ashamed of *his* conduct in the test awaiting him, but that *God* will allow him to be put to shame before the forces of evil ranged against him.[7] He will ultimately triumph over evil because his hope is in the Lord.

His victory, however, is not dependent on acquittal at the trial. Instead, he will not be ashamed, and Christ will be exalted in him "whether by life or by death." Even if his appearance before a Roman tribunal results in condemnation and death at the hands of an executioner, Paul contends that he will not have been put to shame by his enemies (cf. Ps. 25:2) and that the Lord will be exalted. His physical circumstances are out of his hands, and it may look perhaps to some as if they are out of God's as well, but the apostle knows that despite appearances God is still sovereign over the affairs of his life and that God will see him safely through to ultimate, eternal vindication.

---

6. Josephus, *Bellum Judaicum* 3.264 (3.7.26). The translation belongs to the Loeb Classical Library edition of Josephus' works.

7. Cf. O'Brien, *Philippians*, 114; Fee, *God's Empowering Presence*, 738 n. 21.

**Death a Gain, Life a Fruitful Labor** (1:21–26). Paul explains more fully the reason for this remarkable indifference to his physical fate in the second part of the passage. Whether he lives or dies, Paul says, he will be with Christ, although he believes that he will live since he is convinced that the Philippians need his guidance in order to progress in the faith.

Paul explains this understanding of his destiny through a series of contrasts between death and life and the results of each. Thus life is Christ, but death is gain. Living in the flesh means fruitful labor, but death is better by far since it is a departure to be with Christ. Life, however, is more necessary for the Philippians (vv. 21–24). Each result is so desirable that Paul finds himself on the horns of a dilemma about which to "choose" (vv. 22–23). He finally decides that although dying and being with Christ would be "better by far" (v. 23), the Philippians' "progress and joy in the faith" would be better served by his continued work among them; therefore, that becomes his "choice" (v. 25).

The most important statement in this series of contrasts is the first: To Paul, life means Christ (v. 21a). Statements like this are common in Paul's letters. Everything that might have usurped the place of Christ in Paul's life he has considered rubbish that he might gain Christ (3:8). Paul has been buried together with Christ so that just as Christ was raised, Paul might live a new life (Rom. 6:4; cf. 6:8, 11; 14:7–9; 2 Cor. 5:14–15; 1 Thess. 5:10). He has been crucified with Christ so that Christ lives in him (Gal. 2:20). His life *is* Christ (Col. 3:4).[8] Such statements can only mean that Paul's relationship with Christ was so close that his entire existence derived its meaning from his Lord.

Paul's account of his circumstances prior to verse 21 and his perspective on the future after this verse both demonstrate what his close relationship with Christ means in practical terms. Prior to verse 21, even imprisonment by the unbelieving authorities and ill will from fellow believers could not dampen the joyful character of Paul's life, for God was advancing the gospel of Jesus Christ through these hardships (1:12–18a). After verse 21, Paul looks ahead and comments that death is gain, for it will mean the closest possible union with Christ.[9] In the same way, continued life is fruitful labor because

---

8. Many ancient copies of Colossians read "Christ, who is *your* life" at Col. 3:4 (see the NIV) instead of "Christ, who is *our* life." In either case, the point of the verse is that Christ is the believer's life, and Paul would surely include himself in this description.

9. The term Paul uses for "depart" (*analuo*) is a mild word that could be used of a ship weighing anchor or of a group of soldiers breaking camp. Paul uses it, much as he uses the euphemistic term "those who fall asleep" (*hoi koimomenoi*) in 1 Thess. 4:13, to indicate that for believers death is not the final and terrible thing that it is for "the rest of men, who have no hope" (cf. 2 Tim. 4:6). On the use of the term *analuo* outside the Bible see Henry George

it means that Paul will be able both to preach the gospel (1:7) and strengthen the Philippians' faith (1:25).[10] Such a perspective on the hardships of the present and the possibilities of the future is possible for Paul only because Christ lives within him and gives him strength (4:13).

The thrust of 1:18b–26, then, is clear, but the way Paul expresses himself poses a problem. Why does the apostle seem to entertain the real possibility that his imprisonment will end in execution in verses 20b–23, but then in verses 24–26 appears to be convinced that he will remain for the benefit of the Philippians' spiritual advancement? Some commentators have suggested that Paul underwent a change between the composition of these two units—that he perhaps received a divine revelation about his fate, or that a judge handed down a favorable verdict, or that Paul thought more deeply about God's purposes for him.[11]

When Paul claims to "know" that he will remain in the flesh in verse 25, however, he does not shut out the possibility that he will be executed. Indeed, the possibility of his martyrdom surfaces again in 2:17. Instead, Paul states his own difficult decision, based on his confidence that remaining in the body would be better for the Philippians, to choose life. The ultimate choice of life or death throughout the passage, as Paul surely knows, lies with God. Paul speaks here, therefore, not of certainties but of what he would do if the choice were his and of what he believes God's own desire may be.

But why does he do this? Why does he debate before the Philippians his personal preference in circumstances whose outcome he cannot control? The answer lies in Paul's desire to serve as a model for the Philippian church. Paul urges the Philippians twice in the letter to look to him and to others like him as examples (3:17; 4:9). Here, then, Paul provides an example to the Philippians of what it means to put "the interests of others" above one's "own interests" (2:4), an admonition that the disunited Philippians needed to hear (2:14; 4:2). Although Paul's personal preference is unquestionably to depart and be with Christ, he is convinced that his acquittal and freedom to return to Philippi would result in "progress" for the Philippians in the faith and in the kind of joy that characterizes Paul himself (vv. 25–26). This joy, as we have seen, is connected not with outward circumstances but with the advancement of the gospel. Like Christ in 2:6–8, Timothy in 2:20–21, and Epaphroditus in 2:30, Paul has put the interests of others ahead of his own interests, and the interests of the gospel above all.

---

Liddell and Robert Scott, *A Greek-English Lexicon*, 9th ed., rev. and aug. Henry Stuart Jones (Oxford: Oxford University Press, 1940), 112; O'Brien, *Philippians*, 130.

10. On the relationship of 1:21 to its immediate context, see Bonnard, *Philippiens*, 28–29.
11. See the list of positions in Martin, *Philippians*, 79.

Paul's mention of the Philippians' "progress" (*prokope*) in the faith in verse 25 echoes his claim in verse 12 that his own circumstances had served "to advance" (*eis prokopen*) the gospel. He thus brings the discussion of his own circumstances to a close and introduces the topic of the Philippians' circumstances. As we have seen, Paul's discussion of his own circumstances is actually a discussion of the advancement of the gospel within those circumstances. So, when Paul turns to the Philippians, his primary concern will be with how, in the give and take of life in Philippi, the gospel might progress by means of the Philippian church.

IN MOVING THIS text out of Paul's context and into our own we should remember that verses 18b–26 form the second part of a larger section in which Paul gives the Philippians news, probably eagerly awaited, of his own circumstances. Throughout these two parts, however, Paul speaks of his own affairs only as they touch on the progress of the gospel. Paul is in prison, but that "has really served to advance the gospel" (v. 12). Rival preachers are attacking him, "but what does it matter?" Christ is being preached (v. 18a). He may live or die, yet he does not know what to choose, for living is Christ and dying means being with him (vv. 21–22). He thinks he will live, however, because that will encourage the "progress" of the gospel among the Philippians (vv. 25–26). As we bring the second part of Paul's report on his own circumstances out of his context and into ours, then, we should keep in mind that the most significant theological feature of the entire section is Paul's absolute devotion to the gospel.

We should also keep in mind the breathtakingly comprehensive nature of Paul's devotion to the gospel and to the Christ proclaimed in it. Every major feature of his life at the time when he wrote the letter—his physical comfort, the opinions others have about him, his position with respect to the secular authorities, and the question of whether he lives or dies—are molded by his commitment to the advancement of the gospel. Paul expects the Philippians to have the same perspective—their progress and joy in the faith, he implies in verse 24, should mirror his. The culture of the Western world at the turn of the twenty-first century, with its elevation of personal freedom and individual rights above virtually every other ideal, does not provide a friendly environment for the development of the notions that Paul expresses here, and we who are products of that culture will have to resist the temptation to soften the impact of this passage.

The difference between verses 12–18a and 18b–26, then, lies not in a change of the section's overall theme, but in a change in Paul's temporal orientation. In verses 12–18a he was concerned with the progress of the gospel in his present circumstances. In verses 18b–26 he is concerned with the future. Two aspects of Paul's future emerge as particularly important. One is the shape of his confidence in his future salvation, the other the shape of his confidence in the outcome of his imprisonment. Both contain important theological elements that our own culture has conditioned us to ignore; thus, the message of both aspects needs careful attention.

**Salvation, Prayer, and the Supply of the Spirit.** Paul is sure that he will be saved on the final day, but he views his impending opportunity to testify to the gospel before his accusers as an important step on his way to that final destination. Moreover, he is dependent on the Philippians' prayers, particularly their prayers that God will supply him with the sustaining presence of the Spirit, so that he may take this step successfully.

Paul frequently asked the churches to which he wrote for their prayers that he would be kept safe (Rom. 15:30–31a; 2 Cor. 1:10–11; 2 Thess. 3:2; cf. Philem. 22), that his apostolic labor would progress unhindered (Rom. 15:31b–32; 2 Thess. 3:1; cf. 1 Thess. 5:25), and that he would proclaim the gospel clearly (Col. 4:3–4) and fearlessly (Eph. 6:19).[12] Only in Philippians 1:19, however, does he speak of prayer for his ultimate salvation. This is a difficult concept for many Christians to grasp, and indeed if grasped incorrectly could lead to the notion that Christians can somehow distribute salvation through their prayers—that they hold the keys to the kingdom and can give or deny them at will. Such a notion, of course, is utterly foreign to the Paul who wrote elsewhere that "God has mercy on whom he wants to have mercy, and he hardens whom he wants to harden" (Rom. 9:18).

On the other hand, it is important to recognize that God ordains the prayers of his people as a means through which to accomplish his purposes, including his purposes for the perseverance of Christians in the faith and for their ultimate salvation. Paul's own prayers for the sanctification and final salvation of the believers to whom he wrote (1 Cor. 1:4–9; Eph. 1:15–23; 3:14–21; Phil. 1:3–11; Col. 1:9–14; 2 Thess. 1:11–12) show how seriously he took this duty, and Philippians 1:19 shows that he expected his churches to take it seriously on his behalf as well. Although it grates against Western notions of the autonomy of the individual, Paul did not conceive of sanctification and ultimate salvation as solely private enterprises. Individual Christians need the prayerful intercession of their brothers and sisters for their spiritual well-being so that they "may be pure and blameless until the day of Christ" (1:10).[13]

---

12. Cf. O'Brien, *Philippians*, 110.
13. See the sage comments of Silva, *Philippians*, 78–79.

The Philippians' prayers, as we saw in our study of the original meaning of the passage, are closely linked in Paul's mind to "the supply of the Spirit of Jesus Christ" (v. 19, KJV), and this concept too is difficult to grasp. Does Paul's statement mean that the Spirit came and went in his life? Does it mean that one believer can pray for another to receive the Spirit? Paul could hardly be clearer elsewhere that the Spirit dwells within every believer. "You . . . are controlled not by the sinful nature," he wrote to the Romans, "but by the Spirit, if the Spirit of God lives in you. And if anyone does not have the Spirit of Christ, he does not belong to Christ" (Rom. 8:9). It is unlikely, then, that here Paul suddenly reverts to the notion that he can be deprived of the Spirit and may need the prayers of other Christians to restore it.

On the other hand, many Christians today believe that the Spirit is more inactive than Paul's language allows. Paul can speak of the Spirit being given to the Thessalonians (1 Thess. 4:8) and being supplied to the Galatians (Gal. 3:5), he commands the Ephesians to be filled with the Spirit (Eph. 5:18), and he tells Timothy to fan the gift given to him (probably the Spirit) into flame (2 Tim. 1:5).[14] All believers have the Spirit all the time, but they sometimes experience the Spirit's presence in greater power and abundance than at other times. Thus Luke tells us that Peter was "filled with the Holy Spirit" when he bore witness to the gospel before a hostile Sanhedrin (Acts 4:8), that the persecuted Jerusalem community was "filled with the Holy Spirit" and spoke God's word boldly (4:31), and that Stephen, prior to his martyrdom, was "full of the Holy Spirit" (7:55). Paul was similarly "filled with the Holy Spirit" when he confronted the magician Elymas (13:9), and despite the persecution that Paul and Barnabas left in their wake when they departed Pisidian Antioch, the disciples there were "filled with joy and with the Holy Spirit" (13:52). The Holy Spirit lived within each of these people prior to these occasions (see, for example, 6:5), but each apparently received an unusual abundance of the Spirit's infilling during a time of special testing. Paul awaited such a time when he wrote Philippians 1:19, and he hoped that through the prayers of the Philippians on his behalf, the Spirit would be supplied to him in such measure that he would witness boldly to the gospel before his accusers. In the words of Henry Barclay Swete:

> He was confident that, as his converts prayed, a fresh abundance of the Spirit which was in Jesus Christ and had been sent by Him would be poured into his heart, making for his final salvation whether the present captivity should result in life or death.[15]

---

14. Fee, *God's Empowering Presence*, 741–42, 785–89.
15. Swete, *The Holy Spirit in the New Testament*, 228.

It is appropriate and desirable that believers today should in a similar way pray for their fellow believers that, especially in times of trial, God will fill them with his Spirit in unusual abundance so that they may stand firm and even be strengthened in the faith.

**The Choice to Live, a Difficult Choice?** The second major aspect of this passage that can easily go unnoticed in our own culture is that Paul genuinely considers his choice to live rather than to die to be the more difficult and sacrificial choice. We live in a culture that thinks of physical death with such dread that society's highest goal is the postponement of death as long as possible. When it finally occurs, it is something of an embarrassment. On the other hand we are so obsessed with physical life that we are willing to deny it to countless unborn children too small and weak to defend themselves in order to improve "the quality of life" for the strong who can. Those of us who are products of such a society will inevitably find Paul's notion that remaining alive is a sacrifice and execution a gain difficult to understand.

The implications of this passage are undeniable: Physical life or death are not of ultimate importance to Paul. Living means carrying out his calling to preach Christ (v. 21a) and dying means both the gain of conformity with Christ's death (v. 21b; 3:8—11) and fellowship with Christ (1:23). He hopes for the outcome that, in his opinion, will most clearly advance the preaching of Christ. This can only strike us as strange in the modern church if we have allowed the comforts of our present physical existence to usurp the place of Christ in our lives as our chief priority. If we are to let this passage speak to us on its own terms, we will need to stare Paul's astonishing indifference toward death squarely in the face and ask ourselves whether our attitude toward death imitates his.

Paul, however, may find our need to do this puzzling; he seems to have assumed that his is the only attitude for a slave of Christ Jesus to take. He has another point primarily in mind in this section of his letter, for he hopes to demonstrate for the Philippians the principle that he will articulate more clearly in 2:4, "Each of you should look not only to your own interests, but also to the interests of others." This is a principle that we in the modern church should take away from this passage as well. In matters as momentous as life and death, Paul is willing to put the interests of the Philippians ahead of his own. We, on the other hand, are too often ready to destroy the church's unity over whether to place the new piano on the left or the right side of the sanctuary. Along with the Philippians in times past, we need to look to Paul as a model. Christ is more important than life itself to him, and the joy and progress of his fellow Christians more important than departing to be with Christ.

**Two Minor Confusions.** We should not leave our study of how to apply this section to the modern church without commenting on two minor issues that occasionally disturb modern readers. First, verse 23 sometimes appears in the debate over "soul sleep," or the idea that at death the soul loses consciousness or "sleeps" until it is reunited with the body at the final resurrection. Advocates of this position claim that because the soul is not conscious during the interval between death and resurrection, Paul can say in verse 23 that when he dies he goes to be with Christ, as if that happens immediately. The difficulty this verse poses to the notion of soul sleep, however, is insuperable. Death certainly would not have been "better by far" to Paul had he been conscious of any interval when he would not be with the Lord between his physical death and his physical resurrection. When we add to this Paul's clear teaching in 2 Corinthians 5:8 that at death he will leave the body but dwell with the Lord, the case against "soul sleep" appears closed.[16]

Second, some readers might mistake Paul's statement in verse 26 to mean that Paul had an inflated view of his own importance. The NIV has appropriately translated the verse in a way that shows that this is not the case. But translated more literally, verses 25–26 read this way:

> And since I am confident of this, I know that I will stay and remain on with all of you for your progress and joy in the faith, in order that your boast might abound in Christ Jesus in me through my coming again to you.

Is Paul saying here that he thinks he will be released to return to the Philippians so that they might be able to boast about him? The answer to this question lies in looking carefully at Paul's grammar. The Philippians' boast will abound not in Paul but "in Christ Jesus." The phrase "in me through my coming again to you" simply explains that Paul's return to the Philippians will provide an opportunity for the church to give glory to Christ Jesus. Paul's return will provide clear evidence that God is able to advance the gospel among the Philippians despite human attempts to keep it in fetters, and that is certainly appropriate grounds for giving glory to Christ.

Far from revealing a self-absorbed Paul, this statement shows the apostle's clear-headed reckoning of his own place in God's plans to advance the gospel. All glory belongs to Christ, but Paul understands that just as God's work among his churches provides others with the opportunity to give grateful praise to God (2 Cor. 9:11–15; cf. Phil. 2:16), so God's work in his own

---

16. See the concise definition of "soul sleep" and the lucid summary of the arguments for and against it in the article by E. K. Harrison in *The Evangelical Dictionary of Theology*, ed. Walter A. Elwell (Grand Rapids: Baker, 1984), 1037–38.

life sometimes provides the opportunity for his churches to give glory to Christ and to God (cf. 2 Cor. 1:10–11).

NEARLY EVERY THEOLOGICAL principle that lies beneath this passage challenges the modern church of the West. Paul's unmistakable feeling of dependence on the prayers of his fellow believers in Philippi urges evangelical Christians to temper their emphasis on the autonomy of the individual with an appreciation for the interconnectedness of the church. The notion that salvation lies in the future and that those who enter it may pass through times of testing on their way reminds Reformed Christians to make their calling and election sure. Paul's desire that the Philippians should ask God to supply him with the Spirit should prompt those who are not Pentecostals to reexamine their static notions of the Spirit's role in the believer's life. Paul's request that this special abundance of the Spirit might come to aid him amid a particularly strenuous trial challenges the "health-and-wealth" wing of Pentecostalism to reexamine its notion of the victorious Christian life. No sector of Christianity in the comfort-conscious West is exempt from the implicit rebuke of Paul's attitude toward death. It will be a rare believer indeed who can read this passage, grapple with it seriously, and come away satisfied that he or she is following Paul's example.

**The Character of Our Intercessory Prayers.** This passage challenges the modern church both to pray for others and to pray for the perseverance and eventual salvation of believers. We should not assume in a culture that emphasizes the rights of the individual as heavily as Western culture that believers will automatically think it necessary to pray much for others, except as their prayers for others somehow meet some need of their own. We tend to spend much of the time we devote to prayer asking God for things that will make our lives more pleasant, and since seeing friends and family members in difficult circumstances is unpleasant for us, we sometimes pray for their deliverance from hardship. But even so, our prayers are often self-centered. The first step in applying this passage to ourselves, then, may simply be to ask God to give us a genuine love for other Christians and an understanding of their need for our prayers.[17]

Even if we have an unselfish desire to pray for other Christians, we may seldom think to pray for their salvation. Among Christians who trace their

---

17. See the valuable discussion of this issue in Richard Foster, *Prayer: Finding the Heart's True Home* (San Francisco: HarperSanFrancisco, 1992), 201.

theological roots to John Calvin, this notion may seem especially foreign. The Westminster Confession, which many of us who are Presbyterians have been taught from our youth, contains an entire chapter on "... the Perseverance of the Saints," the first paragraph of which reads this way:

> They whom God hath accepted in his Beloved, effectually called and sanctified by his Spirit, can neither totally nor finally fall away from the state of grace; but shall certainly persevere therein to the end, and be eternally saved (17.1).

The guiding documents and confessions of other Reformed denominations contain similar statements.[18] The doctrine was never intended by those who drafted these theological summaries to encourage the notion that formal church membership guaranteed a secure eternal destiny or that believers could pay little attention to the development of their spiritual lives. But the doctrine, in attenuated form, has sometimes had these effects. A vivid illustration of this recently appeared in my own state when a teenager was accused of complicity in the murder of a young woman. When his friends, who had actually committed the murder while he stood by, claimed that he had taught them the satanic rituals that led to their evil deed, the local newspaper claimed that he responded, "I'm no Satan worshipper. I've been saved and baptized."

There can be little doubt that Paul believed in the ultimate salvation of those who truly follow Christ. Only a few sentences before verse 19 he expressed his confidence in God's ability to bring to completion the good work begun in the Philippians (1:6; cf. 1 Cor. 1:1–9; 1 Thess 5:23–24). There can be equally little doubt, however, that Paul thought that those who have truly believed can tear down rather than build up their faith by the way they live (1 Cor. 8:1–13; Rom. 14:1–23) and that those who persist in grave sins may have never experienced a real conversion at all (1 Cor. 5:1–13; 10:1–12).[19] So far was Paul from presuming upon his own standing before God on the final day that he could say, "I beat my body and make it my slave so that after I have preached to others, I myself will not be disqualified for the prize" (1 Cor. 9:27). Whether the prize here is salvation, as some interpreters believe, or the glory that Paul will receive at the final day, as others hold, the statement shows that Paul refused to use his assur-

---

18. See, e.g., Article 11 of the Canons of Dort and Article 5 of *The Baptist Faith and Message*.

19. See the definitive study of this issue in Judith M. Gundry Volf, *Paul and Perseverance: Staying In and Falling Away* (Louisville, Ky.: Westminster/John Knox, 1990), esp. 283–87.

ance that he would persevere to the end as an excuse to relax his efforts in the service of Christ and the gospel.[20]

This, of course, is why he coveted the Philippians' prayers during his present time of testing. This is also why we should be as vigorous in our prayers for the perseverance of other believers as we are in other aspects of our intercessory work for them. One of the prayers for perseverance in the old Presbyterian *Book of Common Worship* (1906) provides a particularly good model to follow:

> O God, who hast willed that the gate of mercy should stand open to the faithful; look on us, and have mercy upon us; that we, who by Thy grace are following the path of Thy will, may never turn aside from the ways of life; through Jesus Christ our Lord. Amen.

**Our Understanding of the Spirit's Work.** The modern church also needs to learn from this passage that the work of the Holy Spirit is not some easily contained and static operation but powerful and dynamic. The church has historically taken a cautious attitude toward claims that the Spirit is at work in some new and powerful way. Sometimes this caution sprang from a disobedient conservatism, as when the earliest Christians resisted the notion that Gentiles should be admitted to the people of God without first becoming Jewish proselytes. At other times it was well advised, as when the church rejected the claims of Montanus and his followers in the second century that the Holy Spirit had led them to accept extreme forms of asceticism.[21] The reason for the caution is clear: Anyone can claim to be possessed with the Spirit's power, and many have used this claim deceptively for their own advancement or erroneously, imagining themselves to be led by the Spirit of God when they were not. The danger that such claims can lead believers astray is real.

The biblical approach to claims that the Spirit is at work in unusual ways will, of course, try to avoid the disobedient conservatism of the "circumcision party" on one hand and the gullible permissiveness of Montanism on the other. Philippians 1:19 will not provide all of the guidelines we need to test the spirits, but it does provide two important ones. (1) We should expect the Spirit to come upon Christians with surprising power. The Spirit's work is not limited to creation, to producing the miracles of the apostolic age, and

---

20. For the arguments on either side of the issue see Gordon D. Fee, *The First Epistle to the Corinthians* (Grand Rapids: Eerdmans, 1987), 438–41; Gundry Volf, *Paul and Perseverance*, 233–47.

21. For the rejection of Gentiles in the early church, see Acts 10:14; 11:2; 15:1; for the rejection of Montanism see, e.g., Hippolytus, *Philosophoumena*, 26.

to the inspiration of those who wrote the Word of God. The Spirit comes upon believers today for surprising purposes and sometimes in ways that do not fit comfortably into Western notions of the superiority of the empirical and rational. Some Christians, for example, speak in tongues, and an entire library of books by people dedicated to the belief that the Bible is the infallible Word of God has appeared to claim that this ecstatic speech cannot really be from God's Spirit. Every argument that tries to exclude ecstatic utterances such as speaking in tongues from present-day manifestations of the Spirit's power, however, crashes against the plain reading of the relevant passages. When those who speak in tongues follow the rules and adopt the attitude expressed in 1 Corinthians 12–14, then the church neglects the lucid command of 1 Corinthians 14:39 at its own peril: "Do not forbid speaking in tongues."

(2) This passage teaches us that we should pray for and expect the Spirit to come with unusual abundance on Christians who are undergoing suffering, particularly suffering for their faith. Paul does not desire a special supply of the Spirit in this passage so that he might be ushered onto a higher spiritual plane than the ordinary believer. He certainly does not desire the Spirit's anointing so that he might experience health and wealth. Instead, he hopes that the Spirit's abundant presence will lead him to bear courageous and clear testimony to the gospel so that whether he is spared or executed by the Roman authorities, "Christ will be exalted" (v. 20).

**Our Attitudes Toward Life and Death.** It has often been observed that death is an embarrassment to modern Western culture. Prior to the first half of the twentieth century, when extended families often lived near each other and even in the same house with one another, it was not uncommon for children to observe death firsthand and to learn to cope with it from older family members around them. Today, however, people die in hospitals more frequently than in homes, bodies are quickly removed from hospital to morgue, and the embalmer's art rapidly restores the body of the deceased to a lifelike appearance.[22] Death is the worst possible event for those who believe that they have an inalienable right to "life, liberty, and the pursuit of happiness," and our way of coping with it seems to be to deny its existence.

Paul, however, faced death with the same firm resolve that marked his approach to life, for both death and life to him meant service to Christ, and service to Christ was his primary goal. Perhaps more than at any other time in history, the church today needs to adopt Paul's perspective on life and death. With most in the world around us refusing to talk about the subject out of stark terror, and with the philosophers who do speak of it often claim-

---

22. See William E. Phipps, *Death: Confronting the Reality* (Atlanta: John Knox, 1987), 1–9.

ing that the notion of life after death is only wishful thinking, it is tempting for the believer to live as if there were nothing beyond the grave. This can only cause us to clutch our material possessions more tightly for the security they can give and keep us from risking our lives in the service of God.

Many Iranian believers, on the other hand, have learned Paul's perspective on death, and they, like him, provide an example for Westerners. Mehdi Dibaj, for example, was imprisoned by the government of Iran in 1984 on charges of "apostasy," since he had converted from Islam to Christianity. The penalty for this crime according to the Islamic law that ruled Iran was death. Mehdi languished in prison for ten years before his case came to trial; when it did, his written statement of defense was a simple and straightforward reaffirmation of commitment to Jesus Christ. The last few lines of that defense contain this remarkable paragraph:

> [Jesus Christ] is our Saviour and He is the Son of God. To know Him means to know eternal life. I, a useless sinner, have believed in His beloved person and all His words and miracles recorded in the Gospel, and I have committed my life into His hands. Life for me is an opportunity to serve Him, and death is a better opportunity to be with Christ. Therefore I am not only satisfied to be in prison for the honour of His Holy Name, but am ready to give my life for the sake of Jesus my Lord. . . .

On December 12, 1993, the court before whom this defense was made sentenced Mehdi to execution. Then, under intense pressure from people in the West who knew of the case, including the U. S. State Department, the Iranian government arranged Mehdi's release in January 1994. Seven months later, he was found dead "under suspicious circumstances" in a Tehran park, the third Christian murdered in Iran after his release from prison. Some Christian groups suspected the complicity of the Iranian government.[23]

The test of faith that Paul experienced nearly two millennia ago is repeated in the modern church still. We in the West are insulated from it, but it remains a reality for believers who live under anti-Christian totalitarian regimes. If we are to be as faithful in our commitment to the gospel and to the church as Paul expected the Philippians to be, we need to be aware of the needs of our suffering brothers and sisters, pray that God will supply them with an unusual abundance of the Spirit of Jesus Christ, and learn from their single-minded devotion to the gospel, in life and in death, how we should live in the service of the gospel in our own time and place.

---

23. See "Christian Found Dead, Iran Says," *The Boston Globe* (July 6, 1994), 8; "Prominent Church Leaders Slain," *Christianity Today* (August 15, 1994), 54.

# Philippians 1:27–2:4

WHATEVER HAPPENS, CONDUCT yourselves in a manner worthy of the gospel of Christ. Then, whether I come and see you or only hear about you in my absence, I will know that you stand firm in one spirit, contending as one man for the faith of the gospel [28]without being frightened in any way by those who oppose you. This is a sign to them that they will be destroyed, but that you will be saved —and that by God. [29]For it has been granted to you on behalf of Christ not only to believe on him, but also to suffer for him, [30]since you are going through the same struggle you saw I had, and now hear that I still have.

[2:1]If you have any encouragement from being united with Christ, if any comfort from his love, if any fellowship with the Spirit, if any tenderness and compassion, [2]then make my joy complete by being like-minded, having the same love, being one in spirit and purpose. [3]Do nothing out of selfish ambition or vain conceit, but in humility consider others better than yourselves. [4]Each of you should look not only to your own interests, but also to the interests of others.

**Original Meaning**

WITH THE PHRASE "Whatever happens, conduct yourselves in a manner worthy of the gospel of Christ," Paul turns a critical corner in the argument of the letter. His own affairs drop from view to reemerge only briefly at two places in the rest of the letter (2:19–24 and 4:10–14, 18, 22). The Philippians' circumstances, on the other hand, come to the fore. Paul had opened the previous section of the letter in verse 12 with a reference to his circumstances (or, in a literal rendering of the Greek, "the things about me"). He opens the new section in verse 27 in a similar way but now with a reference to the Philippians' circumstances ("the things about you," as the Greek literally says). Just as verse 12 signaled to the Philippians that Paul would give them information about himself, so verse 27 shows that he now intends to devote a section of the letter to them. The command "conduct yourselves in a manner worthy of the gospel of Christ" confirms this. It is the first command of a long string of commands that appear throughout the rest of the letter, and it demonstrates that Paul is now turning his full attention to the Philippians' own "progress ... in the faith" (1:25).[1]

In 1:27–2:18 Paul's primary concern is with the Philippians' attitudes toward one another. Two prominent members of the church and valuable coworkers in Paul's ministry, Euodia and Syntyche, were quarreling with one another (4:2), and their dispute had probably infected the rest of the church (2:14). In the first part of this new section, then, Paul concentrates on encouraging the church to put the interests of others ahead of their own (1:27–2:4), to follow the example of Christ's humility (2:5–11), and to avoid the error of the disobedient and discontented Israelites during the days of their desert wanderings (2:12–18). Paul does not leave the theme of unity entirely behind after 2:18, but this section devotes more attention to it than any other.

The two paragraphs that make up 1:27–2:4 form the first part of this larger section. Paul's concern here is to admonish the Philippians to remain steadfast in the midst of persecution from the outside (1:27–30) and then to urge them not to succumb to the destructive forces of disunity that have already arisen within the church (2:1–4).[2] The conjunction "therefore" (*oun*), which does not appear in the NIV, joins the two paragraphs and shows that Paul's admonition to unity in 2:1–4 is closely connected with his claim that he and the Philippians share a common struggle for the advancement of the gospel (1:30).[3] If the Philippians are to make a contribution to that struggle, Paul says in 2:1–4, then they must be "like-minded, having the same love, being one in spirit and purpose" (2:2).

**Standing United Against Opposition from Outside (1:27–30).** In 1:27–30 Paul compares his own struggle against inimical outside forces, just recounted in 1:18b–26, with the Philippians' struggle against outside opposition, a theme that will reappear in 2:15–16a and 4:4–9. He also introduces the theme of the Philippians' unity, a concern that reappears in 2:6–18 and 4:2–3. This paragraph, then, allows the themes of the previous section to mingle with the themes of subsequent sections, providing a skillful transition between these two major parts of the letter.

Paul begins with a statement that stands as a topic heading over all of 1:27–2:18: "Whatever happens, conduct yourselves in a manner worthy of the gospel of Christ" (v. 27). Just as he has conducted himself in a way worthy of the gospel of Christ despite opposition both from outside and from within the Christian community, so Paul urges the Philippians to cope with

---

1. Beginning with 1:27, verbs in the imperative mood are scattered evenly throughout the letter (2:2, 5, 12, 14, 29; 3:1, 2, 15, 16, 17; 4:1, 3, 4, 5, 6, 8, 9, 21).

2. O'Brien, *Philippians*, 164, 166.

3. Cf. Witherington, *Friendship and Finances in Philippi*, 61.

the problems of persecution and dissension in a way consistent with the gospel. The word that the NIV translates "conduct yourselves" (*politeuesthe*) is unusual and probably carries a deeper significance than is immediately apparent from most English translations. It occurs only twice in the New Testament, once here and once in Acts 23:1. In other ancient Greek literature it sometimes means to "have one's citizenship" or "home" in a certain city or state, to "rule" or "govern the state," or simply to "live, conduct oneself, or lead one's life."[4] Does it merely mean "conduct oneself" in Philippians 1:27, or does it have more political overtones?

Several pieces of evidence show that Paul probably chose the word specifically because of its political nuance. (1) In Acts 23:1 the word apparently bears political overtones. There Paul is addressing the Jewish chief priests and Sanhedrin at the request of a Roman military commander. Roman soldiers had arrested Paul after a riot broke out near the Jerusalem temple over the claim that he was an apostate and had defiled the temple (Acts 21:27–36). "This is the man," they claimed, "who teaches all men everywhere against our people and our law and this place. And besides he has brought Greeks into the temple area and defiled this holy place" (21:28). Paul responds to this charge in Acts 23:1. "My brothers, I have fulfilled my duty [*pepoliteumai*] to God in all good conscience to this day." In light of the political nature of the charge against Paul, he probably chose this word carefully. He claims to have conducted himself properly as a citizen of God's commonwealth and not to have violated its customs.[5]

(2) As we have already seen in the introduction to the commentary, the Philippians were conscious of their status as citizens of Rome and proud of it. This word would probably not have been unknown to them as a term for living as a citizen of Philippi should live.

(3) In this paragraph, Paul is concerned with the Philippians' steadfastness amid persecution from their fellow citizens who are not believers and who may feel that participation in a Jewish sect is incompatible with citizenship in Philippi (cf. Acts 16:20–21).[6] If the word does have political connotations,

---

4. Walter Bauer, *A Greek-English Lexicon of the New Testament and Other Early Christian Literature*, 2d ed., trans., adapt., and rev. William F. Arndt, F. Wilbur Gingrich, Frederick W. Danker (Chicago: University of Chicago Press, 1979), 686.

5. Cf. U. Hutter, "πολιτεύομαι," *Exegetical Dictionary of the New Testament*, ed. Horst Balz and Gerhard Schneider, 3 vols. (Grand Rapids: Eerdmans, 1990–93), 3:130.

6. Others have suggested that the persecution originated in the Philippians' unwillingness to participate in the worship of the emperor, an expression of civic loyalty known to be popular in the region during the first century. See Pheme Perkins, "Philippians: Theology for the Heavenly Politeuma," *Pauline Theology. Volume I: Thessalonians, Philippians, Galatians, Philemon*, ed. Jouette M. Bassler (Minneapolis, Minn.: Fortress, 1991), 93.

then Paul is telling the Philippians to govern their lives according to the gospel rather than according to society's requirements for being a good citizen of Philippi. Although the temptation may be strong to compromise with "those who oppose" them (v. 28), their first consideration should be loyalty to the standards of God's commonwealth as they are summarized in the gospel.

If the Philippians are to do this, Paul continues, then they must present a united front against their opposition.[7] They should "stand firm" and "contend" for the gospel "in one spirit" and "as one man." The phrase "one man" is literally "in one soul," and most translators and commentators have understood the two phrases "one spirit" and "one soul" to be parallel to each other. This means that just as "soul" is a reference to the human soul, so "spirit" is a reference to the human spirit, not to the Holy Spirit. Paul, they believe, is asking the Philippians to be united in spirit and soul.[8] Since he uses the precise phrase "in one spirit" elsewhere to mean "in the one Spirit of God" (1 Cor. 12:13; Eph. 2:18), however, it is likely that in verse 27 the phrase carries at least some allusion to God's Spirit.[9] Paul is probably saying that the Philippians should be united in spirit (because they have all experienced the work of God's Spirit) and united in soul.

Turning their attention outward, Paul next says that the Philippians should not fear their opponents, and then gives two results of the opposition they are experiencing, both of which should encourage the Philippians to persevere. (1) The Philippians should not fear those who oppose them because this very opposition is a "sign to them" that in the day of Christ (cf. 1:10) their

---

7. In his stimulating work *Seek the Welfare of the City: Christians as Benefactors and Citizens* (Grand Rapids: Eerdmans, 1994), 81–104, Bruce W. Winter observes that when ancient political theorists such as Dio Chrysostom (ca. A.D. 40–after 112) spoke of how citizens should behave (*politeia*), they often emphasized the necessity of concord among a city's citizenry and between different cities. To behave properly as a citizen in ancient times meant to strive for unity and peace.

8. See, for example, Hawthorne, *Philippians*, 56; Silva, *Philippians*, 94. If this interpretation is correct, it does not mean that Paul distinguished sharply between the human soul and the human spirit. The term "soul" (*psyche*) in Paul usually means "purposeful life" (cf. 2:30; Rom. 16:4; 2 Cor. 12:15; 1 Thess. 2:8). The term "spirit" (*pneuma*) has a number of meanings in Paul, but frequently refers to human feeling (1 Cor. 16:18; 2 Cor. 2:13; 7:13). If "spirit" refers to the human spirit here, then it is probably added primarily for rhetorical effect. See also 1 Thess. 5:23, where the phrase "through and through" shows that Paul's emphasis lies on the whole person, not on the division of the person into three parts.

9. Cf. Eduard Schweizer, "ψυχή," *Theological Dictionary of the New Testament*, ed. Gerhard Kittel and Gerhard Friedrich, 10 vols. (Grand Rapids: Eerdmans, 1964–76), 9:649; Bonnard, *Philippiens*, 34; Fee, *God's Empowering Presence*, 743–46. O'Brien, *Philippians*, 150, believes that some reference to the Holy Spirit may lie beneath Paul's use of the word, but denies that it is explicit.

---

opponents will be destroyed. The NIV's phrase "sign to them" can be understood to mean that the Philippians' opponents will somehow perceive their own doom in the courageous faithfulness of their victims (cf. REB; NRSV).[10] Paul's Greek, however, indicates only that the sign is related in some way to the opponents; thus we might translate the relevant phrase, "This is a sign, with respect to them, of destruction." Paul probably means that the opposition the Philippians have encountered is a sign to any who are able to perceive it, and especially to the Philippian Christians, that God will destroy those who persecute his people. As Paul says in a different context, "If anyone destroys God's temple, God will destroy him; for God's temple is sacred, and you are that temple" (1 Cor. 3:17).

(2) Paul says that the Philippians should remain unfrightened by the persecution they are experiencing because it is a sign of their salvation. Again, the NIV (cf. REB, NRSV) can be understood to mean that the fearlessness of the Philippian Christians amid the fires of persecution will show their opponents that the Christians will be saved. But Paul's Greek probably means instead that the Philippians' perseverance in the face of persecution serves as a sign to the Philippian believers of their own salvation.[11] In verse 28, then, Paul encourages the Philippians to view their perseverance amid persecution as a double-sided token of God's verdict at the final day: It is a sign of their opponents' destruction, but of the Philippian believers' salvation, on that day.[12]

Paul concludes this thought with the phrase "and that by God," indicating that both the Philippian believers' salvation and the assurance of salvation that comes to them through the patient endurance of persecution originate with God.[13] In the next phrase (v. 29) he explains the divine origin of their assurance of salvation in greater detail: Their suffering for the faith, he says, is a gift. This startling statement probably has two characteristics of Christian suffering in view, one that Paul has just explained and the other which he will explain later in the letter. (1) Suffering is a gift because, when successfully endured, it confirms the future salvation of the believer (cf. v. 28b). (2) It is a gift because through it we become identified with Christ's suffering (3:10), a suffering that was redemptive and issued in the resurrec-

---

10. See also Beare, *Philippians,* 68.

11. O'Brien, *Philippians,* 144, has captured the meaning precisely by translating v. 28, "in no way letting your opponents intimidate you. This [state of affairs] is a sure sign, with reference to them, of perdition, but of your eternal salvation."

12. Paul adopts a similar perspective in 2 Thess. 1:3–10.

13. In the Greek text the NIV's "that" is actually "this" (*touto*). It is also in the neuter gender, revealing that its antecedent is not simply salvation, which would have required the feminine pronoun (*haute*), but also the double-sided sign of perseverance amid persecution.

tion.[14] Just as grace abounded in the suffering of Christ (Rom. 5:20–21), so when believers suffer for him, grace abounds as well (cf. 2 Cor. 4:7–12).

Paul closes the paragraph with an encouraging equation of his own suffering in the cause of the gospel with the Philippians' experience with their oppressors. They had seen the hardship Paul endured for the sake of the gospel when he came to Philippi. He and Silas had been stripped, beaten, and jailed for "throwing [Philippi] into an uproar" over the Christian message (Acts 16:19–24). After the arrival of this letter, the Philippians will have heard both from Epaphroditus and from Paul's own pen (1:12–26) of the hardship that he was presently enduring in prison for the advancement of the gospel.

Now Paul applies the perspective he has adopted on his own suffering to the suffering of the Philippians. Their suffering and his are part of the same struggle to advance the gospel.[15] Thus just as Paul was more concerned about the advancement of the gospel than about his own imprisonment (1:12–14), just as he was more concerned that Christ was being preached than that those who preached Christ sometimes opposed Paul (1:18a), and just as he was more concerned that Christ be magnified than that he live or die, so the Philippian Christians should concern themselves with conduct worthy of the gospel in the midst of their own time of testing.

**Standing United Against Dissension from Within (2:1–4).** Paul's next paragraph turns from the problem of withstanding persecution from the outside to healing the wounds of strife within the Philippian church itself. In 1:30 he had described the Philippians' united stand against their adversaries as participation with him in the great struggle to advance the gospel. He now picks up the theme of unity announced in 1:27b and claims that if the Philippians are to participate successfully with him in this struggle, then they must be unified in mind, love, and soul and must humbly place the interests of their fellow believers above their own. Paul shows the connection between the struggle for the gospel (1:30) and the internal unity of the Philippian church (2:1–4) with the word "therefore" (*oun*), which begins the new paragraph.[16] The word is left untranslated in the NIV. Literally, 2:1 reads,

> If, *therefore*, there is any encouragement in Christ, if any comfort of love, if any fellowship of the Spirit, if any compassion and mercy. . . .

---

14. On the second, see the comments of O'Brien, *Philippians*, 160.

15. On Paul's notion that his ministry was a great struggle for the gospel, a struggle in which he expected his churches to join, see 1 Cor. 9:24–27 and Victor C. Pfitzner, *Paul and the Agon Motif: Traditional Athletic Imagery in the Pauline Literature* (Leiden: Brill, 1967), 114–19.

16. Meyer, *The Epistles to the Philippians and Colossians and to Philemon*, 60. Cf. Fee, *God's Empowering Presence*, 749–50.

The two paragraphs, then, are closely tied together and make the point that internal unity is necessary for holding back the destructive forces that would hinder the progress of the gospel.

Three questions arise from Paul's opening sentence. (1) Why does Paul express himself in such a highly rhetorical style? (2) In what sense does he use the word "if"? (3) Why does Paul choose precisely these qualities for his list? The first two questions can be answered quickly. Paul uses this rapid series of conditional clauses in order to make a heart-felt appeal to the Philippians. He is their friend as well as their apostle: They are his "joy and crown" (4:1), they fill Paul with joy whenever he remembers them in prayer (1:4), and their unity with one another will only complete the joy he already has on their account (2:2). The rhetoric of his appeal, then, is not intended to be harsh but precisely the opposite. John Chrysostom, who spoke ancient Greek fluently, comments on 2:1, "See how earnestly, how intensely, with how much sympathy he speaks!"[17]

The word "if" does not mean that the Philippians' possession of the qualities that Paul lists is hypothetical. The Greek word for "if" used here (*ei*) can sometimes mean "since." Because Paul does not doubt that the Philippians have experienced, for example, the "encouragement" and "comfort" of Christ, the word clearly has this meaning here. Paul's appeal, then, is based both on his friendship with them and on the blessings that belong to them because they belong to Christ.

But why does Paul mention these particular blessings? The answer to this question probably lies both in the immediately preceding paragraph (1:27–30) and in Paul's appeal in this paragraph to his and the Philippians' mutual affection (2:2). In 1:27–30 Paul has equated his suffering for the gospel with the Philippians' suffering and considered both to be part of the great struggle to advance the gospel. Thus he wants them to stand as firmly in the faith as they would if he were present with them (1:27), and he reminds them of the similarity between their suffering for the faith and the trials they know he has endured (1:30). The "encouragement" (*paraklesis*) they have in Christ, then, is the "comfort" (*paraklesis*, cf. 2 Cor. 1:3–7) that God gives to both Paul and the Philippians amid their suffering.

The "comfort of love" (2:1, lit. trans.) is probably not the comfort of Christ's love, as the NIV understands the phrase (the translators have added "his"), but the mutual affection that Paul and the Philippians have for one another and to which Paul appeals when he urges his readers to make his joy complete (2:2). The "fellowship with the Spirit" is the fellowship Paul and the Philippians experience because the Spirit who helps believers in their weak-

---

17. See Vincent, *Philippians*, 53.

nesses (Rom. 8:26) indwells them both. "Tenderness and compassion," likewise, probably refer to the affection that Paul feels for the Philippians and that the Philippians feel for him. Thus, Paul urges his readers to act on the relationship they have with one another because of what the Lord has done for them all.[18]

Paul describes this action as making his joy complete through cultivating a single mind. He then shows the Philippians how they can accomplish this unity of purpose with a list of brief clauses. Literally translated, Paul's list looks like this:

having the same love
[being] united in soul
thinking one thing
[doing] nothing from selfish ambition
[doing] nothing from empty conceit
but
considering others better than yourselves
each one not looking out for his own interests
but
each one also [looking out for] the interests of others

Two clear interests emerge from this list: that the Philippians be united, and that they achieve this unity through promoting the interests of others rather than their own interests. The term "selfish ambition" (*eritheia*) sums up the attitude Paul wants the Philippians to avoid. In literature prior to the New Testament, the term appears only in Aristotle's *Politica*, where, in the course of discussing the various causes of political revolutions, the philosopher identifies one cause as the greedy grasp for public office through unjust means.[19] No trace of this connection with politics appears in the New Testament's use of the term, but the notion of a greedy attempt to gain the upper hand through underhanded tactics is clearly present. Paul had seen this quality at work in his own situation (1:17), and he urges the Philippians in this passage not to let it take hold in theirs. Instead, he hopes that their relationships with one another will demonstrate a "humility" that promotes the good of others even at personal expense (2:4). This attitude should characterize the believer's relationship with fellow believers, he will say in the next section, because it is the chief quality of Jesus' relationship with us.

---

18. For this understanding of 2:1, see Fee, *God's Empowering Presence*, 747–50.

19. See *Politica*, book 5, chapter 3, p. 1302b in the standard Greek text of Aristotle's works. See the discussion in Bauer, *Greek-English Lexicon*, 309.

**Bridging Contexts**

As we interpret this passage for the modern church, we should remember the transitional role that the passage plays in Paul's argument. It moves from the theme of the gospel's advancement in Paul's ministry, despite hardship, to the theme of the Philippians' unity. The twin themes of suffering and unity should, in turn, occupy our efforts to apply the passage to the contemporary situation.

**Suffering for the Gospel.** Paul's comments on suffering in 1:28–29 constitute the most difficult portion of the passage to convey from his world into ours. There are two reasons for this. First, believers in modern Western democracies know little or nothing of the kind of suffering Paul describes in these verses, and so the temptation is strong to make them more generally applicable than they are. Paul's statement that the Philippians should not be frightened by those who oppose them can too easily within our culture be stretched to cover someone's opposition to the new church building program, rejection of some fine point of our theology, or disavowal of our favorite Christian teacher. Yet Paul's language meant nothing of the kind; it was rather intended to encourage people who stood as a tiny island of commitment to the gospel amid a raging sea of pagan antagonism. The suffering of which Paul speaks is suffering for "the gospel faith" (v. 27, REB), not suffering in general, and certainly not opposition to some personal agenda.

Does this mean that we should shelve Paul's advice and hope that we never need to consult it? A clear-headed interpretation points in another direction. Although we may not be able to obey directly the command to contend "as one man for the faith of the gospel" amid intense societal persecution, we can stand together with our brothers and sisters across the globe who suffer for the faith in circumstances similar to those of the Philippians. Paul stood united with the suffering Philippians across the miles, and the Philippians did the same for Paul. The contemporary church in the West, then, should follow their example and unite itself in practical ways with its suffering brothers and sisters in other cultures.

In addition to this, the principles in this passage are relevant both to the occasional direct opposition that Christians experience for their convictions even in the free West and to the more subtle ways in which modern, technologically sophisticated societies deny the reality of God. Although oppression of Christians is not officially sanctioned in our culture, Christian convictions are not infrequently ridiculed in the workplace or subtly berated as "unprogressive" in academic circles and in the news and entertainment media. The intense materialism of modern culture, moreover, trivializes the spiritual realm and puts subtle pressures on believers to view their answers to life's most profound questions as unimportant and slightly backward. This can lead believers, even in places where religious freedom is respected, to feelings of isolation and depression. When this happens, it is no less important for them to heed Paul's advice not to be frightened by the forces ranged against them.

Paul does not expressly say how we should avoid "being frightened," but he probably means that the courage and joy that God supplies to Christians should sustain them even when they know that the people in power over them and the prevailing ideologies do not agree with what they think and do. Paul had experienced the fear and depression that come to the believer who suffers because of obedience to God. He had been afraid in Corinth when his preaching met opposition, and God had responded with the encouraging words, "Do not be afraid; keep on speaking, do not be silent. For I am with you and no one is going to attack and harm you, because I have many people in this city" (Acts 18:9–10). He had come near despair in Ephesus because of his suffering, and the Lord had comforted him in some unknown, and perhaps less dramatic, way (2 Cor. 1:3–11). If Paul wrote Philippians from this Ephesian imprisonment, perhaps Philippians 1:28 is an example of how God's compassion and comfort amid intense suffering overflowed from Paul to others who were experiencing trouble (2 Cor. 1:4). God had comforted him in his time of trial, and the Philippians should not be afraid since God will help them also.

Within our own context it is helpful to observe that Paul, in agreement with the rest of the New Testament and the early Christian apologists, does not suggest that the Philippians engage in an aggressive offensive against their persecutors. Paul suggests instead that they maintain their composure and await the day when God will destroy those who oppose the gospel. "Do not take revenge, my friends," he says elsewhere, "but leave room for God's wrath, for it is written: 'It is mine to avenge; I will repay,' says the Lord" (Rom. 12:19; cf. Matt. 5:43–45). In the meantime, according to the rest of the New Testament, believers are to respond to opposition only with kindness and exemplary behavior (Rom. 12:20–21; cf. 1 Peter 4:19), so that their opponents may be shamed into silence (Titus 2:8) and even won to the faith (1 Peter 2:12, 21–23; 3:1, 16).

The early Christian apologists, eager to persuade the Roman emperor that a policy of Christian persecution was unjust, picked up this theme. They never tired of pointing out to their detractors the exemplary lives of Christians and their unwillingness, out of love, to retaliate against those who wronged them. In the late second century, for example, the Christian philosopher Athenagoras pleaded with the emperors Marcus Aurelius and Lucius Aurelius Commodus to stop their policy of persecuting Christians.

Both emperors encouraged the study of philosophy within their realm, and Athenagoras made the most of this in his plea. At one point he asked the emperors to consider whether any philosophers of their acquaintance, despite their good educations and quick minds, "have so purified their own hearts as to love their enemies instead of hating them; instead of upbraiding those who first insult them (which is certainly more usual), to bless them; and to pray for those who plot against them." Then, in a memorable passage, he described the demeanor of the persecuted Christians:

> With us, on the contrary, you will find unlettered people, tradesmen and old women, who though unable to express in words the advantages of our teaching, demonstrate by acts the value of their principles. For they do not rehearse speeches, but evidence good deeds. When struck, they do not strike back; when robbed, they do not sue; to those who ask, they give, and they love their neighbors as themselves.[20]

Both within the New Testament and among early Christian writings outside the canon, Christians who are persecuted echo the words of Jesus in their perspective on persecution:

> Do not resist an evil person. If someone strikes you on the right cheek, turn to him the other also. And if someone wants to sue you and take your tunic, let him have your cloak as well. If someone forces you to go one mile, go with him two miles. . . . Love your enemies and pray for those who persecute you, that you may be sons of your Father who is in heaven (Matt. 5:39–45).

Christians who suffer for the gospel today should take an equally restrained, loving, and courageous approach.

Second, Paul's claim that suffering is a gift can easily be misunderstood to mean that suffering itself is good. A historically tragic misinterpretation of Paul's discussion of suffering here and elsewhere in his letters has led some Christians to seek suffering or to inflict it upon themselves, under the impression that suffering itself somehow purifies them of sin or is for other reasons pleasing to God. It has led others to speak of the value of suffering to those in pain in a glib way that only increases the hurt. It has sometimes caused those who suffer to view God as a cruel tyrant, one who gives gifts that nobody wants.

---

20. Athenagoras, *A Plea Regarding Christians*, 11 (from the translation of Cyril C. Richardson in *Early Christian Fathers* [New York: Macmillan, 1970], 310). Cf. *Letter to Diognetus*, 5.9–17; Justin Martyr, *First Apology*, 12, 15–17.

When Paul speaks of suffering as a gift, however, he does not mean that God is its author. The Philippian pagans of Philippi who persecuted their newly converted neighbors were sinning, and God is not the author of sin. These pagan persecutors, out of their own fallen will, chose to make the fledgling church in their midst suffer. The suffering was their fault, not God's, and God justly held them responsible for it. But Paul can describe this suffering as a gift from God because God in his sovereignty used this suffering to serve his own good purposes. In the words of Joseph to his brothers, "You intended to harm me, but God intended it for good to accomplish what is now being done, the saving of many lives" (Gen. 50:20). In some mysterious way, unfathomable for finite and fallen human minds, Joseph's brothers did evil, but that evil did not lie outside the sovereign rule of God—God "intended" it in order to bring good results.[21]

What are these good results? As we have already seen in our discussion of this passage's original meaning, suffering for Christ can have two positive effects: It gives assurance of salvation, and it identifies the believer with the suffering of Christ. In this passage Paul dwells on the assurance of future salvation that comes to the believer who suffers for the faith.

Paul's claim that the opposition the Philippians experience serves as a double-sided token indicates one aspect of the gift-character of suffering for Christ. Such suffering provides clarity about who stands with God and who does not. It is unlikely that anyone whose commitment to the gospel is inauthentic will be willing to endure the fiery trials of physical discomfort and emotional pain that persecution brings. In such a crisis, inquirers who have been walking the border between commitment to and rejection of the gospel must finally make a decision, and those who have professed loyalty to the church for ulterior motives finally decide that their deception no longer pays. Those who remain, as a result, have the assurance that their commitment is real. And this, as Paul says elsewhere, is cause for rejoicing:

> We ... rejoice in our sufferings, because we know that suffering produces perseverance; perseverance, character; and character, hope. And hope does not disappoint us, because God has poured out his love into our hearts by the Holy Spirit, whom he has given us (Rom. 5:3b–5).

In other words, the testing of the believer's mettle in the fires of persecution produces assurance of salvation and reduces the visible church to something more like its true, invisible number. The confidence and fellow-

---

21. See the lucid and helpful discussion of the biblical evidence for God's sovereignty over evil in Carson, *How Long O Lord? Reflections on Suffering and Evil*, 199–227; also in Carson's longer work, *Divine Sovereignty and Human Responsibility: Biblical Perspectives in Tension* (Atlanta: John Knox, 1981).

ship that result are gifts from the God so powerful that he can even make evil do his bidding.

**Unity Within the Church.** Paul's advice to the Philippians about Christian unity is more directly and universally applicable to the modern church. Although it is connected specifically with the suffering of the church in 1:27, in 2:1–4 it takes on an independent significance that any church can readily appropriate. In both passages Paul refers to the role of the Spirit in this unity. The Philippians are to stand firm in the Spirit (1:27), and their unity with one another should flow in part from their own experience of the fellowship that the Spirit effects (2:1). The unity Paul hopes the Philippians will experience, then, originates with God's Spirit.

This does not mean, however, that the Philippians are to adopt a passive posture, waiting on the Spirit to impel them forward into the practical deeds of love that produce unity. The Philippians are commanded to be "like-minded," to have "the same love," and to unite in "spirit and purpose" (2:2). They are to avoid "selfish ambition" and are to "look ... to the interests of others" (2:3). Thus, on the one hand the Philippians' unity appears to flow from the Spirit; on the other it seems to come from the hard work of the Philippians themselves.

The same tension will appear later in 2:12–13, where Paul tells his readers to "continue to work out your salvation with fear and trembling, for it is God who works in you to will and to act according to his good purpose," and in Ephesians 2:8–10, where he emphasizes the gracious character of salvation and then says that God has created believers "to do good works, which God prepared in advance for [them] to do" (Eph. 2:10). It is probably as impossible to understand precisely how these paradoxical truths fit together as it is to understand how God's intention can somehow stand behind the evil of the Philippians' suffering. The two-sided nature of the paradox shows, however, that God both holds us responsible for the unity he commands and refuses to give us any credit for achieving it. At first this seems unfair, until we understand how thoroughly tainted with sin we are as fallen creatures and that if we are ever to obey God, he must give us both the will and the ability to do it. That he does this is cause for rejoicing in his mercy, not for complaint against his sense of fairness.[22]

But how, exactly, is the church today supposed to obey Paul's command to be "like-minded" and to be "one in spirit and purpose," or, to follow the Greek more literally, "think the same thing, having the same love, united in soul, thinking one thing" (2:2)? Does this mean that Paul supports some rigid set of detailed norms to which everyone must conform, in thought as well

---

22. See Carson, *How Long, O Lord? Reflections on Suffering and Evil*, 210–11.

as in deed? In order to understand Paul's intention it is necessary to look at the context in which the crucial phrases "think the same thing" and "thinking one thing" appear. As the literal translation shows, two defining terms are sandwiched between these phrases: Paul wants the Philippians to think the same thing by having a mutual affection for one another and by being soulmates. In the next two verses (2:3–4) he explains that this means subordinating our own interests to those of others.

Paul does not, therefore, imagine that the church is a group of automatons, walking in lockstep with one another. Instead, he sees it as a group of individuals who, despite their differences, are willing to show love for one another through putting the well-being of others first. This will always mean speaking the truth and acting on the truth, but doing so in love. It will also mean having the humility to admit when we have spoken or acted amiss and then to mend our ways. As each believer lovingly looks out for the interests of fellow believers, all will move forward toward the "attitude ... of Christ Jesus" (2:5) and will begin to approximate what Paul means when he speaks of "thinking one thing."[23]

 SINCE EARLIEST TIMES the church of Jesus Christ has struggled with precisely what its relationship should be to the broader social order. During its first three centuries the church faced hostility from people in political power, and the emphasis lay on the depth of corruption within the social order. The authorities had crucified Jesus, outlawed the preaching of the gospel, executed James, imprisoned Peter and Paul, confiscated Christian property, and demanded that Christians worship them.[24] Later, matters went from bad to worse as the official regime fed Christians to the lions, burned them at the stake, and destroyed their Scriptures.[25] Supposedly their nontraditional notions about an unseen God and a crucified Lord threatened the order of the empire.[26] In such a situation the New

---

23. For a simple and practical guide to this kind of unity, Bonhoeffer's *Life Together*, 90–109, is unsurpassed.

24. See, for example, Acts 4:17–18; 12:2–3; 16:23; 1 Cor. 2:8; Heb. 10:34; Rev. 13:1–8.

25. *The Martyrdom of Polycarp*, for example, speaks of Christians being thrown to the wild beasts and describes how Polycarp, bishop of Smyrna, was burned at the stake. Lactantius, *De Mortibus* 12, tells how in the year 303 the emperor Diocletian, among other atrocities, burned the Holy Scriptures. See W. H. C. Frend, *Martyrdom and Persecution in the Early Church: A Study of a Conflict From the Maccabees to Donatus* (Oxford: Basil Blackwell, 1965), 491.

26. See, for example, the comments of Celsus in his work *Alethes Logos* (written between 178 and 180), as quoted in Origen's *Contra Celsum*, 55–56.

Testament writers and early Christian fathers wisely stressed the alien status of the believer within the world. Christians were citizens of a different, eternal commonwealth. They were neither Jews nor Greeks but a third race, and this world was not their home.[27]

When official persecution subsided in the early fourth century, however, the way was open for the development of different approaches to the social structures within which the church had to live. Sometimes the governing authorities were viewed as divinely appointed keepers of the social order who occasionally needed to hear the advice of the church (as in the Catholic and Orthodox traditions), sometimes as the guardians of the kingdom of this world whose affairs were wholly separate from those of the church (as in the Lutheran tradition), and sometimes as sinful authorities over sinful social structures both of which the church was called upon to reclaim for the God of all creation (as in the Calvinist tradition).[28]

Many believers today are heirs to one of these three traditions and are perhaps predisposed to view the biblical evidence in the light of their own heritage. In the complicated network of alliances and tensions between the church and the social order at the turn of the third millennium, however, it is important not only to appreciate the traditions of the past but to look again at the biblical evidence in order to gain direction for our own time and culture. Philippians 1:27–30 offers some help.

It is now widely recognized that in the last half of the twentieth century, Christian notions have been increasingly excluded from debates over public policy, especially domestic policy, and this development parallels during the same period the gradual marginalizing of Christian theology in the halls of academic power. A small piece of evidence that illustrates the point is the history of the term "fundamentalist" in the academic and popular press. This word was used in the first part of the twentieth century to describe Christians bent on resisting the accommodation of traditional Christian teaching to the spirit of the age.[29] But in the closing decades of the century it has been used repeatedly in the news media and in academic circles to refer both to conservative Christians and to grenade-wielding Islamic terrorists, despite few clear reasons for associating the two other than that both are interested in purifying their religion of modernist incursions and both promote a conser-

---

27. See, for example, Phil. 3:20; 1 Peter 2:11 (cf. Heb. 11:1; 13:13–14); also the *Letter to Diognetus* 5. This stance toward the world was preserved in later church history in the Anabaptist tradition.

28. See the useful discussion of the differences among these traditions in Nicholas Wolterstorff, *Until Justice and Peace Embrace* (Grand Rapids: Eerdmans, 1983), 3–22.

29. See George M. Marsden, *Fundamentalism and American Culture: The Shaping of Twentieth-Century Evangelicalism 1870–1925* (Oxford: Oxford University Press, 1980), 3–4.

vative public policy.[30] As a result, the term has become so forbidding that groups who in the 1920s would have happily used it of themselves now desperately attempt to dissociate themselves from it. Once used as a self-designation, the word has been transformed into a virtual slur, and in the process a large number of Christians have been marginalized.[31]

At first all of this may seem irrelevant to Christians who do not consider themselves fundamentalists and agree to a large extent with the wary attitude of the secular press and the academy toward the fundamentalist movement. The critical point, however, is that many non-Christians within these secular institutions fail to make the fine distinctions between Christian groups that Christians usually understand instinctively. To many, fundamentalist Christians demonstrate the social and political tendencies of Christianity generally, and the fundamentalists only provide an excellent illustration, in their view, of why Christians cannot do good scholarship and should not be involved in politics unless they somehow sequester their religious thinking from their scientific and political thinking.[32]

Although this is a far cry from the intense level of persecution that the Christians at Philippi endured, Philippians 1:27–30 nevertheless provides perspective for marginalized believers in Western democracies. Since these verses stress the citizenship of the believer in the kingdom of God, the eschatological perspective of awaiting the time when God will separate believers from their persecutors, and the courage that believers should show in the face of persecution, it seems unlikely that Paul would approve of a Christian "anti-defamation league" or a "Christian Democratic Party"

---

30. Perhaps the crowning example of this trend is the massive *Fundamentalism Project*, ed. Martin E. Marty and R. Scott Appleby, 4 vols. (Chicago: University of Chicago, 1991–94), which discusses North American Protestant fundamentalism alongside Roman Catholic, Jewish, Islamic, Hindu, and Buddhist "fundamentalism."

31. For other examples of the exclusion of both Protestant and Roman Catholic Christians from public policy debates and from the academic enterprise, except when they are viewed as supporters of a left-leaning political agenda, see William J. Bennett, *The De-Valuing of America: The Fight for Our Culture and Our Children* (New York: Summit, 1992), 205–29; Stephen L. Carter, *The Culture of Disbelief: How American Law and Politics Trivialize Religious Devotion* (New York: Basic Books, 1993), 1–43; and the comments of Thomas C. Oden, *Requiem: A Lament in Three Movements* (Nashville, Tenn.: Abingdon, 1995), 135.

32. The reasons for this state of affairs are ably recounted and addressed in George M. Marsden, "The Soul of the American University: A Historical Overview," *The Secularization of the Academy*, ed. George M. Marsden and Bradley J. Longfield (New York: Oxford University Press, 1992), 9–45. On the danger that the exclusion of Christian thinking from public and academic discourse poses to a just society, see Alasdair MacIntyre, *After Virtue: A Study in Moral Theory*, 2d ed. (Notre Dame, Ind.: University of Notre Dame Press, 1984); for a similar argument from a British perspective see Duncan B. Forrester, *Beliefs, Values and Policies: Conviction Politics in a Secular Age* (Oxford: Oxford University Press, 1989).

designed especially to protect Christian interests and to fight back against detractors. As Karl Barth says in commenting on this passage, "Christians do not strive 'against' anybody (nor *for* anybody either!), but *for the faith.*"[33] The Christian way is to refuse retaliation and to live such exemplary lives that our persecutors not only become ashamed of their conduct but want to become believers themselves.[34]

On the other hand, precisely because the situation in Western democracies is not exactly parallel to the situation of the first Christians, it does not seem appropriate simply to focus on God's coming kingdom and neglect the opportunity believers in democratic societies have to show mercy to their neighbors by working for just policies. Since God commands us to love our neighbors as ourselves, and since our neighbors include not only God's people but others as well, it seems proper to seek ways of upholding God's vision for public justice by relieving oppression, effecting peace, and alleviating suffering within society. When we do this, we are following the biblical model of leaving the work of retaliation to God, focusing on our citizenship in his kingdom, and living such other-centered lives that those around us want to become citizens of that kingdom as well.[35]

The same human tendency that urges us to retaliate against our detractors leads us to assert our own interests over those of other believers, to climb the ladder of "selfish-ambition" at the expense of others. This tendency is deeply ingrained in the modern psyche. Americans, for example, are taught from their youth that they are "endowed by their Creator with certain unalienable Rights, among these are Life, Liberty and the pursuit of Happiness."[36] Much modern social and psychological theory is indebted to the notion that members of the human species, like all other animals, are involved in a relentless quest to dominate others in order to survive.[37] So we not only enter the church with the belief that we deserve to be made happy but often with the notion that our pursuit of happiness at the expense of others is inevitable.

Among pastors the temptation is sometimes strong to march upward from a smaller church to a larger one, beating out the competition along

---

33. Barth, *Philippians*, 47.

34. See J. Christiaan Beker, *Suffering and Hope: The Biblical Vision and the Human Predicament* (Grand Rapids: Eerdmans, 1994), 82–86; Stanley Hauerwas, *The Peaceable Kingdom: A Primer in Christian Ethics* (Notre Dame, Ind.: University of Notre Dame Press, 1983).

35. A thoughtful proposal for the Christian position on modern political and social issues can be found in John Stott, *Issues Facing Christians Today* (Basingstoke, Eng.: Marshall, Morgan & Scott, 1984).

36. The American "Declaration of Independence" (Philadelphia, 1776).

37. See, for example, the Pulitzer Prize-winning volume by Ernest Becker, *The Denial of Death* (New York: Macmillan, 1973), 1–8.

the way with little thought for God's priorities. Among Christian colleges, universities, and seminaries, decisions are also sometimes made on the basis not of what is best for the kingdom of God but what is best for the institution's survival. Christian organizations have sometimes exaggerated their financial need in order to depict a crisis that will garner greater support and put them a step ahead of the competition, and at other times have overstated their impact on society or the quality of their programs for the same reason.

Against all of this Paul commands, "Each of you should look not to your own interests, but also to the interests of others" (2:4). This command stands in the tradition of Jesus' own teaching that the road to greatness among Christians is service to others, that "whoever wants to be first must be slave of all" (Mark 10:43–44; cf. 9:35; Matt. 20:27; 23:11; Luke 22:26–27).[38]

How, practically, can we curb the temptation to assert our rights over others? In his superb essay on how Christians should live together, Dietrich Bonhoeffer supplies seven principles for eradicating selfish ambition from Christian communities. Christians, he says, should:

- hold their tongues, refusing to speak uncharitably about a Christian brother;
- cultivate the humility that comes from understanding that they, like Paul, are the greatest of sinners and can only live in God's sight by his grace;
- listen "long and patiently" so that they will understand their fellow Christian's need;
- refuse to consider their time and calling so valuable that they cannot be interrupted to help with unexpected needs, no matter how small or menial;
- bear the burden of their brothers and sisters in the Lord, both by preserving their freedom and by forgiving their sinful abuse of that freedom;
- declare God's word to their fellow believers when they need to hear it;
- understand that Christian authority is characterized by service and does not call attention to the person who performs the service.[39]

---

38. Beare, *Philippians*, 73, comments appropriately, "Paul does not suggest that anyone is claiming for himself honours that are undeserved; the point is precisely that we must not insist on receiving even the honours that we entirely deserve. For the law of the Christian life is renunciation, not self-assertion; concern for others, not concern for ourselves and our precious rights."

39. Bonhoeffer, *Life Together*, 90–109.

Within the modern Western context, perhaps Bonhoeffer's final point is the most important. The temptation to follow personalities rather than Christ is strong in the modern church. Today's Christians can buy the albums of their favorite Christian singer in the same stores that carry the music of popular secular "idols"; they can hear their favorite Christian teachers weekly on the radio, see them daily on television, and even join them for luxurious cruises to Alaska. If we are to put the interests of others ahead of our own, however, we must relinquish our fascination with personalities, including our own, and get busy with the unimpressive tasks of helping our brothers and sisters at their points of need. Bonhoeffer puts it well:

> Every personality cult that is concerned with important qualities, outstanding abilities, strengths, and the talents of someone else—even though these may be thoroughly spiritual in nature—is worldly and has no place in the Christian community. Indeed, it poisons that community. The demand one hears so often today for "people of episcopal stature," for "priestly men," and for "powerful personalities" springs too often from the spiritually sick need for the admiration of people, for the erection of visible structures of human authority, because the genuine authority of service seems too unimportant.[40]

Instead of following the latest Christian personality, our gaze should be fixed on Jesus. And this is Paul's point in Philippians 2:5–11.

---

40. Dietrich Bonhoeffer, *Deitrich Bonhoeffer Werke*, vol. 5, *Gemeinsames Leben, Das Gebetbuch der Bible*, ed. Gerhard Ludwig Müller and Albrecht Schönherr (Munich: Chr. Kaiser Verlag, 1987), 91. Cf. *Life Together*, 108.

# Philippians 2:5–11

YOUR ATTITUDE SHOULD be the same as that of Christ
Jesus:
⁶Who, being in very nature God,
    did not consider equality with God something to be
grasped,
    ⁷but made himself nothing,
        taking the very nature of a servant,
        being made in human likeness.
    ⁸And being found in appearance as a man,
        he humbled himself
        and became obedient to death—even death on a
cross!
    ⁹Therefore God exalted him to the highest place
        and gave him the name that is above every name,
    ¹⁰that at the name of Jesus every knee should bow,
        in heaven and on earth and under the earth,
    ¹¹and every tongue confess that Jesus Christ is Lord,
        to the glory of God the Father.

**Original Meaning**

THESE SEVEN VERSES have received more attention from New Testament scholars and Christian theologians than any other passage in Philippians and easily qualify for inclusion among the most hotly debated passages of the Bible. The reasons for all this ferment lie both in what the passage says about Christ and in the way the passage says it.

Philippians 2:6–11 is among the most informative statements in the Bible on the nature of Christ's incarnation. At least on the traditional reading of the passage, it speaks of Christ's preexistence, his equality with God, his identity with humanity, and the costly nature of that identity. The passage also provides insight into Christ's status after his incarnation and into the future submission of all created beings to his authority.

The way in which the passage makes these statements, moreover, has led most scholars to believe that it is an early Christian hymn, taken over and perhaps modified by Paul at this point in his argument. If that is true, then the hymn provides a window into the shadowy but critical period of Christian history between the resurrection of Jesus and the composition of Paul's letters. It provides a glimpse of the earliest Christians at worship and tells us what they thought about Jesus.

The breadth and depth of the discussion on this passage has had both advantages and disadvantages for the student of Philippians. One clear advantage is that virtually every term in 2:5–11 has been subjected to painstaking scrutiny, and advances have been made in understanding the meaning and inner logic of the passage as a result. A disadvantage of all this scrutiny, however, is that scholarly efforts to understand the passage often isolate it from its broader context in Philippians and the body of Paul's letters. Students of the passage can become so bogged down in the details of scholarly hypothesis and counter-hypothesis about the form, origin, and meaning of the hypothetical hymn that little energy remains for clarifying precisely how it serves Paul's own argument.[1] With these results of the debate over this passage, both negative and positive, in mind, we will first look at two important questions that have emerged from the debate and then examine the passage in light of Paul's wider concerns in the letter.

**Critical Preliminary Questions.** Perhaps the most important question in the interpretation of Phil. 2:5–11 is whether the consensus that verses 6–11 comprise a previously composed Christian hymn is correct. Advocates of this position point to two particularly important pieces of evidence for their view. (1) The section has certain poetic characteristics. Like other known hymns about Christ in the New Testament (Col. 1:15–20; 1 Tim. 3:16), it begins with a relative pronoun ("Who"), its two main sections (vv. 6–8 and 9–11) are neatly balanced, and its language is rhythmical. Some believe in addition that the passage is arranged in parallel statements similar to that found in Hebrew and other Semitic poetry. (2) The passage has an uncommon vocabulary. Three crucial terms in the hymn appear nowhere else in the New Testament: the Greek term that the NIV translates "very nature" (*morphe*) in verses 6 and 7, the word that stands behind the phrase "something to be grasped" (*harpagmon*) in verse 6, and the word for "exalted . . . to the highest place" (*hyperypsoo*) in verse 9.[2]

These arguments, however, do not constitute an airtight case.[3] Although it is true, for example, that the passage begins with a relative pronoun just as

---

1. Even the printing of the passage in verse form in many modern translations, a step directly indebted to the scholarly discussion of vv. 6–11 over the last seventy years, puts the passage in bold relief and separates it from the surrounding argument.

2. On these and other unusual features of the passage's style, see O'Brien, *Philippians*, 199–200. The Greek word *morphe* appears in Mark 16:12, but the oldest and most reliable manuscripts of the New Testament omit Mark 16:8–20.

3. As, for example, is argued by Bonnard, *Philippiens*, 48. He comments, "That these verses originated with Paul, as an integral part of his argument, does not strike us as a defensible position."

two other New Testament hymns about Christ do, in those two other instances the relative pronoun has no antecedent, so that the hymn clearly stands apart from the surrounding context. Here, however, the relative pronoun "who" refers unambiguously to "Christ Jesus" in verse 5. This is perfectly good Pauline Greek, and the relative pronoun does not therefore indicate the beginning of an interpolated hymn.

In addition, the notion that the passage is a discreet piece of poetry that can be detached from its surrounding context is thoroughly modern. This idea appeared for the first time in 1899 and gathered support from a number of prominent scholars in the 1920s.[4] If the section is a hymn, it is surprising that no Greek- or Syriac-speaking commentator of the ancient church recognized its poetic character.[5]

Moreover, although everyone seems agreed that the passage has unusual stylistic features, many different proposals for how the hymn should be divided and the precise nature of its supposedly poetic features have appeared. One scholar divides it into six stanzas, another into five, another into three, and another into six antiphonal couplets. Some believe that the phrase "even death on a cross" is Paul's addition to the original hymn, others that the phrase was part of the original. This wide variation in the scholarly analysis of this section casts a shadow over the entire hymn thesis.

Indeed, it is difficult to see how, in ancient terms, the passage can be considered either a hymn or poetry at all. "Hymns" in both ancient Greek and Hebrew literature were songs of praise to the gods or to God, but Philippians 2:6–11 is not a song of praise.[6] The style of the passage, moreover, is fully compatible with Paul's prose style elsewhere. Paul makes a series of statements about Christ (vv. 6–8), draws an inference from these statements (v. 9), and describes the result of this inference (vv. 10–11). This is typical Pauline argumentation, not poetry in the ancient sense.[7]

---

4. Ralph P. Martin, *Carmen Christi: Philippians 2:5–11 in Recent Interpretation and in the Setting of Early Christian Worship*, rev. ed. (Grand Rapids: Eerdmans, 1983), 24–25.

5. Syriac is a slightly later form of Aramaic, the language from which some scholars believe that the hymn was translated. See, for example, Martin, *Carmen Christi*, 38–41; P. Grelot, "Deux notes critiques sur Philippiens 2,6–11," *Biblica* 54 (1973): 169–86; Joseph A. Fitzmyer, "The Aramaic Background of Philippians 2:6–11," *Catholic Biblical Quarterly* 50 (1988): 470–83. Neither John Chrysostom (ca. 347–407) nor Theodore of Mopsuestia (ca. 350–428), both of whom grew up in Antioch, spoke Syriac and Greek, and wrote commentaries on Philippians, mention the hymnic quality of Phil. 2:6–11 in their comments on the passage.

6. Stephen E. Fowl, *The Story of Christ in the Ethics of Paul: An Analysis of the Function of the Hymnic Material in the Pauline Corpus* (Sheffield: JSOT Press, 1990), 31–45.

7. Gordon D. Fee, "Philippians 2:5–11: Hymn or Exalted Pauline Prose?" *Bulletin of Biblical Research* 2 (1992): 29–46 (here 31–32).

Finally, despite the few unusual terms, the passage is intricately woven into its surrounding context. In 2:1–4 Paul tells the Philippians to be "like-minded" (*phronete*) and united "in purpose" (*phronountes*, v. 2), just as he says in verses 5–11 that they should have the same "attitude" (*phronete*) as Christ (v. 5). He urges them to "consider" others better than themselves "in humility" (v. 3), just as he says that Christ did not "consider" equality with God something to be exploited (v. 6) but "humbled himself" (v. 8). He also connects verses 5–11 with his argument in verses 12–18 by the strong connective word "therefore" (v. 12) and echoes the reference to Christ's obedience (v. 8) when he speaks of the Philippians' obedience (v. 12).[8]

All of this places a bold question mark against the long-standing thesis that Philippians 2:5–11 is a pre-Pauline hymn that affords a glimpse into the understanding of Christ in the earliest church. Other passages in Paul's letters show that the apostle was capable of producing careful, rhetorically sophisticated prose to advance his arguments.[9] Here he seems to have followed this same strategy in order to convince the Philippians that they should seek the interests of others ahead of their own, drop their quarrels, and become unified with one another.

The way in which the passage advances this argument, however, has also been the subject of dispute among interpreters. Two principal lines of thought have been popular: the "ethical" interpretation and the "kerygmatic" interpretation. Those who advocate the "ethical" understanding of the paragraph's function believe that Paul is presenting Christ as an example that the Philippians should follow. Just as Christ had an attitude of humility, self-sacrifice, and obedience, so the Philippians should invest themselves with these qualities as a means of achieving unity.[10] According to the more recent "kerygmatic" interpretation, however, the passage simply recounts the story of Jesus' incarnation, death, and exaltation. Paul quotes it not to provide an example for the Philippians to follow but to remind them that they are "in Christ" and that obedience is appropriate to this status.[11]

---

8. See Morna D. Hooker, "Philippians 2:6–11," in E. Earle Ellis and Erich Grässer, eds., *Jesus und Paulus: Festschrift für Werner Georg Kümmel zum 70. Geburtstag* (Göttingen: Vandenhoeck & Ruprecht, 1978), 151–64 (here 153).

9. Fee, "Philippians 2:5–11: Hymn or Exalted Prose?" 32 n. 11, cites as examples 1 Cor. 1:22–25, 26–28; 6:12–13; 7:2–4; 9:9–22. See also the list of passages treated in Eduard Norden, *Agnostos Theos: Untersuchungen zur Formengeschichte Religiöser Rede* (Leipzig and Berlin: Verlag B. G. Teubner, 1923), 240–63.

10. Until recently, this was the standard interpretation of the place of the passage in Paul's argument. See, for example, Vincent, *Philippians*, 78–79; Michael, *Philippians*, 83.

11. See Ernst Käsemann, "A Critical Analysis of Philippians 2:5–11," *Journal for Theology and the Church* 5 (1968): 45–88 (esp. 45–59, 83–88); Martin, *Carmen Christi*, 84–88.

The decision about which of these interpretations is the best hangs largely on the answer to three questions. (1) Is the passage a hymn? Advocates of the kerygmatic view generally believe that the passage is a hymn since they hold that Paul is simply summarizing the gospel the Philippians believed. What better way to do this than to appeal to a Christian psalm, perhaps already known at Philippi, which told the story of Jesus? Supporters of the ethical interpretation sometimes view the passage as a previously composed hymn, but several are comfortable with the notion that Paul himself designed the passage to say precisely what needed to be said about Christ in order to portray him as an appropriate example for the Philippians to follow.

(2) How should verse 5 be translated? A literal translation demonstrates the problem: "Have this attitude among yourselves which also in Christ Jesus." The confusion about how to understand this verse arises from the absence of a verb in the second clause ("which also in Christ Jesus"). Did Paul intend for the reader to supply the same verb in this clause that appeared in the first clause ("Have this attitude among yourselves which *you* also *have* in Christ Jesus")? This is the view of those who adopt the "kerygmatic" interpretation, according to which the Philippians should have the attitude among themselves that is required of those who are "in Christ"—that is, those who have believed the gospel that the following hymn summarizes. But it is equally possible that Paul intended his readers to supply the verb "was" in this clause ("Have this attitude among yourselves which *was* also in Christ Jesus"). Those who believe that the "ethical" interpretation of the passage is correct tend to adopt this understanding of the sentence. Paul would then be admonishing the Philippians to follow Christ's example of humility, obedience, and self-sacrifice.

(3) What is the role of verses 9–11? Those who hold to the kerygmatic view claim that the passage tells the story of Christ's descent and exaltation and therefore summarizes the gospel that the Philippians believed and in the light of which they should conduct their lives. The details of the story, such as the exaltation of Christ, they claim, are not important to Paul's exhortation because his point is not that the Philippians should imitate Christ's example. Rather, the hymn provides a summary of what the Philippians believed. Supporters of the ethical interpretation find verses 9–11 more difficult to explain and have advanced a number of theories about why Paul would include an account of Christ's exaltation in a summary designed to provide the Philippians with an example of humility.

Nevertheless, on balance, the "ethical" interpretation of the passage seems more likely to be correct. As we have already suggested, the passage is probably not a pre-Pauline hymn, but Paul's own prose composition intended to advance his argument that the Philippians should agree with one another, avoid selfish ambition, and in humility put the interests of others ahead of their own (2:1–4). The word "this" at the beginning of verse 5 in Greek ("This think among yourselves which was also in Christ Jesus"), then, probably refers to the quality of humility that Paul has just described in verses 1–4. "Think in this way," he says, "just as Jesus Christ thought in this way." Paul is calling the Philippians to follow the example of Christ's selflessness (vv. 6–7), humility (v. 8), and obedience (v. 8).[12]

It is true, as advocates of the kerygmatic view claim, that Paul does not usually derive Christian ethics from the pattern of Christ's life but from the believer's participation in Christ's death and resurrection (Rom. 6:1–14; cf. 1 Cor. 6:11–20; Col. 3:1–4) and from the indwelling power of the Holy Spirit (Rom. 8:1–17; Gal. 5:16–26). Nevertheless, the use of Christ's conduct as an example to believers of how they should conduct themselves is certainly not unknown in Paul (Rom. 15:3, 7–9; 1 Cor 11:1; 2 Cor. 8:9; Eph. 5:1–2; Col. 3:13; cf. 1 Tim. 6:13–16), and in a letter that twice entreats its readers to imitate other Christians (3:17; 4:9), an admonition to imitate Christ does not seem unlikely.

But what about verses 9–11? How does a description of Christ's exaltation provide an example for the Philippians to follow? This passage is probably best understood as a pointer, again through Christ's example, to the Philippians' own future if they remain faithful. Just as God exalted Christ to the highest place in response to his obedience, so the Philippians, if they remain steadfast in the faith through enduring persecution and seeking unity with one another, will be glorified. This thought is consistent with Paul's emphasis in 1:9–11 on the eschatological goal of the Philippians' sanctification. There Paul prays that the Philippians "may abound more and more in knowledge and depth of insight, so that [they] may be able to discern what is best and may be pure and blameless until the day of Christ." It is also consistent with his statement in 3:21 that those who follow Paul's example rather than the example of the "enemies of the cross of Christ" will experience the transformation of their "lowly bodies [lit., body of humility] so that they will be like [Christ's] glorious body" (3:21). As with Christ Jesus in 2:9–11, their faithfulness amid hardship and their humble obedience will one day be transformed into glorification.[13]

In summary, 2:5–11 is an integral part of Paul's argument from 1:27 forward that the Philippians should "conduct" themselves "in a manner worthy

---

12. Cf. 3:15, where "this" (*touto*) and "think" (*phroneo*) appear together as they do here. In 3:15, "this" refers to the preceding discussion, not to what follows.

13. Hooker, "Philippians 2:6–11," 155, 157.

of the gospel of Christ." Paul composed the passage himself with great care in order to portray Jesus as an example for the Philippians to follow as they reshape their thinking about their mutual relationships.[14]

**An Exposition of the Passage.** The passage can be divided into three parts: an introductory sentence (v. 5), an account of Christ's condescension (vv. 6–8), and an account of his exaltation (vv. 9–11).

Paul begins in verse 5 by admonishing the Philippians to be unified, humble, and unselfish in their relations with one another (2:2–4), just as Christ Jesus was unselfish. His concern is not merely with the inner attitudes of individual Philippian believers, but with the concrete expressions of their attitudes in their day-to-day encounters with each other. The NIV, along with many other translations, is slightly misleading at this point. Its phrase "your attitude" makes Paul's Greek refer to an attitude inside each Philippian believer. Paul says literally, however, "Think this in you," and the words "in you" (*en hymin*) are a common idiom in Greek for "among yourselves."[15] Paul's primary concern, then, is social rather than cerebral: He wants the Philippians to adopt in their mutual relations the same attitude that characterized Jesus. In the remarkable sentences that follow, Paul describes this attitude.

In verses 6–8 Paul describes both Christ's divine status and his willingness not only to empty himself by becoming human but also to humble himself by submitting to a cruel form of death. His first step is to describe Christ's divine status as "being in very nature God" (v. 6). The term the NIV has rendered "very nature" is, in other translations, often rendered "form" (KJV, NASB, REB, NRSV); the Greek word underlying these renderings (*morphe*) frequently referred in classical literature to the different forms that a divine being might take.[16] When Paul uses the term in verse 6, however, he is not interested in the different physical characteristics of a being with a single substance, but in the equality of Christ Jesus with God, as the next phrase explains. Similarly, when Paul uses this same word in verse 7 to speak of Jesus taking the

---

14. In 2:1–4 Paul implies by the use of such terms as "like-minded," "purpose," "consider," and "look . . . to" that the unselfishness he wants the Philippians to show toward one another must flow from an unselfish way of thinking. In 2:5–11 Paul puts flesh and bones on this mental disposition by describing the "attitude" of Christ Jesus (v. 5) as it was displayed in his humility and obedience (vv. 6–8).

15. See Walter Bauer, *A Greek-English Lexicon of the New Testament and Other Early Christian Literature*, 2d ed., trans., adapt., and rev. William F. Arndt, F. Wilbur Gingrich, Frederick W. Danker (Chicago: University of Chicago Press, 1979) 258–59.

16. The word is also used this way in its only other occurrence in the New Testament manuscript tradition. In Mark 16:12 Jesus appears in a different, unrecognizable form to the two disciples who were walking in the country.

form of a slave, he means that Jesus became a slave in his "very nature."[17] Apparently Paul viewed divinity and servanthood as compatible, not contradictory, roles.[18]

Christ's condescension to the form of a slave was made possible, according to verse 6, by his own attitude toward equality with God: He did not consider it "something to be grasped." This phrase is notoriously difficult because it represents a Greek word (*harpagmos*) that appears nowhere else in the Greek Bible and occurs only rarely in secular Greek. Its few secular occurrences carry the meaning "robbery" or "rape," and so the KJV translated the phrase "thought it not robbery to be equal with God." Careful research has shown, however, that the word *harpagmos* could be used synonymously with the much more frequent word *harpagma*, and that both words appear in expressions similar to the one in Philippians 2:6 to mean "an advantage." The early Christian historian Eusebius, for example, used both words in similar sentences to mean the same thing:

And Peter considered death by means of the cross *harpagmon* on account of the hope of salvation (*Eis to kata Loucan Evangelion*, 6).

Some [persecuted Christians] ... regarded death as *harpagma* in comparison with the depravity of ungodly men (*Historia Ecclesiastica* 8.12.2).[19]

The point of both passages is that Peter and the persecuted Christians viewed death as something of which to take advantage. Paradoxically, they considered it not a dreaded evil, but a windfall.

This is the sense in which Paul uses the same idiom in Philippians 2:6. Because Christ was in very nature God, he did not consider equality with God "something to be exploited" (NRSV), something of which he should take advantage. His equality with God led him to view his status not as a matter of privilege but as a matter of unselfish giving. This is the character of the biblical God, and this was the character of Christ Jesus as well.

An attitude, however, is abstract and remains unknown until it is expressed in some concrete way. In verses 7–8 Paul tells us that Christ acted

---

17. See W. Pöhlmann, "μορφή," *Exegetical Dictionary of the New Testament*, ed. Horst Balz and Gerhard Schneider, 3 vols. (Grand Rapids: Eerdmans, 1990–93), 2:442–43.

18. Compare C. F. D. Moule, "Further Reflexions on Philippians 2:5–11," *Apostolic History and the Gospel*, ed. W. Ward Gasque and Ralph P. Martin (Grand Rapids: Eerdmans, 1970), 264–76.

19. Roy W. Hoover, "The Harpagmos Enigma: A Philological Solution, *Harvard Theological Review* 64 (1971) 95–119, here at 108. On this issue, see also N. T. Wright, *The Climax of the Covenant: Christ and the Law in Pauline Theology* (Edinburgh: T. & T. Clark, 1991) 62–90.

on his way of thinking in two ways in verse 7. First, as to verse 7, Paul emphasizes that Christ "made himself nothing" by "taking the very nature of a servant, being made in human likeness." Three aspects of this verse are essential for grasping its meaning. (1) The phrase "made himself nothing" is an appropriate translation of the Greek that says, more literally, "he emptied himself" (NASB, NRSV). The verb "empty" (*kenoo*) appears only four times elsewhere in the New Testament. All of these occurrences are in Paul's letters, and all use the term, not literally to refer to emptying something of qualities it possesses, but figuratively of nullifying something, making it of no account.[20] It is unlikely, then, that the term is used in a literal sense here in verse 6. This is confirmed by the rest of the verse, where Paul uses two participial constructions to specify precisely how Christ emptied himself. He did so both by "taking the very nature of a servant" and by "being made in human likeness." Christ did not literally empty himself of any divine attribute; instead, he metaphorically emptied himself by revealing the form of God in the form of a slave and in human likeness.[21]

(2) The term "servant" in the NIV represents the Greek word for "slave" (*doulos*). A number of proposals about the possible background for the term have been advanced: Does it refer to the Servant of the Lord in Isaiah (42:1–4; 49:1–6; 50:4–9; esp. 52:13–53:12)? Does it refer to God's righteous servants who suffer at the hands of the ungodly in later Jewish tradition (e.g., 2 Macc. 7:34)? Does it point to Christ's role as slave of all during his earthly ministry (Mark 10:44; John 13:1–20)?[22] Although one or all of these portraits of the unselfish and obedient servant may have contributed to Paul's choice of this metaphor for Christ's condescension, Paul's language is not specific enough to make a primary reference to any of these servant themes plausible. Within the culture shared by both Paul and the Philippians, an unqualified reference to "the very nature of a slave" would have taken its meaning from the ubiquitous institution of slavery. The slave in Greco-Roman society was deprived of the most basic human rights. In the same way, Christ

---

20. Paul uses the term to refer to what would happen to faith if those who lived by the law were heirs to God's promise (Rom. 4:14), to refer to what would happen to the gospel if Paul preached by means of human wisdom (1 Cor. 1:17), to what would happen to his boast about the Corinthians' generosity if they proved unwilling to contribute to Paul's collection when the apostle's fellow workers arrived (2 Cor. 9:3), and to what would happen to Paul's "boast" that he preaches the gospel free of charge if he were to accept payment from the Corinthians (1 Cor. 9:15).

21. Bruce, *Philippians*, 46; O'Brien, *Philippians*, 218.

22. Various proposals are summarized and evaluated in Martin, *Carmen Christi*, 165–96; O'Brien, *Philippians*, 218–24.

refused to exploit the privilege of his deity and, giving up that right, became a slave.[23]

(3) The term "likeness" in Paul's claim that Christ emptied himself by "being made in human likeness" does not indicate a difference between Christ and humanity, but an essential identity. On first examination, Romans 8:3 seems to argue against this understanding of the term. There Paul uses the word "likeness" to stress the difference between Jesus and others who possessed sinful human flesh. Unlike them, his sinful flesh did not succeed in leading him to sin. Thus, to show that this one difference remained between Christ and humanity, Paul qualifies his reference to the Incarnation: God, he says, sent "his own Son in the likeness of sinful man to be a sin offering."

The phrase "being made in human likeness" in Philippians 2:7, however, stands parallel to the phrase "taking the very nature of a slave." Just as the term "very nature" (*morphe*) stresses the essential identity of Christ Jesus with a slave, so the term "likeness" (*homoiomati*) in the parallel phrase emphasizes the essential identity of Christ Jesus with humanity. A better analogy than Romans 8:3 to Paul's use of "likeness" here in Philippians is Romans 5:14. There Paul says, "Death reigned from Adam until Moses even over those who had not sinned in the likeness (*homoiomati*) of Adam's transgression" (pers. trans.). Paul's point is that some people had not sinned *exactly* as Adam had sinned. Similarly, in Philippians 2:7, Christ Jesus became human in the *exact* sense, in every sense that makes one truly human.

In verses 6–7, then, Paul both states the equality and the substantial unity of Christ with God and then describes one way in which Christ expressed his deity. He did not exploit this status but manifested it in humble service by becoming a slave and a human being. To use the words of Jesus himself, "For even the Son of Man did not come to be served, but to serve, and to give his life as a ransom for many" (Mark 10:45; cf. Matt. 20:28).

In verse 8 Paul describes a second way in which Christ expresses his deity: He humbled himself by being found in appearance as a man and by suffering death by crucifixion. There is little difference between the statement that Christ emptied himself by becoming a slave and a human being and that "being found in appearance as a man, he humbled himself."[24] But Paul does not end the second statement with a reference to Christ's self-imposed

---

23. Moule, "Further Reflexions on Philippians 2:5–11," 268–69.

24. The expression "being found in appearance as a man" does not mean that Jesus only appeared to be a man. Rather, it means that in every way recognizable to anyone else, he was a man. This is clear from the parallel statements "taking the very nature of a servant" and "being made in human likeness," which govern the meaning of this phrase. "As" does not have to indicate a difference between Jesus and humanity but can refer to the typical essence of something, as in 2 Thess. 3:15. See O'Brien, *Philippians*, 226, esp. n. 139.

humility. Instead, he takes the second statement further by saying that Christ Jesus "became obedient to death—even death on a cross." Christ emptied himself by taking the form of a slave, but he stooped even lower when his human condition and his obedience led him to the cross.

In the world Paul shared with the Philippians, this was the lowest that one could stoop socially. Crucifixion was the cruelest form of official execution in the Roman empire, and although a Roman citizen might experience it if convicted of high treason, it was commonly reserved for the lower classes, especially slaves.[25] The second century B.C. Latin playwright Plautus, for example, says that slaves had been executed by crucifixion "from time immemorial."[26] Partly because crucifixion was not the conversation of polite company and partly because the cruel creativity of executioners was allowed wide latitude, the specifics of the process are not frequently described. Generally, however, the victim was first tortured in various ways and then fastened to a cross by impaling, nailing, binding with ropes, or some combination of all three. Death often came slowly over a period of days as the victim experienced increased blood loss, thirst, hunger, the attacks of wild animals, and suffocation.

Thus it is no surprise that Paul found the message of the cross to be "a stumbling block to Jews and foolishness to the Gentiles" (1 Cor. 1:23; cf. 1:18), that Christian apologists in later centuries had constantly to explain to their detractors the meaning of this offensive, yet central, part of their proclamation, and that some who called themselves Christians tried to play down its significance or to eliminate it altogether with the claim that their Savior did not actually die on the cross. When Paul adds to the statement that Christ emptied himself by taking the form of a slave the comment that he humbled himself by becoming obedient to the point of death on a cross, therefore, he has taken the nature of Christ's selfless denial of his rights to new depths. Christ went from the highest position imaginable to the lowest precisely because such selfless love was an expression of his deity.

To summarize, in the second part of this passage (vv. 6–8) Paul has described Christ's deity in terms of his selfless denial of his rights. This selfless denial entailed two steps, making himself nothing (or emptying himself) by becoming a human being and a slave, and humbling himself by becoming obedient to the point of suffering a slave's death, death on the cross.

The third part of the passage (vv. 9–11) stands in stark contrast to the second. In verses 6–8 Christ Jesus is the focus, and God stays in the background

---

25. This account of crucifixion is drawn from Martin Hengel's comprehensive study, *Crucifixion* (Philadelphia: Fortress, 1977).

26. Quoted in Hengel, *Crucifixion*, 52.

as the one whose form Christ possesses, with whom Christ is equal, and whom Christ obeys. In verses 9–11, however, God takes center stage, and Christ is the recipient of his action.[27] The section can be divided into two parts: The first (v. 9) describes God's response to Christ's obedience, the second (vv. 10–11) describes the result of that action.

Verse 9 begins with the two Greek words *dio kai* ("Therefore also"), a strong way of showing that in what follows Paul describes a response to the selfless humility and obedience depicted in the first part of the passage. God responded to Jesus' obedience in two ways: He "exalted" Jesus "to the highest place," and he "gave" to Jesus "the name that is above every name." Occasionally scholars have thought that the first response meant that "Christ would receive a condition or authority greater than that which he possessed before his condescension."[28] But since it is difficult to imagine a station higher than that of "being in very nature God" and "equality with God" (v. 6)—the place Christ occupied before his condescension—the term *exalted* is better understood as a reference to God's exaltation of Jesus to a position of recognizable superiority over all creation. Although he was acting in a way that was fully consistent with his divine status when he humbled himself, his resurrection and ascension to the Father's right hand make his superiority more fully evident to the creation over which he rules.[29]

Paul describes this exaltation more specifically when he says that God gave to Jesus "the name that is above every name." Since Paul does not say precisely what name God gave to Jesus, interpreters have made a variety of suggestions. Pelagius thought that it was "Son of God." An early Latin commentator believed that it was "God." More recent suggestions have included simply the human name "Jesus."[30] Most students of this letter are surely right, however, in claiming that it is the name "Lord," for in verse 11 this title appears for the first time in the passage and is added to the name "Jesus Christ," used before (v. 5). It is not insignificant, however, that Paul leaves the precise name vague in verse 9. His emphasis is not on the name itself but on the status of the name as "above every name." This can only mean that at Christ's exaltation the process began by which the equality with God that Jesus always possessed would be acknowledged by all creation.

---

27. O'Brien, *Philippians*, 232.

28. Bonnard, *Philippiens*, 46.

29. In the Greek translation of the Old Testament, this term is used in Psalm 97:9: "For you, O LORD, are the Most High over all the earth; you are *exalted* [*hyperypsothes*] far above all gods." See Bauer, *Greek-English Lexicon*, 842.

30. See the list in Meyer, *The Epistles to the Philippians and Colossians and to Philemon*, 81. For an intriguing argument that God gave to his Son the name "Jesus," see Moule, "Further Reflexions on Philippians 2:5–11," 270.

Why did God exalt Jesus and grant him the name above every name? At first glance God seems to have done this as payment for Christ's obedience. Christ was "obedient to death—even death on a cross," Paul says, "and therefore God exalted him to the highest place and granted to him the name above every name" (pers. trans.). The key to understanding this sentence, however, lies in noticing that God takes the initiative. Jesus does not force God's hand, nor is the exaltation and granting of the name a payment for deeds performed. Instead God initiated the exaltation of Jesus and "freely gave" (*echarisato*) to him the most superior of names.[31]

Paul next describes the result of this exaltation (vv. 10–11). Every knee of every created being, he says, will bow before him (v. 10), every tongue confess his splendid name, and God will be glorified (v. 11). Two questions have troubled students of this final part of the passage. (1) Who are the creatures "in heaven and on earth and under the earth"? Are they every creature in the universe? Or are they the spiritual forces ranged against Christ who will be forced to submit to his conquering power? If the two phrases "every knee" and "every tongue" indicate the identity of these beings, it seems clear that Paul refers not merely to forces opposed to Christ, but to every creature. (2) Does this passage imply that all will confess Christ willingly or only that all will acknowledge him, some willingly and others unwillingly? The key to answering this question lies in realizing that verses 10b–11a refer to Isaiah 45:23–24:

> Before me every knee will bow;
>> by me every tongue will swear.
> They will say of me, "In the LORD alone
>> are righteousness and strength."
> All who have raged against him
>> will come to him and be put to shame.

In this passage, some of those who bend the knee and confess the greatness of the Lord are opponents who will now be put to shame. If this passage informed Paul's thinking as he penned verses 10–11—and the clear echoes of Isaiah 45:23 show that it did—then it would be unwise to assume that, according to this passage, all those who will bow before Jesus at the final day and confess his Lordship will do so gladly.

It would also be unwise, however, to leave the impression that Paul's emphasis lay on Jesus' triumph over his enemies. Paul's lack of specificity on this point shows that his concern lay not in Jesus' victory over those who opposed him but in Jesus' sovereignty over all creation. One day, Paul says,

---

31. On this issue, see Paul D. Feinberg, "The Kenosis and Christology: An Exegetical-Theological Analysis of Phil 2:6–11," *Trinity Journal* 1 NS (1980): 21–46 (here 42).

the universe will acknowledge what the small, persecuted community at Philippi confesses in its worship—"Jesus Christ is Lord."

Beyond this, Paul still portrays Christ as the Philippians' example in this passage. Certainly they cannot experience the unique exaltation of the One who is "in very nature God," but if they are faithful as he was faithful, then they too will be found "pure and blameless" at that day, "filled with the fruit of righteousness" (1:10–11), having reached "the goal," and having gained "the prize of the heavenly call of God in Christ Jesus" (3:14).[32] None of this will be earned as payment for services performed—God will work within them to ensure their faithfulness (2:13), and he will freely grant his approval out of his own sovereign will. But the Philippians can be assured that just as Christ's faithfulness will lead to the universal acknowledgment of his position, so their faithfulness will lead to identity with Christ and resurrection from the dead on the final day (3:10–11). They can also rest assured that precisely because Christ has been exalted and stands in authority over all things, one day the body of their humility will be transformed to be like his glorious body (3:20–21).[33]

In 2:5–11, then, Paul places the example of Christ before the divided Philippian community. They should pursue humility and the interests of others (2:4), just as Jesus refused to exploit the power that his equality with God gave to him and instead demonstrated his deity in the role of a slave. They should also pursue obedience (2:12), just as Jesus was obedient to the point of suffering a slave's dreadful death. If they are faithful as Jesus was faithful, then the final day will mean the fulfillment of their deepest longings.

*Bridging Contexts*

BECAUSE PHILIPPIANS 2:5–11 has attracted the attention both of historians interested in the development of Christianity between Jesus and Paul and theologians interested in the biblical witness to the incarnation and divinity of Jesus, the passage has gained a significance of its own apart from its place in the argument of Paul's letter. Faced with the mass of literature on the passage, it would be easy to forget two commonsense principles, one historical and the other theological. Historians who look to the passage for evidence of the development of ideas about

---

32. Perhaps vv. 9–11 also contain a subtle admonition to the Philippians that they will one day bend the knee before Jesus Christ and give an account of their relationships with fellow believers. Cf. Paul's use of Isa. 45:23 in Rom. 14:11 to remind the divided Roman community that they will one day render account for their actions to God. I am indebted to Professor Klyne Snodgrass for bringing this point to my attention.

33. Hooker, "Philippians 2:6–11," 155, 157.

the nature of Christ and his incarnation in the early church prior to Paul tend to assume that the passage is a pre-Pauline hymn. This thesis, however, is far from certain, and at the end of the day all we can know for sure is that Paul placed this passage in his letter to the Philippians. From the historical perspective, then, the primary issue for students of Philippians should be how the passage functions in Paul's argument, not how the passage may have functioned in some hypothetical worship setting in the period prior to Paul.

From the theological perspective, understanding the passage primarily within its Philippian context is even more important. The church did not canonize Philippians 2:6–11 as a separate document, a kind of New Testament psalm in praise of Christ. Indeed, as we have seen, the fathers of the church, who spoke Paul's language as their native tongue, appear to have been unaware of any hymnic qualities in the passage at all. Thus they canonized these verses only as part of Paul's letter to the Philippians, and the passage therefore has no independent authority for the believer apart from the role it plays in the argument of this canonical letter. As we bring Philippians 2:6–11 out of its original setting and into the contemporary church, therefore, we must not forget that verse 5 binds it to Paul's previous admonitions in verses 1–4, and that verse 12a binds it to the subsequent appeal in verses 12b–16. Philippians 2:6–11 is a significant step, but only a step, in Paul's wider argument.

In addition to this general interpretive stumbling block, four narrower aspects of the passage have often provoked intense debate and serious misunderstanding: the nature of the imitation that the passage requires of its readers, the character of God's response to Christ's obedience, the extent to which the passage claims that Christ "made himself nothing," and whether or not the passage teaches Christ's deity and preexistence.

(1) The biblical notion of the imitation of Christ has suffered under a variety of misinterpretations. It became especially prominent in the thirteenth century through the influence of Francis of Assisi and the ecclesiastical orders he founded. In a famous step, Francis renounced his large family inheritance and lived a life of simplicity and poverty in imitation of his understanding of Christ's life. He begged for bread, kissed lepers, and responded in absolute obedience and simplicity to the call of God. In 1224, two years before his death, Francis reportedly was praying at his mountain retreat in Tuscany when he saw a mysterious vision of the crucified Christ and found himself scarred, like the Christ in his vision, with nail prints in both hands and feet and inflicted with a continuously bleeding wound in his side. His followers reported that Francis suffered with this condition until his death, and they understood this period as a prolonged identification with Christ

crucified.[34] For Francis and his followers, then, the imitation of Christ involved an attempt to reproduce as nearly as possible within their own contexts Christ's life of wandering poverty and, at least in the case of Francis, a near repetition of Christ's passion.

Much later, and for widely different reasons, the imitation of Christ also became popular in nineteenth- and early twentieth-century liberalism. Much of the worth of Christianity, it was thought, lay in the sublime ethical example of the simple Galilean rabbi, Jesus of Nazareth. Stripped of his miracles, which were considered largely the creation of naive and uneducated followers of Jesus in the early church, Jesus became significant because of his ethic of peace and love.[35] Paul obscured this simple ethic with his thoroughly Hellenistic and mystical understanding of baptism and the Lord's Supper. These were magical elements that could have no enduring connection with the modern world.[36] But where the simple message of Jesus' life and teaching is rediscovered and followed, it was said, something of enduring worth has been found.

Scholars who have reacted against the "ethical" interpretation of Philippians 2:5–11 at times seem to have done so in order to avoid giving credence to such notions as these about the imitation of Christ. Fascination with the imitation of Christ, these scholars believe, supports ethical idealism and leaves out the central doctrine of justification by faith through God's grace.[37] Resistance to such notions is surely valid. If our lives are consumed with a rote attempt to mimic the actions of Christ as they are revealed in the Gospels, then we stand in danger of forgetting that salvation comes by faith alone apart from works of the law. Similarly, we stand in danger of thinking that "the fellowship of sharing in his sufferings" (3:10) is a matter solely of identifying our physical pain with Christ's death on the cross.

On the other hand, we should not allow abuses of the notion of the imitation of Christ so to govern our understanding of Paul that we miss the intention of this text. The verbal connections between 2:6–11 and the argument both before and after it show that Paul is describing Christ's incarnation and

---

34. See William R. Cook, *Francis of Assisi* (Collegeville, Minn.: Liturgical Press, 1989), 19–49, 94–114.

35. See, for example, Adolf von Harnack, *What Is Christianity?* (Gloucester, Mass.: Peter Smith, 1978), 1–151. Harnack gave the lectures on which this book is based at the University of Berlin during the winter of 1899–1900.

36. See, for example, the quotation from the early twentieth-century German scholar Wilhelm Heitmüller in Werner Georg Kümmel, *The New Testament: The History of the Investigation of Its Problems* (Nashville, Tenn.: Abingdon, 1972), 257.

37. See Ernst Käsemann, "A Critical Analysis of Philippians 2:5–11," 50–51, who argues against the ethical interpretation in part because it excludes the doctrine of the justification of the impious. Cf. Barth, *Philippians*, 59–68.

exaltation as an example of the humility and obedience which he wants the Philippians to display in their relations with one another (2:3, 7–8, 12). For the Philippians, the imitation of Christ could not have involved a literal mimicry of his incarnation and certainly could not be equated with some mystical identification with his death on the cross. Paul's focus instead is on the imitation of Christ's "attitude" (v. 5).[38] In Thessalonica this meant faithfully suffering for the gospel as Christ had suffered (1 Thess. 1:6; 2:14–15). In Corinth it meant not exercising rights within the church when to do so would cause another's stumbling and destruction (1 Cor. 11:1). In Philippi it meant being loving, united, humble, and willing to put the interests of others ahead of one's own (Phil. 2:2–4).

The way in which the believer imitates Christ's attitude will vary from situation to situation. At times the church surely needs the reforming influence of those who, like Francis of Assisi, follow Christ's selfless regard for the poor and sick in radical ways. But the imitation of Christ should not be an attempt to relive the particulars of his life and death. It should instead lead each believer within his or her own context to "live a life of love, just as Christ loved us and gave himself up for us" (Eph. 5:2).

(2) A second pitfall that has sometimes stood in the way of a proper application of this passage is the claim that in verses 9–11 Paul describes the reward God has given to Christ for his obedience. As we have already seen in our study of the original meaning of the passage, Paul does not describe in these verses a reward Christ earned by his efforts to do good but honors God freely chose to confer on his Son in response to obedience. Both the obedience and the exaltation came at God's initiative for Christ, just as they do for us (2:12–13).

Occasionally, however, the attempt to avoid any notion of reward in this passage has led to one-sided interpretations and opened the door for inappropriate applications. Karl Barth, for example, claimed that there was no difference between the exalted Christ of verses 9–11 and the humble Christ of verses 6–8. Christ, said Barth, is exalted in the form of the suffering and obedient servant. The crucial "therefore," which marks the division between the two parts of the passage, does not mean

> that he who was humbled and humiliated was afterwards exalted, was indeed ... rewarded for his self-denial and obedience. But what it says is, that precisely he who was abased and humbled even to the obedience of death on the cross is also the Exalted Lord.[39]

---

38. Fee, "Philippians 2:5–11: Hymn or Exalted Prose?" 38.
39. Barth, *Philippians*, 66.

In other words, Christ remains crucified even in his exaltation.

If we were to take this approach, however, we would not only be doing violence to the text, where the "therefore" clearly means that a shift in Christ's state has occurred in response to his obedience, but we would also be ignoring a theme that runs throughout Scripture and be placing too great an emphasis on Christ's suffering. Throughout Scripture the biblical writers affirm that God exalts the humble, and this theme often comes as a word of comfort to those who are suffering under the oppression of the powerful. Certainly the exalted Christ is the crucified Christ and, as Barth comments, the old paintings of Christ enthroned in heaven with the wounds of his crucifixion still visible are appropriate. Nevertheless, Christ exalted is Christ triumphant, and he will come the second time not in humility but riding the white horse of the Apocalypse (Rev. 19:11–21). At that time he will put an end to suffering and injustice and welcome into his company those who have faithfully suffered for the gospel under the oppressing hand of tyrants. Philippians 2:9–11, then, stands as a word of comfort to those who are oppressed, especially to those who, like the Philippians (1:27–30), are oppressed for the sake of the gospel.[40]

(3) A third stumbling block to understanding this passage is the unfortunate role it has played in efforts to claim that Christ emptied himself of complete divinity when he became human. In the nineteenth century a view of Christ's incarnation became popular that claimed he had either given up or restricted some element of his divinity at the time of his incarnation. Advocates of this position often appealed to the statement in Philippians 2:7 that Christ "made himself nothing" (lit., "emptied himself") as evidence for their thesis, and, because the relevant Greek term is *ekenosen* (from the verb *kenoo*), such notions became known as "Kenotic" theories of the Incarnation.[41] As we have already seen in our study of the original meaning of the passage, however, when Paul uses the term *kenoo* elsewhere, he uses it metaphorically, and nothing indicates a different use here. The text cannot serve as evidence, then, that at his incarnation Christ literally emptied himself to some extent of his divinity.

On the other hand, concern to deny any connotation within the passage that Christ emptied himself of his divinity should not lead us to the opposite error of playing down the passage's emphasis on the humiliation of Christ. The passage clearly says that Christ became not merely a man but a

---

40. See Fowl, *The Story of Christ in the Ethics of Paul*, 90–91.

41. See the useful overview of and response to Kenotic theories of the Incarnation by Eugene R. Fairweather, "The 'Kenotic' Christology," in Beare, *Philippians*, 159–74; see also Erickson, *The Word Became Flesh*, 78–86.

slave and that he died the dreaded death of a slave. This does not mean, of course, that he literally was one of the millions of slaves that peopled the Roman empire in the first century. But it probably does carry connotations of his low social station. He was part of a conquered and oppressed people, and within that people was so poor that he had no place to put his head (Matt. 8:20; Luke 9:58) and had to be supported in his work by the kindness of others (Matt. 27:55; Luke 8:3). As remarkable as it may seem, Paul affirms that such a lowly position was not incompatible with Christ's divinity but was in some way a manifestation of it. When we play down the human and lowly side of Jesus, then, we are damaging his divinity as well.

(4) A final understanding of the passage claims that the preexistence of Christ is not taught in this passage and that instead these verses presuppose a fully human Jesus whom God exalted precisely because he refused the attempt to gain equality with God. The most popular form of this thesis claims that the passage implies a contrast between Christ and Adam.[42] Christ was in the "form" of God in the same sense that Adam was in the "image" of God, but unlike Adam he did not consider equality with God something to be grasped. Instead, he took the path of humility and self-service. God, in response, exalted him to a place higher than he had before and conferred great honor on him.

It is far from clear, however, that a comparison with Adam stands behind this passage. Despite complex arguments to the contrary, "image" in Genesis 1:26 is not fully synonymous with "form" in the Greek translation of the Hebrew Scriptures, and the fault of the first woman and man lay in their craving for the kind of knowledge God had, not in a craving for equality with God himself.[43] Indeed, it seems impossible to deny plausibly that the passage presupposes the equality of Christ with God and his existence prior to the Incarnation. How could Christ refuse to exploit equality with God if he never possessed it? How could he possess it without an eternal existence? And why would Paul speak of Christ "being found in appearance as a man" if he never existed as anything but a man?[44]

---

42. See, for example, James D. G. Dunn, *Christology in the Making: A New Testament Inquiry Into the Origins of the Doctrine of the Incarnation* (Philadelphia: Westminster, 1980), 114–21. Not all who find a contrast between Adam and Christ in the passage, however, deny that the passage teaches Christ's preexistence or equality with God. See, for example, Wright, *The Climax of the Covenant*, 90–92, who argues that the parallel between Christ and Adam need not be exact, and indeed cannot be, if the task Christ accepted was to undo the damage of Adam's sin.

43. See Erickson, *The Word Became Flesh*, 477; Vincent, *Philippians*, 86; especially O'Brien, *Philippians*, 263–68.

44. Cf. O'Brien, *Philippians*, 267.

In bringing Philippians 2:6–11 out of Paul's world and into our own, then, it is essential to comprehend the full height and depth of the passage. Paul affirms that Christ was fully God and entitled to all the privileges of God, but he also expressed his deity in humility and obedience of the lowliest type. If this is so, Paul seems to say, no sacrifice of our own comparatively paltry rights as human beings seems too great to make in order that the gospel might be advanced.

What, then, is the message that Philippians 2:5–11 speaks to the church at the turn of the twenty-first century? (1) It reminds us of the character of God. He is not only, in the words of the Westminster Shorter Catechism, "infinite, eternal, and unchangeable, in His being, wisdom, power, holiness, justice, goodness, and truth" (A. 4), but he also identifies with the weak and powerless to the extent that he has suffered their fate. Unwilling to use his privileges as God for selfish ends, Jesus expressed his deity in lowly and humble service. (2) The passage calls on us to take the daring step of conforming our own character to this aspect of the character of God. Just as Jesus expressed his divine character in his unselfish obedience to God, so we should express our Christian character by placing the interests of others ahead of our own in obedience to God's Word. (3) The passage reminds us of the final day, when God will respond to the lives of his obedient servants with commendation, just as he responded to Christ's obedient life. All of us will one day give an account to God for our stewardship of the time and resources he has given us (Rom. 14:10; 1 Cor. 3:15; 2 Cor. 5:10). Paul's hope throughout this letter is that both he and his readers will, on that day, stand before God pure and blameless (Phil. 1:10; cf. 2:16; 3:11–14). By telling the story of Jesus' incarnation, humiliation, and exaltation, this passage shows the path we should follow as we await that final day.

FROM THE MOMENT of birth, people urge others to meet their needs. The infant cries until Mom comes to feed or change her. The toddler misbehaves until Dad stops playing with little sister and has to give full attention to him. At older ages siblings often demand privileges in at least equal proportion to, and preferably in greater amounts than, their brothers and sisters. Adults often seek the highest paying jobs, the most comfortable homes, the most prestigious cars, and the most extravagant vacations possible, and are willing to go to considerable trouble to achieve these ends. What begins as a survival instinct quickly becomes an expression of fallen human nature, but for people to live successfully in community with other people this instinct must be restrained in numerous ways. Many of the rules laid down in a well-functioning family and many of the laws in any larger society are attempts to restrain and channel the human desire to dominate others. The drive is so strong and so universal that the community that does not effectively accomplish this task of restraint self-destructs.

The incarnation of Christ Jesus represents the antithesis of this human drive to dominate. Although he had access to all the privilege and power to which his identity with God entitled him, and although he could have exploited that privilege and power to dominate his creatures, Jesus considered his deity an opportunity for service and obedience. His deity became a matter not of getting but of giving, not of being served but of serving, not of dominance but of obedience. The difficult part of all this for the twentieth-century believer is that Paul did not leave his description of Christ's astounding refusal to dominate in the realm of abstract speculation. Instead, he advised the church at Philippi, and through them the church of today, to follow Christ's example. This means that the church and the believer must adopt an "incarnational" demeanor.

Yet this is extremely difficult to do in modern Western societies. Great, even ultimate, value in these societies is often attached to wealth, glamour, power, and prestige, and the accepted ways of achieving these ends often involve dominance over others. Thus advertising involves far more than the simple announcement of a product's availability and benefits to the potential consumer. It frequently communicates subtle and powerful lies. The attractive and virile twenty-year-old on the billboard has a cigarette dangling from her mouth as she rides high and carefree on the shoulders of a handsome young man. She says nothing verbally, but the image of social acceptance that she powerfully represents tells the young people who drive by that one of the deepest longings of the human heart can be met if they smoke the advertiser's brand of tobacco. The people who produced the advertisement are sophisticated enough to know that the required warning running along the bottom of the billboard is true. Smoking may or may not lead to social acceptance, but it often leads to addiction and painful, premature death. Through the use of a powerful image, the advertisement dominates and abuses, and those who produce it get rich.

With our minds assaulted by this kind of abusive use of power day after day, it is easy for us and the churches we represent to think that in our own way it is acceptable to dominate others in order to achieve our ends. It is easy to see this in advocates of the "prosperity gospel" who enrich themselves by preying on the fears and superstitions of their followers about withholding or giving money to God. But we should probably ponder whether the same principles are at work in some church building campaigns and membership drives. Are these genuine efforts to see the gospel advance, or are they ways of enhancing the prestige and comfort of our own group?

Several diagnostic questions might help in determining whether such programs originate in good motives or in motives unworthy of the gospel:

- Is this strategy designed to meet the need for every sector of human society to hear the gospel or only for those parts of society with which I feel comfortable?
- Would the poorest person in the city assume that the new church building was a place for him or her, or would that thought probably not even occur?
- Do evangelism teams give more effort to affluent neighborhoods than to poverty-stricken communities?

If honest answers to questions like these reveal that we are building and recruiting for our own social group, then it becomes difficult to tell whether at the deepest level our concern is for the advancement of the gospel or only for making our own lives more comfortable by providing ourselves with more pleasant quarters and gaining legitimacy among our peers. The strategies for dominance within the world have so thoroughly permeated the Western church that if the Word became flesh today, many churches might not even know of his existence, for according to Philippians 2:7–8, he would be among the poor and disenfranchised.

This passage is not only about how the church as a group can best adopt the character of its Savior, however. It is also about how individual church members act toward one another. That, after all, is the question that prompted Paul to write the passage in the first place. In our mutual relations, Paul says that the hallmark of our lives should be giving rather than getting, service rather than being served, obedience rather than dominance. Most often this is a matter not of choosing whether to build a new church building or of designing an evangelism strategy but of acting in loving ways, hour by hour, toward parents, spouses, children, coworkers, friends, and fellow church members. In the hundreds of ways in which our lives touch the lives of others every week, Paul says, we are to have the attitude of Christ Jesus.

How is this possible for sinful, selfish people? In his classic *Mere Christianity*, C. S. Lewis provides a helpful description of how the fallible believer can be more like Christ amid the give and take of everyday life. It helps, says Lewis, to pretend to be Jesus, just as a child might pretend to be a soldier or a shopkeeper. Just as the child's imaginary games help the child to develop skills that will later be useful as a real soldier or shopkeeper, so the "game" of pretending to be Christ inevitably reveals to the believer places for improvement and guides the believer toward spiritual maturity. Lewis agues that the minute we realize we are dressing up like Christ, we will discover ways in which our pretense could become reality. We will be embarrassed to discover thoughts that Christ would not have had and unfulfilled duties that Christ would not have neglected. Those realizations, he says, should in turn prompt us to more complete obedience.[45]

This is a genuinely Pauline insight. In 1 Corinthians 8:1–11:1 Paul addresses a group within the Corinthian church who thought that they had the right to eat cultic meals in pagan temples despite the fact that some Christians of weaker conscience had lapsed into idolatry as a result. He tells this group that simply possessing a right does not mean that it should be used. Love, not possession of rights, should be the believer's guide. In order to illustrate this, Paul says that he himself had the right to be paid for his missionary work among the Corinthians but chose not to take advantage of the right since to do so might "hinder the gospel of Christ" (9:12). Later, he summarizes his argument: "For I am not seeking my own good but the good of many, so that they may be saved" (10:33); and he concludes the discussion with this admonition: "Follow my example, as I follow the example of Christ" (11:1).

Similarly, in 2 Corinthians 8:1–9:15 Paul urges the Corinthians to give some money to his collection for the poor Jewish believers in Jerusalem. Paul does not want one group of believers to be living in poverty while another flourishes: There should be equality (8:14). As part of his argument that the Corinthians should help maintain the equality of believers, Paul reminds them of what Christ has done for them:

> For you know the grace of our Lord Jesus Christ, that though he was rich, yet for your sakes he became poor, so that you through his poverty might become rich (8:9).

The Corinthians were to imitate Christ by giving to their fellow believers sacrificially, just as Christ in his incarnation had given to them.

In Ephesians 5:25–28 Paul tells husbands to treat their wives as Christ treated the church. Echoing the imagery of God's redemption of Israel in Ezekiel 16:1–14, Paul says that Christ loved the church and gave himself for her in order to make her holy, cleanse her, wash her with the Word, and present her to himself as a "radiant" people. "In this same way," Paul says, "husbands ought to love their wives as their own bodies" (Eph. 5:28).

Paul believed that in the day-to-day affairs of the church and the family we should follow the example of Christ. In matters as mundane as where we eat, what we do with our money, and how we act toward the members of our families, Paul tells us to imitate Christ. Church members would do well to

---

45. C. S. Lewis, *Mere Christianity* (New York: Macmillan, 1943), 161–62.

"pretend" to be Christ when they discuss such divisive issues as the ordination of women, the gift of speaking in tongues, the inerrancy of Scripture, and the relative merits of Calvinist and Wesleyan approaches to theology. Believers united in a deep commitment to the essentials of Christian orthodoxy as they are expressed in the classic ecumenical creeds of the church differ on these issues after making sincere efforts to understand Scripture and to bow before its authority. Surely, in such instances, we should not break fellowship with other believers in the name of the purity of the faith.

This does not mean that such issues are unimportant or that a right answer to the questions that lie behind them does not exist. It only means that since the evidence for the various positions on these issues is ambiguous enough that thoughtful and devout believers can disagree about it, Christians should be willing to listen respectfully to one another during the debate and remain united in spirit afterward. To do this takes the kind of humility Paul ascribes to Christ in this passage. But that is the kind of humility that should characterize every Christian.

God's character, then, is best seen in the selfless service and obedience of Christ. In our own relationships with others, our emphasis should rest on selfless service and obedience, in imitation of Christ. But how do we keep this emphasis central in our relationships? It does, after all, run directly counter to the human tendency to dominate others, and it can easily slip from our grip. We must, of course, always remember that God does not expect us to obey him in our own strength, but works obedience within us. Indeed, Paul will say this explicitly in 2:13. Here, however, his point is different. By finishing his account of Jesus' story with Jesus' exaltation and the eschatological submission of the whole universe to him, Paul reminds us of the final day on which we will have to give an account to God of our mutual relationships, and he implicitly urges us to follow Jesus' example of humility in light of that coming day.

Here, as elsewhere, Paul urges us to focus on the final day not so that we might confute the enemies of the gospel with demonstrations of how Scripture predicted the headlines in this morning's newspaper, or so that we might set the date of Jesus' return, or so that we might convene prophecy symposia in which we anathematize those who do not agree with our own charting of the world's demise. Here and elsewhere, Paul simply reminds us that the final day is coming and that when it comes, we should be found "pure and blameless . . . filled with the fruit of righteousness" (1:11).

For Paul, as for the prophets and Jesus, one of the most important reasons for speaking of the final day was to provide an incentive for ethical behavior. "Woe to you who long for the day of the LORD," says Amos to Israelites who had neglected justice toward their fellow citizens. "Why do you long for the day of the LORD? That day will be darkness, not light ... pitch-dark, without a ray of brightness" (Amos 5:18, 20). In Jesus' parable of the great banquet, he warns the Jews that if they reject him, then Gentiles will fill their places at the coming "feast in the Kingdom of God" (Luke 14:15–24; cf. Matt. 21:45–22:14). Paul likewise reminds the Corinthians that "the Day will bring ... to light ... the quality of each man's work" on the spiritual edifice of the church (1 Cor. 3:13). Philippians 2:9–11 shows again the importance of this aspect of the New Testament's eschatological teaching.

All of us will one day stand before God, just as Jesus did at his exaltation. All of us should be found faithful on that day as he was found faithful. Modern apocalyptic scenarios change, charts must be redrawn and dates revised, but if these two convictions remain firmly fixed in our eschatological thinking, little else matters.

# Philippians 2:12–18

**T**HEREFORE, MY DEAR friends, as you have always obeyed—not only in my presence, but now much more in my absence—continue to work out your salvation with fear and trembling, ¹³for it is God who works in you to will and to act according to his good purpose.

¹⁴Do everything without complaining or arguing, ¹⁵so that you may become blameless and pure, children of God without fault in a crooked and depraved generation, in which you shine like stars in the universe ¹⁶as you hold out the word of life—in order that I may boast on the day of Christ that I did not run or labor for nothing. ¹⁷But even if I am being poured out like a drink offering on the sacrifice and service coming from your faith, I am glad and rejoice with all of you. ¹⁸So you too should be glad and rejoice with me.

**Original Meaning**

PAUL'S PURPOSE IN these two paragraphs is to apply the story of Christ's humble self-emptying and exaltation specifically to the Philippian situation. Thus he begins the new section with the strong conjunction "therefore" and, echoing his reference to Christ's obedience in 2:8, refers in the first sentence of this new section to the Philippians' obedience. The language and themes of the section also show that Paul is turning again to the themes of 1:27–30. He is concerned in both passages that the Philippians live out the implications of their initial response to the gospel, and that they do this whether Paul is among them or absent from them (1:27/2:12). Both passages express concern that the Philippians be unified (1:27/2:14), and that this unity be visible to the unbelieving world outside (1:28/2:15). The two sections also share an interest in the final day (1:28/2:16) and in the experience of suffering for the gospel, which binds the apostle to his friends and apostolic charges in Philippi (1:30/2:17). The concerns of 2:12–18, then, are woven tightly into the fabric of Paul's larger argument that the Philippians should "conduct" themselves "in a manner worthy of the gospel of Christ" (1:27).

The apostle expresses these concerns in three steps. (1) He encourages the Philippians, in light of Christ's example, to continue their good record of obedience (2:12–13). (2) He then becomes more precise about the area of obedience he wants the Philippians especially to address, when he urges them to avoid "complaining" and "arguing" (2:14–16a). (3) He shows how their struggle to remain "blameless" and "pure" is bound up with his own struggle to remain faithful to his calling. In light of this calling, he encourages them to work together with him to present God with an acceptable sacrifice and to experience the joy that comes from doing so (2:16b–18).

**Keep Up the Good Work (2:12–13).** Paul now begins to apply the example of Christ's unselfish humility and obedience to the Philippian situation. His basic meaning is clear: He wants the Philippians to obey as Christ obeyed, and presumably this means to work for unity by avoiding the kind of selfish ambition that leads to dissension (2:1–4, 14). The finer details of Paul's statement, however, are difficult to clarify. To whom does Paul expect the Philippians to render obedience? Does his command to the Philippians to work out their salvation with fear and trembling contradict his emphasis elsewhere on the believer's justification by faith through God's grace? Does it indeed contradict the next sentence, in which Paul says that God creates both the will and the ability of believers to accomplish his desires?

The first question is the simplest of the three to answer. Since Paul speaks of the Philippians' obedience whether in his presence or in his absence, he is probably referring to the obedience they should give to him as the apostle who brought them the gospel and who will have to account for them to God in the Day of Christ (2:16; cf. 1:10). Paul frequently speaks of this kind of obedience in his letters and expresses concern that his congregations be obedient to the teaching he has left with them, whether he is present or absent. Thus in 1 Corinthians 4:14–21 Paul tells the Corinthians that they should imitate him and that he is sending Timothy to them to remind them of his "way of life in Christ Jesus" (4:17). The reason for this admonition and for Timothy's impending visit appears to be that some in Corinth have become "arrogant, as if," Paul says, "I were not coming to you" (4:18). If they do not submit to his authority, he continues, then he will appear among them with a whip rather than "with a gentle spirit" (4:21). Similarly in 2 Corinthians 10:4, Paul tells the Corinthians that he is "ready to punish every act of disobedience" (cf. 13:10).

This notion was not restricted, moreover, to Paul's correspondence with the difficult and wayward Corinthian church. Paul tells his close friend Philemon that he has the authority to demand obedience to his request concerning the slave Onesimus, but that he appeals to him instead on the basis of love (Philem. 8–9, cf. 21–22). He also tells the Thessalonians to "take special note" of anyone who does not obey his admonitions in his letter to them (2 Thess. 3:14). In Paul's absence, the believing community must take responsibility for enforcing obedience to instructions that can only be issued by means of letter.

This does not mean, of course, that Paul expected his churches to obey his personal wishes; rather, he expected them to obey the gospel tradition he handed on to them. He was, after all, their primary access to the teaching of Jesus. Thus the Corinthians, for example, were to obey Paul not by imitating his personal habits but by following his "way of life in Christ Jesus," a pattern of life that Timothy could illustrate as well as Paul and that corresponded to Paul's teaching in all the churches (1 Cor. 4:17; cf. Phil. 3:17; 1 Thess. 1:6). And, not surprisingly, it is as important for the Corinthians to obey Titus, who also bears the gospel tradition, as for them to obey Paul (2 Cor. 7:15). In Philippians 2:12, therefore, Paul is urging his beloved friends to be as obedient in the future to the traditions he has handed on to them as they have been in the past.

The second question is more difficult. The Philippians should pursue obedience, Paul says, by working out their "salvation with fear and trembling." One of the most important themes in Paul's theology is that human effort cannot even cooperate with God's grace to yield a right standing before God on the final day. To Paul, even Abraham, popularly thought to be the most righteous of all Jews, must be considered ungodly when a right standing before God is at issue. Abraham served as Paul's illustration of the principle that "to the man who does not work but trusts God who justifies the wicked, his faith is credited to him as righteousness" (Rom. 4:5). God's people, Paul says, are not chosen because of their works but on the basis of grace, for otherwise "grace would no longer be grace" (11:6). What can Paul possibly mean, then, when he says that the Philippians should "work out [their] salvation with fear and trembling"?

One popular solution to the problem is to understand "salvation" here in the weakened sense of "well-being." Paul is then saying that the Philippians should work toward the well-being of their community. On this explanation, the phrase "fear and trembling" does not refer to an attitude toward God but to an attitude of humility toward one another. Indeed, it is often said that Paul never uses the phrase "fear and trembling" of the relationship between God and people but always of human relationships. The Philippians, then, are to overcome their social discord and so "save" their relationships with one another by adopting a respectful and humble attitude toward each other.[1]

This understanding of the verse fails to be convincing, however, because it assigns an unusual meaning to the term *salvation* and because it has missed

---

1. See, for example, J. Hugh Michael, "'Work Out Your Own Salvation," *Expositor* 12 (1924), 439–50; idem, *Philippians*, 98–103; Hawthorne, *Philippians*, 98–99.

an important nuance in Paul's other uses of the phrase "fear and trembling."
Paul uses the term *salvation* eighteen times in his letters. In fifteen of those
occurrences, it refers to the full-orbed concept of ultimate salvation, and in
two others (2 Cor. 1:6; Phil. 1:19) the usual meaning is arguably the best one.
That would leave the reference here in 2:12 as Paul's only use of the term to
mean "well-being."[2]

Moreover, in the three other occurrences of the phrase "fear and trembling" in Paul's letters, it is far from clear that a reference to God is not in view.
Paul may have come to Corinth in "fear and . . . trembling" (1 Cor. 2:3) not
because of any experience with other people but because of the awesome task
of preaching Christ crucified (cf. 2 Cor. 2:16). The Corinthians received Titus
"with fear and trembling" (2 Cor. 7:15) perhaps as much to indicate their fear
of God in light of their past rejection of Paul, his apostle, as to show to Titus
their willingness to hear him out. Slaves are to submit to their masters with
fear and trembling "just as [they] would obey Christ" (Eph. 6:5). Thus, the
"fear and trembling" to which Paul refers in Philippians 2:12 probably refers
to an attitude that the Philippians should have toward God.

If this is so, then what does Paul mean when he says that the Philippians
should work out their eternal salvation with an attitude of fear and trembling
before God? We must grasp the difference between Paul's use of the term *salvation* and his use of the term *justification* in order to understand this statement
properly. The two terms are not synonymous.[3] When Paul uses the term *justification* and its various forms ( *just, justify*), he refers primarily to a status of
innocence that God confers on the believer and to a condition of peace that
God initiates with him or her. He frequently uses the verb *justify*, therefore,
in the past tense: "You were washed, you were sanctified, you *were justified*," he
tells the Corinthians (1 Cor. 6:11), and he explains to the Romans that we
have peace with God "since we *have been justified* through faith" (Rom. 5:1). This
justification comes entirely through God's grace and not through human
effort (Rom. 4:5; 11:6), and those who have received it can rest assured that
they will one day "be conformed to the likeness of [God's] Son" and be "glorified" in eternity (Rom. 8:29–30).

The terms *salvation* and *save* have a different connotation in Paul. Although
Paul can occasionally refer to salvation as a past event (Rom. 8:24; Eph. 2:5,
8; 2 Tim. 1:9; Titus 3:5), most of his references to it place it in the future, and

---

2. Walter Bauer, *A Greek-English Lexicon of the New Testament and Other Early Christian Literature*, 2d ed., trans., adapt., and rev. William F. Arndt, F. Wilbur Gingrich, Frederick W.
Danker (Chicago: University of Chicago Press, 1979), 801.

3. See especially the discussion of Georg Fohrer, "σῴζω," *Theological Dictionary of the New
Testament*, ed. Gerhard Kittel and Gerhard Friedrich, 10 vols. (Grand Rapids: Eerdmans,
1964–76), 7:970–1012 (here 992–95); Silva, *Philippians*, 137–38.

he often connects salvation with the Day of the Lord (1 Cor. 5:5; cf. 3:15; Rom. 13:11; 1 Thess. 5:9). Those who have been justified can be assured that they will be saved, but their salvation awaits the final day. Romans 5:9 illustrates the difference between justification and salvation in Paul's thinking: "Since we have been justified by [Jesus'] blood," Paul says, "how much more shall we be saved from God's wrath through him!"

When Paul says in Philippians 2:12 that believers must "work out [their] salvation," he does not mean that they should "work for" (JB, NJB) salvation on the final day. He means instead that they should "conduct" themselves "in a manner worthy of the gospel of Christ" (1:27) as they await the final affirmation of their right standing before God at the day of Christ. They should busy themselves with discerning "what is best" so that they "may be pure and blameless until the day of Christ" (1:10). They are to do this "with fear and trembling," because such seriousness is appropriate to the task of living out their commitment to the gospel in a way that demonstrates that they are genuine believers. In other words, Paul's intention in 2:12 is not far from Peter's in 2 Peter 1:10-11:

> Be all the more eager to make your calling and election sure. For if you do these things, you will never fall, and you will receive a rich welcome into the eternal kingdom of our Lord and Savior Jesus Christ.

Paul perhaps recognized the danger, nevertheless, that someone would take his statement to mean that believers cooperate with God in the process of salvation and that if they did their part, God, meeting them halfway, would do his. So in verse 13 Paul explains that salvation comes entirely at God's initiative and that God provides both the will and the ability to accomplish "his good purpose." Paul's emphatic way of putting this ("it is God who works in you" rather than simply "God works in you") and his care in pointing out the divine origin of both the ability and the very will to put this ability at God's service show how concerned he is that his statement in verse 12 not be misunderstood. Although the Philippians must work out their salvation, their salvation does not come at their own initiative. They should work out their salvation with a seriousness appropriate to those who look forward to salvation on the final day, but they should remember at all times that the whole process leading to their acquittal on that Day is theirs neither to initiate nor to complete. It is God's from first to last (cf. 1:6).[4]

---

4. This same understanding of the relationship between human effort and God's grace lies beneath 1 Cor. 15:10: "But by the grace of God I am what I am, and his grace to me was not without effect. No, I worked harder than all [the other apostles]—yet not I, but the grace of God that was with me."

**Redeem the Witness of Disobedient Israel (2:14–16a).** Paul follows this general admonition with a more specific command: The Philippian believers should, he says, stop complaining and arguing (v. 14), so that they may shine as beacons of light within the darkness of a world gone astray (vv. 15–16a) and so that they may join Paul on the final day in the presentation of an acceptable sacrifice to God (vv. 16b–18). Implicit in this command is the assumption that the believing community in Philippi is part of a new people of God that stands in continuity with biblical Israel and should learn from its example.

Paul begins this more specific exhortation with the command that the Philippians should do all things without "complaining or arguing." The term that the NIV translates "complaining" (*gongysmon*) occurs only rarely in the New Testament, and this is its only appearance in Paul's letters.[5] It occurs frequently, however, in the narratives of the Greek Bible that describe Israel's desert wanderings, where the Israelites "complained" against Moses and Moses made clear to them that their complaining was not as much against him as against God (Ex. 16:2–9; 17:3; Num. 11:1; cf. 14:2).

Although some scholars take the parallel too far by claiming that Paul's use of the term means the Philippians were complaining against him or against their "overseers and deacons" (1:1), the peculiarity of the word probably means that Paul intended to echo the biblical narratives of Israel's desert wanderings.[6] If so, his point is not only that the Philippians, although they are Gentiles, constitute part of God's people, but also that as God's people they should learn from the mistakes of their spiritual ancestors. Israel murmured in the desert and suffered a fearful punishment. The Philippians should, in fear and trembling, not presume upon their salvation but instead take measures to quell the dissension in their midst.

In the next four verses, Paul gives two reasons why they should do this. The first reason appears in verses 15–16a. The Philippians, he says, should strive for unity in order that they might be "blameless and pure, children of God without fault in a crooked and depraved generation." Here Paul uses the language of the "Song of Moses" that stands near the end of Deuteronomy (Deut. 31:30–32:37) and describes the unfaithfulness of the wicked

---

5. See John 7:12; Acts 6:1; 1 Peter 4:9; cf. *Barnabas* 3:5; *Didache* 3:6.

6. For the notion that Paul compares the Philippians' attitude to him with the attitude of the Israelites to Moses, see Michael, *Philippians*, 99; for the suggestion that the Philippians' discontent may have been discontent against their leaders in the same way that Israel's discontent was directed against Moses, see Bonnard, *Philippiens*, 51; Silva, *Philippians*, 144. Cf. O'Brien, *Philippians*, 291–92. The first suggestion seems incredible in light of the friendly relationship between Paul and the Philippians that pulses throughout the letter, and the second seems unduly speculative.

generation of Israelites whom God brought out of Egypt. The Greek text of Deuteronomy 32:4–5 can be translated,

> God, his works are truth, and all his ways are right. He is a faithful God, and he is not unjust. Just and pure is the Lord. They sinned, they who were not his *children, full of fault, a crooked and depraved generation* [italics added].

The emphasized words correspond closely to Paul's Greek in Philippians 2:15 and show that here, too, Paul believes that the Philippians stand in continuity with the ancient people of God. Paul hopes that unlike their spiritual ancestors they will prove not to be a crooked, depraved, and blemished generation, but a beacon of light for the truth of the gospel amid a faithless world, a world that can be described in terms the Song of Moses applies to disobedient Israel.[7]

If the Philippians succeed in fulfilling this vocation, Paul says, they will "shine like stars in the universe as [they] hold on to the word of life."[8] This is the vocation that, according to Isaiah 42:6–7 and 49:6, Israel was supposed to fulfill among the Gentiles so that the salvation of God might be brought "to the ends of the earth" (Isa. 49:6). The Philippian believers, as part of the newly constituted people of God, have now inherited this vocation. However, they can only fulfill it if they avoid the mistakes of the past, give up their discord, and present a unified witness to the dark world around them.

**Join Paul in Offering an Acceptable Sacrifice (2:16b–18).** Paul believes that the Philippians' obedience is critical for a second reason: The acceptable nature of their sacrifice to God on the final day depends on it. He begins this thought in verse 16b with a reference to his hope that on the day of Christ he will be able to present the Philippians' blamelessness and purity to God as his "boast." If he is able to do this, he continues, then his apostolic efforts will not have been in vain. Paul describes these efforts with language drawn both from the athletic arena and from the Old Testament. Here and elsewhere, Paul describes his apostolic labor as a race in which he runs and which, if stumbling blocks do not intrude, will result in a prize (1 Cor. 9:24–27; 2 Tim. 4:6–8; cf. Gal. 2:2). These stumbling blocks may include Paul's own

---

7. A more detailed discussion of Paul's use of the biblical narrative of Israel's desert wanderings in this passage appears in Frank Thielman, *Paul and the Law: A Contextual Approach* (Downers Grove, Ill.: InterVarsity Press, 1994), 156–57.

8. The NIV text translates v. 16a, "as you hold out (*epechontes*) the word of life." But the more usual meaning of the term *epecho* is "hold fast," and since the Philippians are enduring persecution at the hands of the "crooked and depraved generation" of which Paul speaks in v. 15 (1:28–30), this more usual meaning is probably the correct one. See the marginal note in the NIV and the thorough discussion in O'Brien, *Philippians*, 297.

faithlessness to his call (1 Cor. 9:24–27), hindrances placed before him by other Christians (Gal. 2:2), or, as here, the faithlessness of the churches whom God has placed in his care.

Paul enriches this metaphor with one drawn from Isaiah. In Isaiah 49:4 the Servant of the Lord expresses dismay that he appears to "have labored to no purpose," to "have spent [his] strength in vain and for nothing"; but he also expresses his confidence that his reward is in the Lord's hands. Later, the prophet promises that in the final day, when God creates new heavens and a new earth, his people "will not toil in vain" (Isa. 65:23).

Paul's language, then, is indebted both to Greek and Hebrew cultural imagery of hard work, which, provided it is not frustrated along the way, ends in reward. Here he expresses the hope that the Philippians will not trip him up in his race or frustrate his labor and prevent him from presenting them before God on that final day as the product of his hard work. On that day, as now, they will be his joy and his crown (4:1).[9]

In verse 17a Paul switches images in order to intensify his emphasis on the necessity of the Philippians' obedience and steadfastness. In language that probably alludes to his death (cf. 2 Tim. 4:6), he describes himself as a drink offering that may be poured out. Drink offerings were a common feature in the sacrificial systems of many ancient cultures, and often the offering was poured over a sacrifice (thus the NIV's rendering, "*on* the sacrifice and service coming from your faith"). Since so much of Paul's imagery in this passage is indebted to the Old Testament, however, he probably has in mind the custom described in such passages as Numbers 15:1–10, where drink offerings are made *in addition to* other offerings. So Paul views the Philippians' continued obedience (2:12) and steadfastness amid persecution (2:15–16a) as an offering to God equivalent to the offering of his own apostolic labors—labors that may end in his death.

Even if this happens, he continues in verses 17b–18, he will rejoice. Moreover, if it happens, he expects the Philippians to join him in rejoicing. Paul's death in prison and their steadfastness despite internal and external hardships will, after all, only mean the accomplishment of their mutual goal. Paul will be with Christ (1:21, 23), and the Philippians will be blameless and pure on the day of Christ (1:10); Paul's apostolic labors will be vindicated, and the Philippians will give glory and praise to God (cf. 1:11).

---

9. See the useful discussion of the imagery in 2:16 in Victor C. Pfitzner, *Paul and the Agon Motif: Traditional Athletic Imagery in the Pauline Literature* (Leiden: Brill, 1967), 102–8.

THE PRIMARY POINTS of this passage are relatively clear and easily applied to the contemporary church. The passage also contains several possible interpretive stumbling blocks that are more difficult to negotiate and several subsidiary points that are easy to miss. The key to applying the passage successfully to the contemporary situation lies in focusing on Paul's major concerns in a way that is sensitive to the less important issues and wary of interpretive errors.

**Primary Points.** Although Paul's difficult admonition in verses 12–13 gets most of the interpretive attention in contemporary discussions of this passage, it is actually a general admonition that he probably intended as an introduction to his specific concern in verse 14: "Do everything without complaining or arguing." As we have already seen in our study of 1:1 (where Paul's address emphasizes the unity of the congregation) and 1:27 (where Paul advises the Philippians to stand firm in the unity of the Spirit), the Philippian community was broken by dissension. The origin of the trouble probably lay in the dispute between Euodia and Syntyche, who (Paul wrote) should agree in the Lord (4:2). If so, their dispute was apparently no minor affair, for it posed a threat to the church serious enough that Paul not only called the primary combatants by name but asked an unnamed friend in the church to "help these women," presumably in the task of reconciliation.

Their dispute and the church's disunity generally also posed a serious threat to Paul's ministry, so serious that he uses extraordinarily strong language to describe their implications. He reminds the Philippians that avoiding the selfishness that stands behind the dissension has eschatological significance. Holding fast to the very word of life is at issue, and therefore their obedience in this matter is a question both of their eternal salvation and of Paul's ability to stand before God on the day of Christ, having completed his assigned task.

Paul reminds them further that the fulfillment of their own commission to complete the task assigned to biblical Israel is at stake. If they do not overcome their internal discord, their witness to the "crooked and depraved generation" surrounding them will be hindered, and they will fail to fulfill their calling to be "light to the Gentiles." Their internal disunity, in other words, will tarnish their external proclamation of the gospel. Holding on to the word of life is more than simply standing firm against persecuting opponents. It is also demonstrating the validity of the gospel to people outside the faith by the way we live.

In addition to this admonition, Paul tells the Philippians both that he rejoices in the privilege of working in his apostolic vocation and that they should rejoice in the privilege of working out their salvation by working for unity and holding on to the gospel (vv. 17b–18). As we have already seen in our study of 1:18, Paul's pervasive concern with joy and rejoicing in this letter is not a superficial claim that Christians should smile, laugh, and at all times appear contented. It is the settled sense of peace that accompanies believers in plenty and in want because they know their lives are devoted to the advancement of the gospel. This allows Paul to rejoice in the prospect of death (v. 17a) and the Philippians to rejoice despite the hard work of retaining their communal unity and the discomfort of holding on to the word of life amid the persecutions they are facing.

It is also why Paul in verse 18 can put the verb "rejoice" in the imperative mood. Smiles and laughter are largely involuntary, but the joy of which Paul speaks comes to those who have committed their lives to the advancement of the gospel and who have decided that they will live in a way, no matter how difficult, that encourages that advancement.

In 2:12–18, then, Paul makes two primary points: Working against disunity is a crucial element in working out salvation before a watching world, and the struggle to work out salvation, since it is a sacrifice to God, should be a cause for rejoicing. Amid the welter of interpretive difficulties that this passage poses, we should not lose sight of these two basic points.

**Subsidiary Points.** We should also not neglect two minor points this passage makes more by means of implication than by direct statement. (1) Paul's assumption throughout this passage that the Philippians stand in continuity with biblical Israel should not go unnoticed. From the description of Philippi and of the few converts mentioned in Acts 16, it is possible to say with reasonable certainty that few or none of the Philippians were Jews. On the Sabbath, instead of following his usual custom of going to the local synagogue, Paul had to go outside the city gate to a place of prayer where he and his companions began speaking with a group of women (Acts 16:13). The only one of these women that is named, Lydia of Thyatira, is called a "worshiper of God"—a technical term for a Gentile who is interested in the Jewish God but who has not yet fully converted to Judaism. Moreover, the charges brought against Paul and Silas, landing them in prison, were that they were upsetting the city *since* they were Jews (16:20). Jews were apparently not welcome in Philippi, and if any were there, they must have formed a small group.

In spite of this, Paul's allusions to the Old Testament in this passage and elsewhere in the letter show that he instructed his new converts in the Jewish Scriptures; the implication is that he considered them as the inheritors of the promises God had made to his people. Christians are thus comparable to the desert generation of Israelites and so should learn from their conduct, and they have assumed eschatological Israel's vocation of being a light to the

Gentiles. They even make sacrifices comparable to the offerings prescribed for Israel in the Mosaic law.

All of this implies an approach to the Old Testament that Christians today should not ignore. The Old Testament remains God's eternally valid Word, but the dawn of the new covenant has radically altered its interpretation. The church is no longer a political entity like biblical Israel, and its boundaries are no longer primarily ethnic boundaries as they were prior to the coming of Jesus. Thus the sanctity of the people of God under the old covenant takes a radically different shape from the sanctity of the people of God under the new. The Mosaic law, since it was intended to govern national and ethnic Israel, is no longer valid.

Nevertheless, the pattern of the believer's relationship with God as defined in the Old Testament remains the paradigm that God's people under the new covenant must follow. Membership in God's people comes at God's initiative, and sanctity is important because it sets God's people apart from the "crooked and depraved generation" within which they live. The element of continuity between the new people of God and the old is strong, and believers today, like the Philippians in their time, have much to learn about God's character and his expectations for his people from the Old Testament.[10]

(2) A second point visible through the primary argument of 2:12–18 is that Paul presents himself as a model for the Philippians to follow here, just as he did in 1:12–26 (cf. 1:30) and just as he will do in 3:4–16 (see 3:17; cf. 4:9). Paul has asked the Philippians in humility to consider others better than themselves (2:3), to put the interests of others ahead of their own (2:4), and to follow Christ's example of humility and obedience (2:5–12). In 2:16b–17 he speaks of his own labor on their behalf and says that he is willing (like Christ Jesus in 2:7–8) even to pour out his life to make the sacrifice of the Philippians' faith complete. This kind of ethical teaching gives definition to the meaning of sanctity under the new covenant. The particulars of the Mosaic law are no longer valid (in 3:7–8 Paul calls them "loss" and "rubbish"). Instead, sanctity within God's newly constituted people is to a large extent a matter of following Christ's example and the example of others who, like Paul, understand the exemplary pattern of Christ's life (1 Cor. 4:16–17; 11:1; Phil. 3:17; 4:9; 1 Thess. 1:6).

**Interpretive Perils.** Several possible pitfalls await us as we attempt to bring this passage out of Paul's setting and into our own, and much of the danger is concentrated in verses 12–13. Because these verses state a paradox in sharp terms, it is easy to place too much emphasis on one side of the para-

---

10. This theme is examined at greater length in Thielman, *Paul and the Law*; on Paul's use of the law in Philippians, see 145–59.

dox at the expense of the other. If we place too much emphasis on verse 12, we may lapse into the notion that salvation is a matter of our own untainted free choice and that by our own efforts we can "work for" (JB, NJB) our salvation with fear and trembling. This was the error of Pelagius in the late fourth and early fifth centuries, and it has reemerged in various forms throughout Christian history. This view has trouble explaining the necessity for Christ's substitutionary death and implicitly denies what Paul affirms in Romans 4:5—that even someone as "righteous" as Abraham appears wicked when standing before God.

If we place too much emphasis on verse 13, however, we stand in danger of retreating into an equally unbiblical quietism that passively awaits an infusion of divine energy before obedience can begin. Although all evangelical Christians owe a great debt to the leaders of the "Second Great Awakening" in the nineteenth century, that movement had an unfortunate spin-off. Under the influence of that event, some claimed that believers must experience a second crisis, akin to their initial conversion, in which the Holy Spirit gained control of their lives and placed them on a higher plane of obedience and Christian devotion than other believers. Any Christian who, under the influence of such thinking, is delaying obedience until he or she experiences what seems to be the Holy Spirit's power, needs to heed the warning of verse 12. Every believer has the Spirit (Rom. 8:9), and God's Word commands every believer to "live by the Spirit" (Gal. 5:16). Anyone who claims to be a believer but is consciously not doing this should probably question the genuineness of his or her commitment to the faith (cf. 2 Cor. 13:5).

How, then, are we to respond to so tensive a statement as verses 12–13? How can we work out our own salvation if God is the one who is at work in us? The answer seems simply to be to work as hard as Paul himself did in his apostolic calling and as diligently as he expected the Philippians to work at their unity, but then, at the end of the day, to recognize humbly that any success we have at doing what God commands comes from God himself. His indwelling Spirit has reshaped our wills so that they may decide to do what he commands, and his Spirit has given us the energy and ingenuity to accomplish God's "good purpose." The result of this is that although at various times we may feel that *we* have put our noses to the grindstone and been obedient even when we did not feel like doing it, we can in the end take no credit. We can make no claim upon God; we can only say, "We are unworthy servants; we have only done our duty" (Luke 17:10).

As we bring this passage into the contemporary church, therefore, we should keep Paul's primary emphases firmly in mind: We should strive for unity, and we should understand that doing so is necessary in order to fulfill our calling of being a light to the dark world around us. Although difficult, we should find joy in completing the task. As we keep these emphases before us, we should remember that the business of living as God wants us to live places us within a venerable tradition that stretches back to biblical Israel; but we should also remember that under the new covenant, Christ himself and the writings of the apostles and their followers set the standard for our sanctity, not the Mosaic law. As we pursue our efforts to stand blameless and pure before God on the day of Christ, we should neither passively await some humanly discernible prior movement of God's Spirit within us, nor should we think, once we have obeyed, that God owes us something, "for it is God who works in [us] to will and to act according to his good purpose" (2:13).

JESUS, IN ONE of his last recorded prayers, asks God to protect the unity of his disciples (John 17:11) and then expands his request to cover those who will believe through their witness:

> I pray also for those who will believe in me through their message, that all of them may be one, Father, just as you are in me and I am in you. May they also be in us so that the world may believe that you have sent me. I have given them the glory that you gave me, that they may be one as we are one: I in them and you in me. May they be brought to complete unity to let the world know that you sent me and have loved them even as you have loved me (John 17:20b–23).

Like Paul, Jesus in this prayer speaks of the unity of believers in the same breath with the effectiveness of the church's testimony to the unbelieving world. The unity both here and in Philippians is, moreover, not merely abstract—a feeling of friendliness or a recognition of common beliefs—but visible. The world must be able to see it and draw conclusions from what they see (John 17:21, 23).[11] The church's unity should be just as clear as a beacon shining in the night (Phil. 2:15). Sadly, the church too often fails to show the world concrete expressions of unity and so obscures an important witness to the gospel. Among large ecclesiastical bodies the visible unity of the church is often compromised by attempts to protect the status quo. A loss of members means a loss of revenue and, unfortunately, for some church leaders, a loss of self-esteem. The result is that when members of one church leave and join another, accusations fly, and the crack in the visible unity of the church widens.

---

11. D. A. Carson, *The Gospel According to John* (Grand Rapids: Eerdmans, 1991), 568.

Sometimes, of course, legitimate concerns over the spiritual health of those who have left come into play. Have they left in anger, producing cracks of their own in the fellowship they have left behind? Have they left a Christian community where the apostolic gospel is preached to join a deviant group whose gospel is really no gospel at all?

Many times, however, affirmative answers to these questions are only deceptive screens to hide deeper and less acceptable reasons for resenting the loss of membership. Thus the so-called "mainline" denominations have suffered large losses of membership in recent years to groups that have broken from them, usually for theological reasons. The temptation of the older, more established churches is to enter into a sophisticated form of name-calling. The break-away churches provide easy "answers" to complex questions, it is said, and have led out of the established churches those who are not interested in theological and intellectual honesty. These churches are more homogeneous, goes the charge; they are unwilling to reach out to women, the poor, and minority groups, so that people who are attracted to them have racist tendencies and are uncompassionate about the plight of the oppressed.

The less-established churches, of course, have their own ways of widening the breech. They sometimes refer to themselves as "the continuing church," implying that the church from which they split retains no continuity with historic Christianity.[12] Those who refuse to join the splinter group are sometimes viewed as immature or uncourageous Christians, if Christians at all, because of their continued affiliation with the old group.

Real differences about what constitutes the gospel exist in both groups, but the most serious of those differences are usually held by the minority who are at the fringes of both groups (although admittedly this minority sometimes holds control of denominational offices). The central majority in both groups, even if they differ on some things, possess enough common ground on the essentials of the faith to make efforts at unity. Jesus and Paul tell us that such efforts are essential proofs of the validity of the gospel to the unbelieving world. It is fairly easy for the various splinter denominations to align themselves with Christians in other such denominations, just as it is fairly easy for the mainline churches to make common cause. Where the church really needs to work at unity, however, and where the world really needs to see it, is among believers in the splinter groups and the groups from which they have come. That would be a miracle, but one the world would recognize as lending credibility to the gospel.

---

12. As in, for example, Frank Joseph Smith, *The History of the Presbyterian Church in America: The Continuing Church* (Manassas, Va.: Reformation Educational Foundation, 1985).

---

The visible unity of the church does not only need to be maintained at the large, institutional level, however, but at the level of individual congregations of believers as well. Here unity is often broken by precisely the verbal kinds of activity that Paul attempts to curb at Philippi: complaining and arguing. At the bottom of this flurry of discontented words is nearly always the desire of each side in the dispute to dominate the other, to see that their concerns are addressed even if the interests of others are neglected. Usually the issue of whose concerns, if anyone's, best advance the gospel is lost in the bitter exchanges and the backbiting, or, even worse, is used as a pious excuse to promote the selfish interests of one party over those of the other. And so the procession continues of ministers who leave their churches because their reputation has been stained by rumor, of congregations torn asunder by leaders who refuse to recognize that they could be wrong, and of church members who quietly never return because they have been shamed by rumor or by an unforgiving spirit.

What is the remedy? Paul's solution is to issue a warning. Those who belong to God's people demonstrate their membership by working out their salvation. Their aim should be to avoid the mistakes of the ancient Israelites, who allowed complaining to stand in the way of their inheritance and whose subsequent historical failure to be a light to the Gentiles meant that God gave this privilege to others. The Philippians should rejoice in working for the advancement of the gospel and consider the energy expended in that work to be a sacrifice to God. The warning implicit in this is that those who find themselves so out of sympathy with these goals that they place their own interest above the unity of the church, and thus the advancement of the gospel, should question whether they belong to God's people at all. Paul would say to them what he said to another group of spiritually immature people:

> Examine yourselves to see whether you are in the faith; test yourselves. Do you not realize that Jesus Christ is in you—unless, of course, you fail the test? (2 Cor. 13:5).

In addition to this strong medicine, Paul implies a remedy to any disunity based on the selfish desire to dominate others: "It is God," he says, "who works in you to will and to act according to his good purpose" (v. 13). Any good that we as believers accomplish is the result of God's work in us. This is a deeply humbling truth, one that should give anyone pause who is bent on having his or her way. We do not deserve to have our own way. We deserve hell. But God in his grace has drawn us to himself by his Holy Spirit and by that same Spirit has worked within us to accomplish his good purpose. If we have grasped the truth that God justifies the impious—that Jesus came not to call the righteous but sinners to repentance—then we will immediately understand how foolhardy it is to break fellowship with others for selfish reasons. "Self-justification and judging belong together," said Dietrich Bonhoeffer, "as justification by grace and serving belong together."[13]

Finally, through its subtle identification of the church with eschatological Israel, this passage issues a challenge to the modern evangelical church to examine its stance on the Palestinian-Israeli question. Many evangelicals have stood with the Israelis and against the Palestinians on the question of who should have sovereignty over the Holy Land. To these Christians Jewish right to the land seems explicitly laid out in the Bible, and Jewish repossession of the land seems a confirmation of the eschatological vision of the prophets. In their euphoria over seeing prophecy supposedly come true before their very eyes, however, many American evangelicals have forgotten that Palestinian Arabs lived in the land of Israel for many centuries and were sometimes brutally treated by Jewish emigrants to Palestine after the United Nations set up an independent Jewish state in the area in 1948. Many of these mistreated Palestinians were Christians, fellow members of Christ's body and part of the newly constituted people of God. Unfortunately, the violence has continued in the decades since 1948, and Palestinian Christians are often at a loss to understand why their believing brothers and sisters in the West seem to ignore or make excuses for Israel's oppressive behavior.[14]

On the most likely reading of Romans 11:25–27, Paul continues to find a special place for ethnic Israel in God's people at the close of the age, and certainly Romans 11:11–24 forbids any triumphalism on the part of Gentile believers over the failure of many Jews to heed the gospel. But these passages should not blind us to Paul's assumption in many places throughout his letters that the church has fulfilled many of the prophetic descriptions of the blessings that have been promised to God's people at the end of time. Even on the dubious thesis that the present state of Israel plays some role in the events surrounding the end of the age, Christians today should not support its policies on the notion that its government and citizens somehow constitute God's covenant people. God's people in the land of Israel are those who, whether Jew, Arab, or neither, believe in Messiah Jesus.

---

13. "Selbstrechtfertigung und Richten gehört zusammen, wie Rechtfertigung aus Gnaden und Dienen zusammengehört," in Bonhoeffer's *Deitrich Bonhoeffer Werke*, vol. 5, *Gemeinsames Leben, Das Gebetbuch der Bible*, ed. Gerhard Ludwig Müller and Albrecht Schönherr (Munich: Chr. Kaiser Verlag, 1987), 78. Cf. *Life Together*, 91; also the comments of Barth on v. 12 in *Philippians*, 71–72.

14. See the gripping analysis of this issue in Gary M. Burge, *Who Are God's People in the Middle East?* (Grand Rapids: Zondervan, 1993), esp. 101–24.

# Philippians 2:19–30

※

I HOPE IN the Lord Jesus to send Timothy to you soon, that I also may be cheered when I receive news about you. ²⁰I have no one else like him, who takes a genuine interest in your welfare. ²¹For everyone looks out for his own interests, not those of Jesus Christ. ²²But you know that Timothy has proved himself, because as a son with his father he has served with me in the work of the gospel. ²³I hope, therefore, to send him as soon as I see how things go with me. ²⁴And I am confident in the Lord that I myself will come soon.

²⁵But I think it is necessary to send back to you Epaphroditus, my brother, fellow worker and fellow soldier, who is also your messenger, whom you sent to take care of my needs. ²⁶For he longs for all of you and is distressed because you heard he was ill. ²⁷Indeed he was ill, and almost died. But God had mercy on him, and not on him only but also on me, to spare me sorrow upon sorrow. ²⁸Therefore I am all the more eager to send him, so that when you see him again you may be glad and I may have less anxiety. ²⁹Welcome him in the Lord with great joy, and honor men like him,
³⁰because he almost died for the work of Christ, risking his life to make up for the help you could not give me.

Original Meaning

AFTER THE THEOLOGICALLY rich language of 2:5–18, we are surprised suddenly to encounter two paragraphs whose primary concern seems to be the travel plans of Paul and his coworkers. Why would Paul include such mundane information at this point in the letter? Why this sudden introduction of a passage which, as Karl Barth says, contains no "direct teaching"?[1] Did Paul, as some scholars believe, intend to end the letter at this point and, following his usual custom, refer to travel plans as part of his concluding remarks?[2] Did he insert the passage, whether by way of con-

---

1. Barth, *Philippians*, 79.
2. See, for example, Collange, *Philippians*, 115; Beare, *Philippians*, 4–5, 95.

clusion or not, in order to assert his authority over the Philippian congregation while absent?[3]

The answers to these questions lie in remembering the emphasis Paul has
placed in his argument so far on discovering conduct that is "worthy of the
gospel of Christ" (1:27) by following the example of others. Paul himself has
provided an example to the Philippians of what it means both to stand firm
amid persecution for Christ's sake (1:12–14, 30) and to submit difficult relational problems among believers to the more important issue of the gospel's
advancement (1:15–18a). Christ has provided an example of the attitude the
Christians in Philippi should have toward one another amid their own relational troubles (2:5–11). Israel has provided a negative example of how
complaining and arguing among God's people can tarnish their witness
before those outside (2:14–15).

It is likely, then, that although Paul wanted to inform the Philippians of
his travel plans in this passage and may have wanted to remind them of his
authority, he nevertheless placed the passage here because he wanted it to
contribute to his list of examples. Both Timothy and Epaphroditus exhibit the
qualities of those who "conduct" themselves "in a manner worthy of the
gospel of Christ" (1:27), especially by looking "not only to [their] own interests, but also to the interests of others" (2:4).

The passage can be neatly divided into two paragraphs, one that explains
why Paul will send Timothy eventually but not now (vv. 19–24), and the
other that explains why Paul intends to send Epaphroditus right away
(vv. 25–30).

**Why Not Timothy? (2:19–24).** Paul begins by telling the Philippians that
he hopes to send Timothy to them "soon" (v. 20), which means, of course,
that Timothy will not be coming right away. This news may have surprised
and disappointed the Philippians, for Paul explains at length in the following verses why Timothy must stay with him until he knows the results of his
trial. When Timothy is finally free to travel, however, Paul says that he will
send him in order to be cheered by news from the Philippians.

Paul's expectation of cheerful news does not mean, as some interpreters
have suggested, that the Philippians were not experiencing problems with

---

3. Robert W. Funk, "The Apostolic Parousia: Form and Significance," *Christian History and
Interpretation: Studies Presented to John Knox*, ed. W. R. Farmer, C. F. D. Moule, and R. R.
Niebuhr (Cambridge: Cambridge University Press, 1967), 249–68. Funk compares Phil.
2:19–24 and 2:25–30 to Rom. 1:8–13; 15:14–33; 1 Cor. 4:14–21; 8:16–23; 9:1–5; 16:1–
12; 2 Cor. 12:14–13:13; Gal. 4:12–20; 1 Thess. 2:17–3:13; and Philem. 21–22. In all of
these passages, he says, Paul attempts to emphasize his authority to his congregations during his absence by speaking of his own or an associate's possible visit.

disunity after all and that those who were seeking their own interests above the interests of others (2:4) were people around Paul at the time he wrote the letter (cf. 1:15–17; 2:21).[4] The statement is instead an example of Paul's commendatory style of exhortation. Just as in 1 Corinthians Paul commends the Corinthian believers for the richness of their speech and knowledge and the abundance of spiritual gifts but then later in the letter issues stern admonitions on precisely these subjects, and just as he commends Philemon for refreshing "the hearts of the saints" (Philem. 7) before asking him to pardon Onesimus, "who," he says, "is my very heart" (Philem. 10–12), so here he takes an optimistic view of the Philippians' ability to stop their feuding.

His statement is both an encouragement to the Philippians not to disappoint his expectations (cf. 2 Cor. 7:14; 9:3–4) and a realistic appraisal of their spiritual maturity. If he had been worried about the Thessalonians' steadfastness amid persecution and then been relieved to hear from Timothy that they were doing well (1 Thess. 3:2–6), and if he had been concerned about the Corinthians' attitude toward him only to hear from Titus that they had repented of their belligerence (2 Cor. 7:5–7), then he had no reason to think that the Philippians would not also respond obediently to his admonitions in this letter.

But Timothy is not bearing the letter. Why? Paul answers this question by telling the Philippians something they already know (v. 22), and something that probably explains why they are eager to see him: Timothy is an exceptional ally in times of trouble. Paul shows this by giving Timothy three commendations. (1) Timothy understands what it means to be united in spirit with other believers, both with Paul and with the Philippians (v. 20). In 2:2 Paul had urged the Philippians to be "one in spirit" (*sympsychoi*), and here he uses a similar term to say that Timothy is of like mind with him (*isopsychos*). The way in which Timothy is like-minded with Paul, however, is that he has a genuine interest in the Philippians' welfare. (2) Timothy stands apart from every other believer whom Paul might have sent to the Philippians because, unlike them, he puts the interests of Jesus Christ above his own interests (v. 21). Like Paul, who was more concerned for the advancement of the gospel than that he was in prison (1:12) or that other Christians were making his hardship more difficult (1:17–18), and like Christ, who put obedience ahead of exploiting the privileges available to him as God (2:6–8), Timothy subordinated his own interests to the "things of Jesus Christ" (pers. trans.). (3) Timothy's mettle had been tested in the difficulty of apostolic service, and both Paul and the Philippians had found him as faithful as a son

---

4. See, for example, Caird, *Paul's Letters From Prison*, 117, 128.

to his father, as willing to slave (*douleuo*; NIV "serve") in the work of the gospel as Paul himself.[5]

It is no wonder that Paul, in light of these qualities, feels that he can send Timothy only after he gains a clear view of the outcome of his imprisonment. With some believers around him having their own interests more at heart than those of the gospel (v. 21) and some seeking to increase his affliction (1:17), it is understandable that Paul would not want to spare this trusted comrade. Eventually he will send him, and Paul expects eventually to come in person, but for the present another messenger must suffice.

**Why Epaphroditus? (2:25–30).** How surprised the Philippians must have been to see Epaphroditus again! They had sent him to Paul not only to deliver a monetary gift from the church (4:18) but also to stay with Paul and minister to his other needs (2:25), something they could not do themselves from such a distance (2:30). Why was he back so soon despite Paul's continued imprisonment? Apparently in order to answer this question and to forestall any ill will toward Epaphroditus for not completing his assigned task, in this paragraph Paul both explains why Epaphroditus has returned and commends him to the Philippians for his diligence.

The basic reasons for Epaphroditus' return are clear. He yearned to be reunited with his friends at Philippi, particularly because they had learned of an illness he had contracted since leaving them (v. 26). There is no need to make light of Epaphroditus' longing as mere "homesickness."[6] Paul uses the same term to describe his own desire to see the Philippians in 1:8, and such expressions of longing for those at home are not unknown in other letters from the period.[7] Epaphroditus had endured a life-threatening illness in order to complete his commission from the Philippian church (vv. 27, 30). Somehow the church had learned of this illness, and Epaphroditus was understandably distressed. Compassion dictated that he be released from his responsibility to care for Paul's needs and be sent home with Paul's blessing.

Compassion also mandated that Paul make clear to the Philippians that they should welcome Epaphroditus back. Paul tries to ensure a hearty welcome for him by the way in which he describes Epaphroditus and his

---

5. Timothy was Paul's most highly valued coworker. Paul frequently referred to him as his son (1 Cor. 4:17; 1 Tim. 1:2, 18; 2 Tim. 1:2), entrusted him with several important missions to his churches besides the one mentioned here (Acts 17:14–15; 18:5; 19:22 [this one may refer to the Phil. 2:19 visit]; 1 Cor. 4:17; 16:10–11; 1 Thess. 3:2–6; 1 Tim. 1:3), and included him in the sponsorship of six letters (1 Thessalonians, 2 Thessalonians, 2 Corinthians, Philippians, Colossians, and Philemon).

6. As does Collange, *Philippians*, 120; cf. Barth, *Philippians*, 88.

7. See Hawthorne, *Philippians*, 117.

service. He first shows how highly he regards Epaphroditus by describing him with two titles of honor, "messenger" and "minister"—titles that rightfully belonged to Paul himself. The term "messenger" (NIV) is more literally "apostle" (*apostolos*), a word Paul often uses in his letters to refer to witnesses of Jesus' resurrection who also carry a special commission to preach the gospel (Rom. 1:1; 1 Cor. 15:7).[8] Paul does not use the term here in this full-bodied sense (cf. 2 Cor. 8:23), but it retains honorable connotations, much in the way that our term "president" is dignified by its use to refer to the chief executive of many republics.

Paul also calls Epaphroditus the Philippians' "minister" (*leitourgos*) to Paul's needs, again a title of dignity. The New Testament uses this term to refer to government officials (Rom. 13:6), to the angels who serve God (Heb. 1:7), and to temple priests (Heb. 8:2). Paul uses it of himself in Romans 15:16 to describe his role as a "priest" of Christ Jesus to the Gentiles.[9] As with the term "messenger," Epaphroditus is not a "minister" in the same sense that Paul is, but Paul gladly lends him the title to demonstrate to the Philippians his esteem for Epaphroditus.

Three other important words are used to describe Epaphroditus: "brother," "fellow worker," and "fellow soldier." Paul can use the term "brothers" in Philippians to refer to believers generally, even to those who oppose him (1:14–15), but most often he uses it with an affectionate nuance (1:12; 3:1, 13, 17; 4:1, 8), and its affectionate connotations resound here. The term "fellow worker" similarly refers to one who has labored beside Paul in the cause of the gospel (cf. 4:3; 2 Cor. 8:23; Col. 4:11; 1 Thess. 3:2; Philem. 1, 24). Although rare, "fellow soldier" also signifies one who has suffered the rigors of service to the gospel along with Paul (Philem. 2; cf. 2 Tim. 2:3).

In verse 25, then, Paul introduces Epaphroditus with a fanfare of complimentary language, leaving little doubt in the minds of the Philippians that their messenger is returning with the apostle's blessing. As if this were not enough, Paul explains to his readers that the illness Epaphroditus suffered was neither minor nor incidental to the mission itself. It almost resulted in his

---

8. Among Paul's 34 uses of the term, the only clear exceptions to this definition are in Phil. 2:25 and 2 Cor. 8:23.

9. C. E. B. Cranfield argues, perhaps correctly, that Paul refers to himself not as a priest but as a Levitical helper to Jesus. Jesus would then be the priest. The argument has some merit since terms closely related to "priest" (*leitourgein* and *leitourgia*) were used in the Greek translation of the Old Testament to refer both to priestly and to Levitical service. Nevertheless, because Paul does not provide us with enough information to determine precisely how he uses the term, it seems best to invest it with its more usual meaning. See Cranfield, *The Epistle to the Romans*, 2 vols. (Edinburgh: T. & T. Clark, 1975–79), 2:755.

death, an event that would have added to Paul's suffering (cf. 1:17), and it happened because Epaphroditus was trying to carry out his commission faithfully (v. 30). Thus, Paul has not sent him back with reservations about his conduct, but eagerly. The Philippians will be relieved to know that he is safe, Epaphroditus will be relieved to be home, and Paul himself will be less anxious about Epaphroditus' well-being (v. 28). For all these reasons, and in spite of their surprise at seeing Epaphroditus earlier than expected, the Philippians should "welcome him in the Lord with great joy" (v. 29).

**Timothy and Epaphroditus as Examples.** Paul's other letters commonly (although not invariably) discuss travel plans near their conclusions. In Philippians, however, Paul has probably moved the discussion forward into the present context because Timothy and Epaphroditus serve as such good examples of the kind of conduct Paul has been urging on the Philippians explicitly since 1:27 and implicitly since the first lines of the letter. The Philippians have been complaining and arguing among themselves (2:14; 4:2). The remedy to this divisiveness, Paul says in the first half of chapter 2, is to squelch selfish ambition and vain conceit, to cultivate unity of spirit and humility, and to put the interests of others first—qualities that Christ himself exhibited.

Now, in 2:19–30, Paul discusses his travel plans to show how Timothy and Epaphroditus have successfully adopted these attitudes as well. Timothy understands the practical meaning of the unity of spirit and purpose that Paul urged on the Philippians in 2:2. He is one with Paul in his concern for the Philippians, a unity that also puts him in unity with the Philippians themselves (2:20). In 2:4 Paul had encouraged the Philippians not to seek their own interests but the interests of others. Timothy seeks the interests of Jesus Christ (2:21), and this goal leads him to seek the best interests of others (2:20). Like Christ Jesus (2:7), he has become a slave to the gospel (2:22).

Similarly, Epaphroditus became a servant to Paul in his need (2:25), and just as Christ Jesus "became obedient to death—even death on a cross" (2:8), so Epaphroditus came near death in faithful service to his commission (2:27, 30). Just as God, in response to Christ's obedience, exalted Christ to the highest place, so Epaphroditus should be welcomed back to Philippi with joy and honor (2:29).

So Paul's discussion of Timothy and Epaphroditus is far more than a mere "travelogue." It is an illustration of how two fellow believers, both well known to the Philippians, can put into practice the principles of conduct that Paul has suggested the Philippians follow. These two coworkers provide tangible evidence that the ethical principles implied in the gospel do not ask more than God gives the power to obey.

Bridging
Contexts

THIS PASSAGE POSES in an especially clear way the primary interpretive problem of all of Paul's letters. How can correspondence intended to address ancient, culture-bound circumstances function as God's eternally valid word? Even if we understand the answer to this question, how is it possible to determine, from our own cultural and chronological distance, precisely what those ancient circumstances were? In this passage one of Paul's primary purposes is to tell the Philippians why Timothy is not coming to them as soon as they expected and why Epaphroditus is coming sooner. But who are Timothy and Epaphroditus anyway, and can we be sure that the scenario suggested above is the correct one? What, moreover, do the travels of two little-known ancient Christians have to do with Christians twenty centuries later? Karl Barth has put the dilemma succinctly:

> Here we have a paragraph that does not contain any direct "teaching." Paul discusses a few points of a purely personal human kind concerning the relationship and intercourse between himself and the Philippian congregation. If we did not know the context, it would be tempting to say that as far as the passage in itself is concerned, it is not absolutely necessary to conclude that the relationship and intercourse in question have any particular connexion with the cause of Jesus Christ.[10]

Specifically, a passage like this presents two stumbling blocks, one exegetical and the other theological. From the exegetical perspective, it is difficult to understand much of the passage because crucial details are missing. Paul could assume that the Philippians would fill in the gaps with their own knowledge of the situation or with information supplied orally by Epaphroditus. None of that information, of course, is available to us, and so the temptation to resort to speculation is strong. Thus some have said that Paul commends Timothy so highly because he expects resistance to his authority from a cantankerous and divided community and knows that Timothy needs his commendation because of his "somewhat spineless character."[11] Others have said the opposite: Paul's expectation of cheerful news from Philippi (v. 19) shows that the community is not divided at all.[12] Some believe that Epaphroditus was so homesick for his friends at Philippi that he

---

10. Barth, *Philippians*, 79.
11. Collange, *Philippians*, 116.
12. Caird, *Paul's Letters From Prison*, 128.

had already left when Paul wrote the letter.[13] Others think that he is "one of the most attractive and heroic characters to be found in the annals of early Christianity."[14] Some believe that Epaphroditus fell ill while with Paul, others that he became sick on the way.[15] Occasionally interpreters even suggest the nature of the illness.[16]

As we seek to bring this passage out of Paul's world and into our own, it seems prudent to base our understanding on the minimum amount of speculation necessary to make sense of the passage. If we do not follow this path, then the points of application we draw from the passage will be as ephemeral as the speculation on which they are based.

We can say with certainty that Timothy and Epaphroditus represent a small part of the complex network of fellow laborers and messengers that surrounded Paul and his churches.[17] Coworkers appear to have always accompanied Paul in his missionary ventures as a means of extending the apostle's efforts. Thus Timothy could be dispatched to Thessalonica to "strengthen and encourage" the church there and to "find out about [their] faith" (1 Thess. 2:2–5). He could also visit Corinth with Paul's full authority to remind the Corinthians of Paul's "way of life in Christ Jesus" (1 Cor. 4:17). Titus and Tychicus apparently functioned in much the same way (2 Cor. 8:16, 24; 12:18; Eph. 6:21–22; Col. 4:7; 2 Tim. 4:12; Titus 3:12).[18]

Paul also recruited coworkers from specific churches to remain in those churches as leaders. He apparently instructed them in the basics of Christian belief and ethics (2 Thess. 3:6–11; cf. 1 Cor. 4:17b; Phil. 3:17), and urged his churches to submit to their authority (Gal. 6:6; 1 Thess. 5:12–13). In Philippi, Euodia, Syntyche, Clement, an anonymous "loyal yokefellow," and Epaphroditus (2:25; 4:2–3) were among these special coworkers; perhaps they were the "overseers and deacons" of 1:1.

Timothy and Epaphroditus, then, stand under Paul's apostolic authority in much the same way as priests and ministers in various Episcopalian and Presbyterian denominations today stand under the authority of their bishops

---

13. Bonnard, *Philippiens*, 57.

14. Michael, *Philippians*, 118.

15. For the first position see Martin, *Philippians*, 121; for the second, Bruce, *Philippians*, 71.

16. Martin, *Philippians*, 121, suggests that it either caused or was accompanied by a nervous disorder and resulted from the rigors of imprisonment with Paul. Barclay, *The Letters to the Philippians, Colossians, and Thessalonians*, 49, suggests that Epaphroditus had caught "the notorious Roman fever which sometimes swept the city like a scourge."

17. See E. E. Ellis, "Coworkers, Paul and His," *Dictionary of Paul and His Letters*, ed. Gerald F. Hawthorne, Ralph P. Martin, and Daniel G. Reid (Downers Grove, Ill.: InterVarsity Press, 1993), 183–88.

18. Ibid., 187.

and presbyteries. Just as a Roman Catholic bishop or an Orthodox metropolitan can, at his discretion, remove a priest from a parish and send him to a new one, and just as a Presbyterian presbytery or synod can bar a minister from serving in churches within its jurisdiction, so Paul could keep Timothy with him and send Epaphroditus back earlier than expected as he thought best.[19]

Once we have understood all of this, however, we still face the question of whether the passage has much to say to us. The Philippians knew Timothy and Epaphroditus, but we do not. These two believers may have been able to serve as illustrations of the qualities Paul has advised the Philippians to cultivate in 2:1–4, and the Philippians may have been heartened to hear that friends whom they knew were doing what Paul considered necessary, but how does that help us? Can we glean from this passage anything more than a repetition of the list of qualities in 2:1–4?

This passage has much to say to us theologically if we are content to dwell on what it implies more than on what it says directly. A rich theological subtext runs, like the road beneath Epaphroditus' feet, throughout this passage. This subtext implies a direct connection between Paul's understanding of the gospel and his day-to-day existence. His theology was hammered out in a pastoral context and retained its connection with that context. In a theological world where statements and confessions of faith have increasingly become objects of intense debate, we would do well to remember that we can come to precisely correct theological conclusions in the abstract and still fall short of what the gospel requires of those who believe it. For Paul, as for James, faith without works lay dead, and knowledge without love was worth nothing.[20]

This is not to say that a carefully considered theology is unimportant— Paul clearly had one, and if a pastoral need had required him to do so, he would probably have written it down in systematic form. But Paul understood that a theology abstracted from the behavior it demanded was distorted and inadequate. Karl Barth, the most influential systematic theologian of this century, said of this passage,

> This is how it looks when a man does not only think these thoughts but, because they are true and necessary thoughts, must live constantly in their shadow and can never get away from them in his concrete decisions.[21]

---

19. See Witherington, *Friendship and Finances in Philippi*, 126, 168 n. 19.
20. See 1 Cor. 8:1–11:1 and James 2:14–26.
21. Barth, *Philippians*, 80.

The passage also highlights a common characteristic of Timothy and Epaphroditus that is not specifically addressed in 2:1–4 but which, if Paul has presented these two believers as models for imitation, is nevertheless important to observe. Both men are faithful to their assigned tasks despite having to fulfill them in the face of hardship. The phrase "But you know that Timothy has proved himself" could be translated more literally, "But his proven worth you know." The phrase "proven worth" interprets a Greek word (*dokime*) that refers to the "character" of one who has remained faithful despite hardship. It is the quality that, according to Romans 5:4, results from perseverance and produces an eschatological hope that God will not disappoint. Timothy certainly had it. He remained with Paul and stood by the gospel from the time Paul first recruited him to be his coworker on the second missionary journey (Acts 16:1–3) to the period when, after Paul's death, he faded from history (Heb. 13:23).

Epaphroditus had it too. Although we know of him only from this brief paragraph and 4:18, his willingness to risk his life to help Paul in the work of the gospel shows that he stands in Timothy's tradition. Paul clearly points out the value of this quality when he tells the Philippians to "honor men like him." As we bring this passage into the contemporary church, we should not ignore this emphasis.

This passage also illustrates how Paul put his theological convictions into action in a delicate interpersonal matter, and, in a letter that advises its readers to follow Paul's example (3:17; 4:9), it is not inappropriate to learn from his actions in this situation. First, we observe Paul doing what he has asked the Philippians to do and what he probably intended the Philippians to see Timothy and Epaphroditus doing as well—he puts the interests of others ahead of his own. Paul could have used the help of both Timothy and Epaphroditus. Epaphroditus had, after all, been commissioned not only to bring him a monetary gift from Philippi but to minister to his needs in ways that the Philippian congregation could not; thus, Paul might have insisted that he stay with him. Instead, Paul not only sent him back in response to Epaphroditus' longing for his countrymen, but he sent him back with a strong commendation. This is the kind of deference that Paul probably hoped Euodia and Syntyche would show each other (4:2) and that the whole congregation would show for their fellow believers (2:14). It is clearly the quality of self-sacrifice that should also characterize modern Christians, particularly those within the church who, like Paul, have authority over others.

Second, the way in which Paul speaks of his plans to send Timothy and to visit Philippi himself is theologically significant. In both verses 19 and 24

Paul says that he has made these travel plans "in the Lord (Jesus)." He probably means by this that although he plans to send Timothy and to come himself, the Lord Jesus may send him in a different direction.[22] This happened frequently in Paul's missionary endeavors. God had directed Paul to Philippi originally in spite of Paul's own plans to minister elsewhere (Acts 16:6–10). Paul had promised to visit Corinth twice on a journey from Ephesus to Macedonia, but God apparently led him not to return after the congregation spurned him on his first visit (2 Cor. 1:12–2:1; cf. 1 Cor. 16:7). He had frequently hoped to visit Rome, but his divinely directed labors in the east had prevented him from doing so (Rom. 1:11; 15:23). Since Paul was a slave of Christ Jesus (1:1), his travel plans were not his own but were made "in the Lord," under the command of his master.

Third, Paul's understanding of hardship is clarified in this passage. Paul tells the Philippians that had Epaphroditus died, he would have experienced "sorrow upon sorrow." Commentators differ about the precise cause of the sorrow that Epaphroditus' death would have increased. Was it Paul's sorrow over his friend's illness? The sorrow that his believing opponents had caused him in prison? The imprisonment itself?[23] The cause will always elude us, but it is nevertheless clear that Paul's joyful attitude in the midst of his adversity did not exclude legitimate feelings of sorrow. The Philippians' joy upon seeing Epaphroditus and the latter's relief at being with his friends again give Paul "less anxiety" (more literally, "less sorrow"), but he is still not entirely without a sense of grief.[24]

Thus, the joy Paul experiences when the gospel makes progress is not a glib happiness that overlooks pain and suffering, but a mature understanding of God's ability to make his purposes prosper even amid human pain. Believers may and should grieve over such pain, but as Paul says elsewhere, they should not "grieve like the rest of men, who have no hope" (1 Thess. 4:13). This hopeful grief falls well within the boundaries of Christian joy.

In summary, this passage reminds us that Paul's theology was a theology for life as he lived from day to day. He had no unhealthy gap between theological convictions and behavior, but a complex interweaving of the two. This is visible not only in the way Timothy and Epaphroditus exemplify what it means to put the interests of Jesus Christ, and therefore of other people, ahead of their own concerns, but also in the way that Paul himself puts the

---

22. See the thorough discussion of this phrase in O'Brien, *Philippians*, 317, 327.

23. See the discussion of options in Meyer, *The Epistles to the Philippians and Colossians, and to Philemon*, 102–3.

24. Ibid., 102.

interests of Epaphroditus first, makes his plans contingent on the Lord's guidance, and, despite the letter's emphasis on joy, legitimizes sorrow over human pain.

 PERHAPS IT IS only during times of persecution that the church has been free from the plague of both clergy and laity who lend intellectual assent to its teaching and go through the motions of its liturgy but who never allow the gospel to soak deeply into their souls and transform their lives. There are professional theologians at leftward-leaning denominational colleges and seminaries who have little connection with the church and who seem unconcerned about their accommodations to a sin-tainted culture. They have counterparts at conservative Christian institutions who are so concerned that everyone confess precisely the same creed that they, like the Pharisees of old, need to "go and learn what this means: 'I desire mercy, not sacrifice'" (Matt. 9:13; cf. 12:7; Hosea 6:6).[25] Some ministers of the gospel can skillfully proclaim God's word in the pulpit, but refuse to take much time away from their sermon preparation schedules for the mundane matters of pastoral service: calling on the sick, helping the needy, and cheering the discouraged. Many lay people attend church services and can recite sections of the catechism, the creed, the liturgy, and the Bible but conduct their day-to-day affairs in ways little different from those around them who lay no claim to Christian commitment. Assent to Christian doctrine is somehow segregated in all of these instances from commitment to Christian behavior.

Against this psychologically and spiritually unhealthy separation of belief from behavior, Philippians 2:19–30 places the examples of Timothy, Epaphroditus, and Paul himself. Because of their commitment to the gospel, Paul and Timothy have adopted the role of slaves (2:22; cf. 1:1), and both have been willing to put the spiritual welfare of the Philippians above their own interests (2:20). Epaphroditus, likewise, has been willing to risk his life to help Paul as he seeks to fulfill his apostolic calling (2:30). Timothy, Epaphroditus, and Paul, then, have understood that Christian commitment means losing one's life in order to find it, forfeiting the whole world but gaining one's

---

25. For a commentary on the state of theological education in some "mainline" denominational seminaries, see Thomas Oden, *Requiem: A Lament in Three Movements* (Nashville, Tenn.: Abingdon, 1995), 40–41. On the conservative side see the complaint of Scot McKnight, "The Nature of the Bodily Resurrection: A Debatable Issue," *Journal of the Evangelical Theological Society* 33 (1990): 379–82.

soul. A divided commitment to the gospel, as Jesus never tired of saying in various ways, is actually no commitment at all.[26]

One of the most important ways in which an undivided commitment to the gospel can be expressed, as Timothy illustrates, is in faithfulness to the gospel and its demands despite the hardship that such faithfulness sometimes requires. Timothy's mettle had been tested over the years of his slave-labor with Paul for the advancement of the gospel, and both Paul and the Philippians valued this quality (2:22)—a quality that is important because it produces assurance that we belong to God's people and will stand before him acquitted on the final day (Rom. 5:4).

It is not a quality, however, that Western, and particularly American, culture presently reinforces. This is most clearly visible in the now well-known statistics on divorce in the United States. Although many who marry promise something similar to the traditional vow to be a "loving and faithful" husband or wife "in plenty and in want; in joy and in sorrow; in sickness and in health; as long as we both shall live," Americans divorce with astonishing frequency. Research published in 1989 predicted that between 50 and 60 percent of all new marriages would end in divorce and that over half of all children would, by the year 2000, become stepchildren.[27] Among social scientists, divorce is often viewed not as a deviation from the norm or as something undesirable, but as "one path in the normal family life cycle."[28] Unfaithfulness to others, it seems, has been replaced by the notion of faithfulness, at all costs, to one's self.

In such a climate, it is not likely that Christians will receive much encouragement from the broader culture to be faithful, in spite of hardship, to their commitment to the gospel. The notion that someone might become a "slave" in the service of anything or risk one's health to fulfill a higher calling appears extraordinary, even abnormal. Yet it is precisely such people that Paul in this passage asks his Philippian readers, and us, to hold in high esteem (2:28). Indeed, the exemplary function of Timothy and Epaphroditus in this passage shows that Paul hopes that all of his readers will, because they are believers, view the commitment of Timothy and Epaphroditus as the norm and not follow the path of those who look out for their "own interests, not those of Jesus Christ" (2:21).

This level of integrated commitment and faithfulness to the gospel will mean that as with Paul, our plans need to be subject to the Lord's sovereign

---

26. See, for example, Matt. 6:24; Luke 9:24; 14:26, 31–33; 16:13.

27. Bryan Strong and Christine DeVault, *The Marriage and Family Experience*, 5th ed. (St. Paul: West Publishing Company, 1992), 508.

28. Ibid., 509; cf. Russell Chandler, *Racing Toward 2001: The Forces Shaping America's Religious Future* (Grand Rapids: Zondervan, 1992), 98.

control. Jesus submitted to death on the cross although he did not want to experience it (Matt. 26:39; Mark 14:36; Luke 22:42; Phil. 2:8). Paul wanted to preach in Bithynia (Acts 16:7) and to visit the Roman church (Rom. 1:13), but submitted to God's call to go elsewhere (Acts 16:7–10; Rom. 15:23). Paul also hoped to visit the Philippians and was confident that he would be able to do so, but knew that his plans were subject to the Lord's control (Phil. 2:24).

Christians throughout the ages have experienced similar divine interruptions of their plans. In June, 1939, Dietrich Bonhoeffer believed that he could help the cause of the struggling Confessing Church—the group of Christians in Germany who refused to compromise with Adolf Hitler—if he visited America. Such a visit, he reasoned, might provide a spiritual bond between the Confessing Church and Christians outside Germany and enable him to avoid his country's inevitable call to military duty for a cause he considered evil.

Bonhoeffer had received several invitations to do various types of church work in America, one of which was to work with German refugees from Hitler's Third Reich. Such an invitation, in order to pass through government censors, had to be worded in a veiled way, and Bonhoeffer misunderstood it. The telegram spoke of a combined task of giving theological lectures and working in college and university summer conferences, but the intention of those who sent it was that Bonhoeffer should work with German refugees for at least three years. When Bonhoeffer arrived in New York and understood the real nature of the invitation, he faced a crisis: Should he remain in America while the Confessing Church he had left behind in Germany struggled to resist the efforts of Hitler to conform the church to Nazi ideals, or should he return to face a bleak personal future? Many good reasons presented themselves for staying in America, but he chose to return. He explained in a letter to Reinhold Niebuhr that the Christian community in Germany would shortly face the terrible alternative of either willing the victory of their country and the destruction of civilization or the survival of civilization and the defeat of their country. He knew what he would choose, he explained, but he could not make that decision in the safe haven of another country.[29]

Bonhoeffer made the hard choice—a choice that left some of his friends in America surprised and disappointed—because he knew it was the choice

---

29. See Eberhard Bethge, *Dietrich Bonhoeffer: Man of Vision, Man of Courage,* trans. Edwin Robertson (New York: Harper & Row, 1970), 559. The details of this critical period in Bonhoeffer's life are narrated on pp. 554–59.

that the advancement of the gospel demanded. He is perhaps the outstanding example from modern times of a theologian who lived his theology, who interrupted the sensible course that the world had mapped out for him in order to respond to God's clear direction. In following Jesus he lost his life, but, in losing it, gained it again.[30]

---

30. Bonhoeffer's dilemma was also faced frequently by prominent Christians in the formerly Communist countries of Eastern Europe. When their witness became too winsome, the authorities frequently imprisoned them, only to find that they had an embarrassingly high-profile prisoner of conscience on their hands. One solution to this dilemma was to offer their prisoner the chance to leave the country. Those to whom the offer was made often chose to stay instead. See Barbara von der Heydt, *Candles Behind the Wall: Heroes of the Peaceful Revolution That Shattered Communism* (Grand Rapids: Eerdmans, 1993).

# Philippians 3:1–11

‍

**F**INALLY, MY BROTHERS, rejoice in the Lord! It is no trouble for me to write the same things to you again, and it is a safeguard for you.

²Watch out for those dogs, those men who do evil, those mutilators of the flesh. ³For it is we who are the circumcision, we who worship by the Spirit of God, who glory in Christ Jesus, and who put no confidence in the flesh—⁴though I myself have reasons for such confidence.

If anyone else thinks he has reasons to put confidence in the flesh, I have more: ⁵circumcised on the eighth day, of the people of Israel, of the tribe of Benjamin, a Hebrew of Hebrews; in regard to the law, a Pharisee; ⁶as for zeal, persecuting the church; as for legalistic righteousness, faultless.

⁷But whatever was to my profit I now consider loss for the sake of Christ. ⁸What is more, I consider everything a loss compared to the surpassing greatness of knowing Christ Jesus my Lord, for whose sake I have lost all things. I consider them rubbish, that I may gain Christ ⁹and be found in him, not having a righteousness of my own that comes from the law, but that which is through faith in Christ—the righteousness that comes from God and is by faith. ¹⁰I want to know Christ and the power of his resurrection and the fellowship of sharing in his sufferings, becoming like him in his death, ¹¹and so, somehow, to attain to the resurrection from the dead.

**Original Meaning**

IN 3:1–11 PAUL enters a discussion of some of the most profound themes of New Testament theology. The passage focuses on the idea that even the most admirable human privileges and achievements fall short of God's requirements for acquittal in the final judgment and that God has provided the means by which people can be rescued from this plight. Just as Paul's circumstantial account of Timothy and Epaphroditus was not devoid of deep theology, so this deeply theological passage was written for practical reasons related to Paul's experiences with false teachers among his churches. Understanding the interplay between the reservoir of Paul's theological convictions and the practical needs of his churches is as important in this passage as it was in 2:19–30.

To review briefly matters that are also discussed in the introduction to the commentary, 3:1–11 probably arises out of Paul's concern that Judaizing missionaries, like those who have invaded his churches in Galatia, will come to Philippi. Their "gospel" mixed the notion of faith in Christ for salvation with the idea that all who want to belong to God's people must accept the yoke of the Jewish law. Gentile believers, in their view, had to become Jews in order to be saved. Paul's strong desire to warn his dearly beloved Philippian brothers and sisters of this theological danger accounts for the change in the letter's tone at 3:2, a change that, although surprising in a letter as cheerful as Philippians, is not out of accord with the straightforward language of 1:17 and 2:21.

Paul's warning can be divided into four paragraphs. The first (v. 1) provides both a transition to the new section after Paul's discussion of travel plans in 2:19–30 and a link to 2:12–18. The second and third paragraphs reveal the true nature of the Judaizers first by contrasting their method and message with the character of true Christians (vv. 2–4a) and then by comparing their theological convictions with those of the pre-Christian Paul (vv. 4b–6). The fourth paragraph describes the great reversal that took place in Paul's own theological convictions when he submitted to the gospel; it implicitly demonstrates the incompatibility of trust in the flesh with faith in Christ (vv. 7–11).

**A Seam in the Letter's Argument (3:1).** Paul introduces this new section of his letter with an admonition to "rejoice in the Lord" (3:1). This command acts as a thread to bind the material in 3:2–4:1 to Paul's discussion of Timothy and Epaphroditus in 2:19–30 and to the argument prior to that discussion in 1:27–2:18. The two previous sections had both concluded with an admonition to adopt an attitude of joy in the midst of difficulty, whether that meant remaining steadfast in the faith rather than capitulating to a quarrelsome spirit or acknowledging the unselfishness of Epaphroditus who nearly lost his life in the service of the gospel (2:18, 29). In 3:2–4:1 Paul describes doctrinal troubles that may face the Philippian community in the future. Amid these trials too, Paul hopes that the Philippians will maintain an attitude of joy.

Here for the first time, however, he follows his admonition to rejoice with the qualifier "in the Lord." The phrase may describe the basis for the Philippians' joy: Because they are united with Christ they rejoice. More probably, it echoes the language of the Psalms that admonishes the righteous to "rejoice in the Lord and be glad" (Ps. 32:11) and to "sing joyfully to the Lord" (33:1). In both of these instances, the psalmist urges the worshiping community to praise the Lord for what he has done for them. This is probably also the intention of Paul's admonition.[1]

After this transitional comment, Paul states why he issues the warnings that follow. Although he is repeating information he has told the Philippians before, he wants to emphasize its importance as a "safeguard." His purpose, then, is to keep the foundation of their faith free from the cracks and weaknesses he has seen develop in the commitment of other churches to the gospel.

**Circumcision, False and True (3:2—4a).** The first step in Paul's warning is to compare the Judaizers with authentic believers. The force of his language is lost in most English translations, both because Paul's rhetoric is almost impossible to duplicate in intelligible English and because the stridency with which he speaks is startling. We can almost capture both the rhetoric and the urgency of the original with the translation, "Beware the curs! Beware the criminals! Beware the cutters!"

Paul calls his opponents "dogs" because, like dogs who intrude where they are not wanted (cf. Ps. 59:14—15), his opponents have insinuated themselves into Paul's churches (cf. Gal. 2:5).[2] They are "men who do evil" because, unlike missionaries of the authentic gospel, they labor in an evil cause (cf. 2 Cor 11:13). They are "mutilators of the flesh" because their confidence lies in circumcision, a physical operation performed on the flesh, rather than in God's gracious work through Jesus Christ (cf. Gal 5:12).[3]

On the other hand, Paul says, believers comprise the true "circumcision." His use of the pronoun "we" shows that he includes himself and the Philippians in this group. Paul, of course, was a circumcised Jew (cf. v. 5), and the Philippian church was probably composed entirely of physically uncircumcised Gentiles. The common ground between them is their commitment to the gospel. As believers, Paul says, they comprise the true people of God, the true circumcision.

How could Paul plausibly make this claim? The Old Testament recognizes that the human heart rather than physical features are God's real concern (1 Sam. 16:7), and it sometimes applies this principle specifically to circumcision. Physical circumcision was a visible mark that identified those who bore it as members of Israel, God's chosen people (Gen. 17). At times, however,

---

1. See Bruce, *Philippians*, 76; O'Brien, *Philippians*, 350.

2. Cf. Robert Jewett, "The Epistolary Thanksgiving and the Integrity of Philippians," *Novum Testamentum* 12 (1970): 40—53 (here 44).

3. The Greek text reveals a play on words that is virtually impossible to reproduce in English. The phrase "mutilators of the flesh" translates *katatome* and the word "circumcision" translates *peritome*. The only difference between the two words is the prepositional prefix, *kata* in one and *peri* in the other.

the Israelites placed such confidence in possession of the physical mark itself that they felt their election was secure even if their hearts strayed after other gods. In these instances, the writers of the Old Testament reminded them that the physical rite should be symbolic of a deeper commitment. They called this commitment "circumcision of the heart," and they looked forward to a time when God would figuratively perform this operation on the hearts of his people so that they might be committed to him (Jer. 4:4; cf. 6:10; 9:25; Deut. 10:16; 30:6). Paul's point in verse 3 is that this time has arrived and that because circumcision of the *heart* is the critical qualification for entrance into God's people in this new era, physical circumcision is irrelevant (cf. Rom. 2:25–29; 1 Cor. 7:19; Gal. 5:6; 6:15; Eph. 2:11; Col. 2:11).[4]

This newly constituted people of God, Paul says, exhibit three characteristics: They "worship by the Spirit," "glory in Christ," and "put no confidence in the flesh." The early Jerusalem church, which was entirely Jewish, was forced to recognize that God had included uncircumcised Gentile believers within his people by placing his Spirit among them (Acts 10:44–48; 11:15–17; 15:7–9). Similarly, when the Gentile believers in Galatia fell under the influence of Judaizers who claimed that they could not be part of God's people until they accepted circumcision, Paul reminded the Galatians that the presence of the Spirit among them was irrefutable proof that they were already members of God's people and needed no additional qualification (Gal. 3:1–5). So here, Paul identifies true circumcision with the work of the Spirit within the worshiping community of both circumcised and uncircumcised believers.

The next two characteristics of the true circumcision are related to one another. We who are truly circumcised, Paul says, "glory in Christ Jesus" and "put no confidence in the flesh." Paul's word for "glory" (*kauchaomai*) can mean "to boast," and, together with two other closely related words (*kauchema* and *kauchesis*), is often used in his letters to indicate the ground of one's confidence. In 2 Corinthians, for example, Paul says that the false apostles who have invaded the Corinthian church and are opposing Paul "commend themselves," but that in contrast he refuses to "boast" in this way (2 Cor. 10:12–13). Similarly, in Romans, Paul concludes his argument that Jews cannot claim exemption from judgment on the final day on the basis of possessing or performing of the law with the statement that "boasting" has been excluded (Rom. 3:27). According to his argument in Romans 1:18–3:26, boasting has been excluded because the Jew, like the Gentile, is sinful and can only escape God's

---

4. Paul believed, however, that physical circumcision could have value for Jewish Christians if, like Abraham, they viewed the rite as a "seal of the righteousness" that comes "by faith" (Rom. 4:11).

wrath by believing in the atoning death of Christ. In Philippians 3:3, then, Paul's point is that the ground of the Christian's confidence is Christ rather than any human social privilege.

Paul follows this with the statement that believers do not put confidence (*pepoithotes*) in the flesh. Two aspects of this statement are interesting. (1) It shows that Paul regards confidence in the flesh and confidence in Christ as mutually exclusive. From his perspective, it is impossible to place one spiritual foot on the foundation of the flesh and one spiritual foot on the foundation of Christ. Both feet must be firmly planted on either one foundation or the other. (2) Paul's term "flesh" has profound significance. Paul probably considered the term especially appropriate to the problem of the Judaizers since they advocated a literal operation on the flesh and since in both the Old Testament and the philosophical literature from Paul's time the term *flesh* often signified human weakness, frailty, and tendency to sin. Simply put, Paul's point is that whereas Christians have placed their confidence in Christ, the feet of the Judaizers rest on a fallen human foundation that will inevitably collapse.

All of this reminds Paul of his own fleshly résumé, and so he concludes this paragraph in verse 4a with a phrase that makes the transition to the next paragraph. If human privilege and attainment could form a stable foundation on which to stand in the final day, he says, then his own pre-Christian foundation was firm indeed.

**Paul's Fleshly Advantages (3:4b–6).** In this paragraph Paul compares the Judaizers' willingness to place confidence in the fleshly rite of circumcision with his own fleshly advantages (*kerde;* NIV "profit") prior to his conversion. These advantages went far beyond mere circumcision and therefore placed Paul in a category by himself (cf. Gal. 1:14). He lists two types of advantages: those that were his by birth and those he attained. In both categories, he excelled. His parents supplied him with impeccable credentials as a member of God's people: circumcision, racial identity with Israel, membership in the Israelite tribe that gave Israel its first king, and the ability to speak the language of his people.[5] Paul supplemented these advantages by observing the law after the manner of the Pharisees and by devoting himself to the law so completely that his zeal led him to persecute the church.

Paul's last statement probably functions as a summary of all of these advantages. He was, he says, "blameless with respect to the righteousness that

---

5. John Chrysostom (A.D. 354–407), whose native language was the language in which Paul wrote, took the phrase "Hebrew of the Hebrews" (*hebraios ex hebraion*) to mean that Paul was raised to speak Aramaic, the language of Palestinian Judaism in the first century. Most modern commentators agree with this understanding of the phrase.

comes by the law" (pers. trans.). This does not mean that Paul thought of himself as sinless prior to his conversion, for his blamelessness would include careful attention to the means of atonement the law provided for those who sin.[6] It means instead that his parents had done everything for him that the law required Jews to do and that he had himself diligently observed the law. Paul trusted that one day this heritage and these achievements would help him to stand acquitted before God.

**Advantage Becomes Disadvantage (3:7–11).** Like a bolt from the blue, however, God apprehended Paul, and he saw that his attitude toward his privileges and attainments was wrong. They had formed the basis of his confidence that on the final day he would be acquitted, "gains" that God would honor and in light of which he would proclaim Paul righteous. But when God apprehended him, Paul saw them for what they were—fleshly and therefore fallible human efforts, tainted with sin and therefore unable to receive God's approval. They could now only be considered "loss for the sake of Christ" (v. 7).

Paul explores the ramifications of this great reversal in verses 8–11. This theologically rich statement is one long sentence in the Greek text. It first restates in a more intense form the fact of the great reversal (v. 8) and then describes its two results (vv. 9–11).

Paul begins by restating in verse 8 in a more intense form what he has just said in verse 7. Instead of referring simply to considering his fleshly advantages as loss, now he says that he considers "everything" to be loss; and instead of saying simply that he did this "for the sake of Christ," he says that he did it "for the sake of the surpassing greatness of the knowledge of Christ Jesus my Lord" (pers. trans.). By saying that he considers everything to be loss, Paul does not mean that his Jewish upbringing, the law, and "everything" else were evil, but that his attitude toward them was evil. At his conversion, he had to drop the notion that he and God were partners in the project of justification and to accept the means for righteousness that God alone provided—the means Paul summarizes in the phrase "knowing Christ Jesus my Lord."

This phrase echoes the Old Testament's use of the term *know* in its various forms to refer to human acknowledgment of and obedience to God's revelation of himself. Isaiah, for example, describes God's future restoration of Israel after the ravages of the Babylonian destruction and exile in the picturesque language of a desert that suddenly turns lush and begins to bloom. God will do this, says the prophet, "so that people may see and know, may consider and understand, that the hand of the LORD has done this, that the

---

6. See Thomas R. Schreiner, *The Law and Its Fulfillment: A Pauline Theology of Law* (Grand Rapids: Baker, 1993), 70–71.

Holy One of Israel has created it" (Isa. 41:20).[7] Jeremiah also prophesies that the time of restoration will be characterized by a spontaneous knowledge of God. In that day, "No longer will a man teach his neighbor, or a man his brother, saying, 'Know the Lord,' because they will all know me from the least of them to the greatest" (Jer. 31:34). When Paul speaks of "knowing Christ Jesus my Lord," then, he means that he has acknowledged God's great act of deliverance in Christ and submitted to Christ's lordship.

Paul next describes two results of this momentous decision. The first is that he might "gain Christ." Paul follows this brief statement with an elaboration of its meaning. For Paul to gain Christ means that he will be "found in him" on the final day when he stands before God to give an account of himself (Rom. 2:1–16; 14:10; 2 Cor. 5:10).[8] On that day, Paul explains, he does not want to be found clinging to the righteousness that is available through the law but to the righteousness that comes from God himself and is appropriated by faith in Christ.[9]

This statement has produced a hornet's nest of controversy, both because the meaning of the term *righteousness* itself is a bone of contention among theologians and because Paul's use of it here is ambiguous. When Paul refers to his own righteousness, does he mean his own "legalistic" efforts to win God's approval? Does he mean simply his former way of relating to God as a Jew without any connotation that his Jewish observance was legalistic? Or does he refer to something else altogether? When he refers to the righteousness that comes from God, on the other hand, does he mean that God regards believers as innocent and therefore acceptable to him? Does he mean that God gives ethical uprightness to believers? Does he mean that God gives a

---

7. For a full discussion of the concept of "knowledge" in the Old Testament, see Rudolf Bultmann, "γινώσκω," *Theological Dictionary of the New Testament*, ed. Gerhard Kittel, 10 vols. (Grand Rapids: Eerdmans, 1964–76), 1:696–701.

8. The reference to the final resurrection in Philippians 3:11 shows that the phrase "be found in him" also refers to the final day. Most commentators understand the phrase this way. See especially the discussion in O'Brien, *Philippians*, 392–83.

9. The phrase "faith in Christ" (*pisteos Christou*) could also be translated "the faithfulness of Christ," and a growing number of scholars believe that both here and elsewhere this is the best rendering (cf. Rom. 3:22, 26; Gal. 2:16, 20; 3:22; Eph. 3:12). If so, they argue, then the phrase refers to Christ's obedience to death (cf. 2:8). The traditional understanding of the phrase is probably correct, however, since Paul never speaks unambiguously of Christ's faithfulness, but frequently speaks in unmistakable terms of believing in Christ (as in Rom. 10:14; Gal. 2:16; Phil. 1:29). Two scholars who pay particular attention to Phil. 3:9 and who take opposing positions in the debate are Morna D. Hooker, "ΠΙΣΤΙΣ ΧΡΙΣΤΟΥ," *New Testament Studies* 35 (1989): 321–42, and James D. G. Dunn, "Once More, ΠΙΣΤΙΣ ΧΡΙΣΤΟΥ," *Society of Biblical Literature 1991 Seminar Papers*, ed. Eugene H. Lovering (Atlanta, Ga.: Scholars Press, 1991), 730–44.

gift to believers that has the power to transform them? Or, again, does he mean something else?[10]

Several texts from the Old Testament and from other Pauline letters help us to find a path through the morass of scholarly discussion on these issues. First, when Paul speaks of "a righteousness of my own," he is not speaking a language foreign to the Old Testament. In Deuteronomy, for example, Israel's own righteousness is her own *inadequate* righteousness, her failed attempts to do what God commanded (Deut. 9:4–29; cf. Dan. 9:7). Similarly, when Paul speaks of his own righteousness, he probably refers to his own inability to keep the Mosaic law. On the final day, when he stands before God, he does not want to be found clinging to this inadequate righteousness.

In addition, Paul contrasts human sinfulness with "the righteousness of God" elsewhere in his correspondence in a way that is helpful for finding out what he means in Philippians 3:9. In 2 Corinthians 5:21 Paul says that God "made him to be sin who knew no sin, so that in him we might become the righteousness of God." God did not, of course, make Christ into a sinner; rather, he regarded him as a sinner. In the same way God does not make the believer an upright person but regards the believer as acquitted. Similarly, in Romans 3:21–26 Paul equates the "righteousness from God" with the atoning effect of Christ's sacrificial death. The "righteousness that comes from God and is by faith" in Philippians 3:9, then, is probably God's willingness to acquit the sinner of his or her guilt on the basis of Christ's atoning death.[11] In summary, the first result of gaining Christ is that when Paul stands before God on the final day, he will not be found clinging to his own defective obedience to God's commands but will be found trusting in God's willingness to consider him acquitted because of Christ's death.

Paul describes the second result of gaining Christ in verses 10–11. It means that Paul's life will take the shape of Christ's death and resurrection. When Paul describes his own life elsewhere as taking the shape of Christ's death, he refers primarily to the suffering he endured as a result of his call to preach

---

10. See the discussion of these issues in Rudolf Bultmann, *New Testament Theology*, 2 vols. (New York: Charles Scribner's Sons, 1951–55), 1:270–85; David Hill, *Greek Words and Hebrew Meanings: Studies in the Semantics of Soteriological Terms* (Cambridge: Cambridge University Press, 1967), 139–62; Ernst Käsemann, " 'The Righteousness of God' in Paul," *New Testament Questions of Today* (Philadelphia: Fortress, 1969), 168–82; Manfred T. Brauch, "Perspectives on 'God's Righteousness' in Recent German Discussion," in E. P. Sanders, *Paul and Palestinian Judaism: A Comparison of Patterns of Religion* (Philadelphia: Fortress, 1977), 523–42; John Reumann, *"Righteousness" in the New Testament: "Justification" in the United States Lutheran–Roman Catholic Dialogue* (Philadelphia/New York: Fortress/Paulist, 1982); Mark A. Seifrid, *Justification by Faith: The Origin and Development of a Central Pauline Theme* (Leiden: Brill, 1992).

11. Bultmann, *Theology*, 1:277.

the gospel to the Gentiles (2 Cor. 4:7–12; 6:4–10; 11:23–29; 12:10). That suffering included the physical dangers encountered during his missionary travels (2 Cor. 6:4–5; 11:23–27), the theological perils of holding at bay the ferocious wolves who were attempting to undermine the infant faith of his churches (2 Cor. 11:26), and the emotional turmoil to which the immature within those churches subjected their father in the faith (2 Cor. 2:1–4; 11:29; cf. Gal. 4:19). Just as Christ's death was the means through which God worked the miracle of the resurrection, so Paul's own suffering in faithfulness to his calling is the means through which God is bringing spiritual life to the congregations of believers he has been establishing (2 Cor. 4:7–11; cf. Col. 1:24). As a result, Paul tells the Corinthians, "death is at work in us, but life is at work in you" (2 Cor. 4:12).

But Paul has more in mind in verses 10–11 than the transformation of people in the present through the resurrection power of Christ's life. These verses also look forward to the final resurrection in which Paul will participate, and the "somehow" that begins verse 11 sounds a startling note of uncertainty after the confident theme of reliance on God that runs through verses 7–9.[12] Paul is certain that God will keep both him and his congregations faithful to their calling and conduct them safely through the final judgment (cf. 1:10; 1 Cor. 1:8–9; 2 Cor. 1:7, 14, 21; 2 Tim. 1:12), but he consistently refuses to relax his own efforts to be faithful to God's call (1 Cor. 9:24–26; 2 Tim. 4:7) and frequently admonishes his congregations not to presume upon their own confidence in God's mercy (e.g., Phil. 1:9–11; Col. 1:21–23; 1 Tim. 6:12). In the next section of the letter this theme will become Paul's primary concern, and the "somehow" that begins verse 11 provides a skillful transition to that important discussion.[13]

The overall purpose of 3:1–11 is to draw a comparison between the pre-Christian Paul and Paul's Judaizing opponents and so to provide the Philippians with a theological rationale for rejecting the Judaizers as completely as Paul rejected his own past when he submitted to the gospel. Both the pre-Christian Paul and the Judaizers rejected the gospel of God's grace. Paul's confidence in his social standing as a Jew and in his own attainments led him not to embrace the gospel of God's grace but to persecute those who did. The

---

12. Some commentators believe that Paul's "somehow" (*ei pos*) contains no element of uncertainty about *whether* he will experience the resurrection, only about *the way* in which he will reach the resurrection—whether by martyrdom, by Christ's coming, or by a natural death (Martin, *Philippians*, 135–36; Bruce, *Philippians*, 92; O'Brien, *Philippians*, 413). Other uses of the phrase in the New Testament, however, show that it voices a fervent hope that only presumption could express as a certainty (Acts 27:12; Rom. 1:10; 11:14). See Silva, *Philippians*, 192–93.

13. See Silva, *Philippians*, 193.

Judaizers are now following the same path by adding a fleshly rite to the spiritual requirement of faith for entry into the people of God. Both the pre-Christian Paul and the Judaizers, therefore, imply that their own human attempts to attain peace with God are necessary for salvation. Against this idea, Paul in this paragraph states that acquittal on the final day must be God's action from beginning to end and that the efforts of fallen human flesh will only result in disaster.

THIS PASSAGE IS so rich theologically that the greatest challenge in interpreting it is to remain within its theological mainstream and to avoid traveling too far down other interesting but tributary brooks. The primary point is clear: Righteousness before God on the final day comes solely from God, and any attempt to add requirements of human invention to what God has freely given amounts to a rejection of the gospel. In Paul's eyes, a Judaizing form of the gospel is equivalent to his own rejection of the gospel, and the Judaizers themselves are as inimical to the church as Paul the persecutor. Those who interpret this passage within the modern context will want to lay particular stress on this equivalency. Anyone who adds requirements to the pure gospel of God's grace, in Paul's view, rejects the gospel in its entirety. Such a gospel, as the apostle says elsewhere, is "a different gospel—which is really no gospel at all" (Gal. 1:6–7; cf. 2 Cor. 11:4).

**Three Cultural Stumbling Blocks.** In order to communicate this primary point with the urgency and meaning that Paul intended to convey to the Philippians, we will have to remove three potential stumbling blocks. First, it would be easy to pass over the stridency of Paul's language in 3:2, since the rhetoric is difficult to reproduce and since, detached from its literary and theological context, Paul's words may sound offensive. The task is made that much more difficult by modern translations that try to remove some of the harshness of Paul's language. One translation, for example, renders the verse, "Be on your guard against those dogs, those who do nothing but harm and who insist on mutilation—'circumcision' I will not call it" (REB). Such a translation misses the staccato rhythm of Paul's rhetoric and therefore fails to communicate the urgency of the statement.

In this verse, however, the medium is an important part of the message— Paul's rhetoric underlines the gravity of the issues at stake in his debate with the Judaizers, and it is important to give Paul's opening salvo all the emphasis in the contemporary context that it had in its ancient context. To call a group "dogs," "men who do evil," and "mutilators" is to use extraordinarily harsh language. This kind of language is typical of the prophet whose message is so urgent that its form is designed to shake his hearers out of complacency. Thus John the Baptist's warning to the Pharisees and Sadducees begins, "You brood of vipers!" (Matt. 3:7; Luke 3:7), and Jesus' sermon to the Pharisees includes the refrain, "Woe to you, teachers of the law and Pharisees, you hypocrites!" The prophetic form of Paul's statement, then, contributes to its meaning and needs to be communicated in the contemporary context.

Second, Paul's primary point in the passage cannot be understood unless we carefully define several difficult terms. The term *circumcision* will puzzle most people today. Since the operation is still often performed on infant boys, many know the physical details of the procedure itself. Few, however, understand why the rite had spiritual significance for the Jews and why it became a bone of contention in the early church. The best textbook on these matters is the Bible itself. Genesis 17 records the institution of the rite, and study of the passage reveals why the Judaizers put such stress on it. There God ratified his promise to Abraham to give him numerous descendants (see Gen. 12:2; 15:5), and God commanded that as a sign of this covenant Abraham should circumcise every male within his household. Whoever does not accept this sign, he says, "will be cut off from his people" (v. 14), and, he continues, the sign is to be "everlasting" (v. 19).

In the early days of the church, the Judaizers were unwilling to recognize that with the coming of the gospel, the literal observance of this rite had been made unnecessary. In a famous incident, a group of them marched off to Antioch to tell the Gentiles there: "Unless you are circumcised according to the custom taught by Moses, you cannot be saved" (Acts 15:1; cf. 11:1–3). Those who understood what Paul calls "the truth of the gospel" (Gal. 2:5, 14) responded to this challenge with clarity: God had given the Holy Spirit to uncircumcised Gentile believers and so had provided undeniable proof that they had been included among his people (Acts 11:15–18; 15:7–11; Gal. 2:11–5:6). Like the Jews, they stood under the law's condemnation, and, like the Jews, the death of Christ on the cross effected redemption for as many of them as believed (Rom. 1:18–5:21; Gal. 2:11–5:6). Other signs of belonging to God's people were unnecessary.

Because the Judaizers were insisting that Gentiles could not be saved apart from accepting circumcision, Paul charges them in Philippians 3:3 with placing confidence in the *flesh*. This term is fraught with possibilities for misunderstanding. Some may not understand the term within this context at all. Flesh to them is a part of human anatomy, and the concept of placing confidence in the flesh is as baffling as the notion that someone would place confidence in "the hair." Others may know that the term has been used figuratively in theological circles to refer to humanity in general or to the created order, but they may believe that Paul is calling God's creation evil. Both groups need to see the connection between Paul's understanding of the flesh and the Old Testament understanding. In the Old Testament the term is sometimes used to refer to the frailty of humanity in comparison with the strength of God (2 Chron. 32:8; Isa. 31:3; cf. Gen. 6:3). It is not a great step from this idea to the notion that humanity, because of its frailty, is prone to sin.

Paul takes this step in numerous passages where the flesh is closely allied with what is worldly and sinful rather than with what is spiritual and good (see, e.g., Rom. 7:5, 18, 25; 8:3–13; Gal. 3:3; 5:13–24). Yet Paul clearly did not believe that the flesh itself is sinful. Sin entered the human scene after the creation of Adam, not at the time of his creation (Rom. 5:12), and Jesus himself could come in "sinful flesh" (Rom. 8:3) but not be tainted by sin (2 Cor. 5:21). In summary, "the flesh" for Paul is humanity in its fallen frailty, unable to help itself and in need of God's redemption. Because it is God's creation, however, it is not sinful in itself.[14]

God's answer to human sin, Paul says in Philippians 3:9, is the *righteousness* that comes from God through faith in Christ. The adjective "righteous" is not commonly used today, and when it is used, it usually means "morally right, just, upright, virtuous, law-abiding."[15] This understanding of the word is derived from the use of the term in classical Greek literature to mean "observant of custom," "fair," "deserved."[16] In the law courts of ancient Greece and Rome and in the law courts of modern Western democracies, the righteous judge condemns the guilty and acquits the innocent in accord with their just desserts. The problem with transferring this understanding into Paul's use of the term without further ado is that "the righteousness that comes from God" might then be understood as God's willingness to suspend his own righteousness as a judge and, by a legal fiction, claim that we "deserved" to be considered righteous when we did not.

Unlike most English speakers, however, Paul's understanding of the term was rooted in the Old Testament. There the term can certainly be used in legal contexts, but even in those contexts the notion of God's covenant with

---

14. On the meaning of the term "flesh" (*sarx*), see W. David Stacey, *The Pauline View of Man* (London: Macmillan, 1956), 154–80; John M. G. Barclay, *Obeying the Truth: A Study of Paul's Ethics in Galatians* (Edinburgh: T. & T. Clark, 1988), 178–81.

15. *The Concise Oxford Dictionary of Current English*, ed. J. B. Sykes, 6th ed. (Oxford: Clarendon, 1976), 969.

16. See Henry George Liddell and Robert Scott, *A Greek-English Lexicon*, 9th ed., rev. and aug. Henry Stuart Jones (Oxford: Oxford University Press, 1940), 429.

his people Israel often lies beneath the surface. The purpose of the covenant was to confirm and guarantee his relationship with his people. A breech of the covenant, therefore, was not merely a deviation from custom or fair play but breaking faith with God—trampling on the relationship God wanted to have with his people. Similarly, the righteousness that God gives to those who have faith in Christ is not a legal shell game but God's willingness to break his relationship with Jesus during the time he was on the cross ("made him who had no sin to be sin for us," 2 Cor. 5:21a) and to establish a relationship with us ("so that in him we might become the righteousness of God," 5:21b).

There is surely a forensic element to all this—Jesus suffers the penalty we deserve—but the relational element between the judge and the accused is equally important.[17] Laying stress on the relational element allows us to understand more clearly the multiple ramifications of the atonement and helps us to comprehend the character of God more fully. The atonement does not only mean that when God looks at us he sees Christ, and it does not only mean that an exchange has taken place between our guilt and Christ's innocence. It means that God acknowledges us to be innocent and, like the father in the parable of the prodigal son, runs to embrace us (Luke 15:11–32).

The passage does not stop with verse 9, however. In verses 10–11 Paul says that he has counted all things loss that he might *know* Christ (cf. v. 8). "Knowing Christ" is often understood as having a personal relationship with the risen, living Christ, of experiencing the presence of Christ in the day-to-day affairs of life. Paul certainly knew Christ in this way, and this passage is properly understood as an expression of the close relationship that Paul had with the crucified and risen Lord (cf. 1:21; Rom. 14:8; 2 Cor. 5:16; Gal. 2:19b–20).

Problems arise, however, when we limit the term *know* to this relational meaning. To know God in the biblical sense is also to be aware of his will and to be willing to obey him. Paul's union with Christ's death, therefore, involved a costly obedience to the commission God had given him to establish and shepherd predominantly Gentile churches (2 Cor. 4:7–12; cf. Rom. 15:17–19; 1 Cor. 9:16–17; Col. 1:24–29). Paul's union with Christ's resurrection, at least in the present, likewise meant God's gracious rescue of Paul from desperate circumstances that the apostle encountered in his efforts to carry out this commission. It also meant God's use of Paul's ministry to produce spiritual life among those to whom he preached the gospel (2 Cor. 4:7–15). In bringing this passage out of Paul's context and into our own, we should

---

17. See Bultmann, *Theology*, 1:272, 277; Paul Achtemeier, *Romans* (Atlanta: John Knox, 1985), 61–66.

stress that knowing Christ means not only feeling his presence but especially living in faithfulness to God and his word day to day.[18]

**Three Transcendent Principles.** After coping with Paul's rhetoric and terminology, we are ready to begin the work of application. Paul's primary concern in the passage is to show that the attempt to make circumcision a requirement for entry into the people of God is equivalent to placing confidence in the flesh rather than in God and is therefore equivalent to rejecting the gospel entirely.

This primary concern implies three basic principles. The first is most important because it is directly related to Paul's chief point, and the other two can be legitimately derived from the first. This principle is simply that any attempt to impose requirements beyond faith in Christ for salvation is a perversion of the gospel. This does not mean that faith in Christ should be left vague and undefined and that anyone who claims to believe in Christ is a Christian. "Faith" means more than intellectual assent or simply mouthing the words "I believe in Jesus." As James reminds us, the demons have that kind of faith (James 2:19; cf. 1 John 3:18). Saving faith is a settled trust that leads to obedience (Rom. 1:5; 16:26). Similarly "Christ" is not a malleable term that can be molded to fit any of the various notions currently in circulation about who Jesus was. "Christ" is the Jesus described in the gospel that the apostles preached and handed down to future generations in the pages of the New Testament (cf. 2 Cor. 11:4; 1 John 1:1–3; 2:22; 4:2; 2 John 9). Once faith in Christ is defined in the way the New Testament defines it, however, any attempt to claim that those who have it must also conform to some other norm in order to be part of God's people is a distortion of the gospel.

It is important to see, moreover, that any proposed extra requirement need not be something that in itself is strange or questionable. Usually it is something that, like circumcision, is good in its proper place but when taken out of that place and elevated to a position equivalent to faith in Christ becomes the most insidious of idols. Philippians 3:1–11, then, should teach us to beware of religious movements that can mount plausible arguments for their position by making good but secondary principles equal in importance to faith in Christ for salvation. We should be no more timid than Paul himself about calling these movements what they are—rejections of the gospel.

Although this is the primary theological principle of the passage, it also implies a second principle. The passage stands as a warning to all who think that they can be at peace with God without submitting to the Christian gospel. The point of Paul's detailed description of his privileges and achievements is that if anyone could be found at peace with God on the final day

---

18. Cf. Eph. 4:20–23, where knowing Christ is defined in ethical terms.

as a result of personal righteousness, Paul could. He was "faultless" with respect to the Mosaic law. What more could God ask? But God could and did ask for something other than obedience to the Mosaic law—he asked for submission to the gospel. This Paul was unwilling to give; thus, had God not apprehended him on the Damascus Road, he would have stood condemned on the final day.

The same is true for all who refuse submission to the gospel today. Other religious systems often contain noble ideals, and people who follow them or who claim to follow no religious system at all often lead exemplary lives. Frequently they believe that whether they follow the "right" pathway to God is ultimately unimportant because God will accept them anyway. What more could God ask than leading a moral life and holding sincere convictions? To all of this Philippians 3:1–11 says that God has asked for submission to the gospel, and anything other than this will end in disaster on the final day. This passage, then, can be used appropriately as an appeal within our own culture for non-Christians to abandon other religious and philosophical systems, no matter how noble they may appear, and to embrace the gospel.

Paul's comments about not placing confidence in the flesh are not only a warning against those who twist the gospel out of shape or reject it entirely. A third theological principle—one applicable to Christians—also lies beneath this passage. It is possible for Christians to shift their focus from Christ and to become concerned with the qualities that the fallen world considers important as ends in themselves—with "the flesh," as Paul calls it. Whenever this happens in the life of a believer or a congregation, the message of this passage needs to be heard. Paul's own privileges and achievements as an unbeliever were without equal from the perspective of his peers (3:4b–6; cf. Gal. 1:13–14), but from the perspective of Paul as a believer, they were stumbling blocks in the way of truth (3:7–8; cf. 1 Tim. 1:12–16). Those who have embraced the gospel need to be reminded that the passage speaks to them as well. It stands as a reminder that the world's definition of success is not God's and that worldly successes, if not handled carefully, can attain an inappropriate level of importance in the thinking and conduct even of believers.

**Three Interpretive Pitfalls.** The interpretation of this passage should not only focus on these three points but should also avoid certain common pitfalls. In making the point that the gospel demands that the believer place confidence in Christ rather than in fleshly privileges and attainments, we must proceed cautiously. Paul did not consider his privileges and attainments to be evil in themselves, nor did he believe that the flesh is evil in itself. The evil lay in Paul's trust in the flesh instead of the gospel, with his willingness to make fleshly privileges and attainments the foundation of his confidence that he would stand acquitted before God on the final day. To speak of Paul's "utter disgust for the Law," as one popular expositor of this passage puts it, then, is to take Paul's language to an extreme he never intended.[19] There is no need to think that in this passage Paul rejects as "rubbish" his parents' faithfulness to the command to have their son circumcised, his Jewish heritage, or the Mosaic law. This would be inconsistent with Paul's approach to his Jewish heritage elsewhere (Rom 7:12; 9:1–5) and would go beyond his teaching in this passage. These privileges and attainments were not evil, but confidence in them was.

Another, and closely related, pitfall is to take this passage as a blast against Judaism generally. Interpreters who take this position sometimes use this passage as evidence that the Jews, and especially the Pharisees, of Paul's day were legalists and that Paul refutes their legalistic religion with an uncompromising statement about God's grace. This error is an ancient one, going at least as far back as Calvin, who in commenting on this passage identified the Roman Catholics of his time with the Pharisees and claimed that both belonged to degenerate religions that believed in salvation by human merit.[20] In more recent times it is not uncommon to read expositions of this passage that claim it describes the standard "Jewish position" that salvation is obtained by "personal human efforts."[21]

The gospels show clearly that some Jews were legalists in the time of Jesus and Paul, and among them were many Pharisees.[22] But there was nothing necessarily legalistic about Judaism generally or Pharisaism in particular in the first century. Luke certainly does not portray Zechariah and Elizabeth, Simeon and Anna, Joseph, Mary, and the boy Jesus this way (Luke 1:6, 59; 2:22–52). After all, first-century Judaism was built on the Old Testament, and the Old Testament is not a legalistic book. God's grace precedes the command to obey in the Old Testament just as it does in Paul (Ex. 20:2; Lev. 11:45; Phil. 2:12–13; Eph. 2:8–10). Philippians 3:4–6 shows clearly that before hearing the gospel, Paul, like the self-righteous Pharisee in Jesus' parable (Luke 18:11), placed confidence in his fleshly privileges and attainments. But Paul's statements about himself are not a sweeping indictment of the Jewish religion as "legalistic."[23]

---

19. Barclay, *The Letters to the Philippians, Colossians, and Thessalonians,* 63.

20. John Calvin, *Commentaries on the Epistles to the Philippians, Colossians, and Thessalonians* (Grand Rapids: Eerdmans, 1948), 271, 274.

21. Lloyd-Jones, *The Life of Peace,* 60.

22. Enough Pharisees were legalists that one could serve as typical of the self-righteous person in Jesus' parable of the Pharisee and the Publican (Luke 18:9–14).

23. On the whole issue of whether or not Judaism in the first century was legalistic, see E. P. Sanders, *Judaism: Practice and Belief 63 BCE–66 CE* (London/Philadelphia: Trinity Press International, 1992). For a different perspective, see Seifrid, *Justification by Faith,* and Schreiner,

Having successfully navigated around this rocky shoal, it is important not to break apart on another one across the channel. Pauline studies have recently experienced a revolution of Copernican proportions, and at the center of the revolution is the question of whether Luther, Calvin, and other Reformers correctly understood Paul's doctrine of justification by faith apart from works of the law. Was Paul interested in freeing the individual from the shackles of trying to work his or her way into acceptance with God by good deeds? If so, did Paul believe that Judaism advocated just such a position? If not, what does Paul's contrast between faith and works mean? Many voices today claim that Paul's contrast between the law and faith is merely a contrast between two religions: Judaism, whose most important religious symbol was the law of Moses, and Christianity, whose most important religious symbol was faith in Christ.[24] Others believe that the contrast represents Paul's opposition to the Jewish notion that one could become a member of God's people only by observing the customs of national Israel that are enshrined in the Mosaic law.[25]

We should approach this "new perspective" on Paul with caution. The new perspective's insistence that second-temple Judaism was not a legalistic religion devoid of an understanding of God's grace is a useful insight and a needed corrective to much sloppy and uncharitable scholarship. Its focus on the need to understand Paul in his own historical context before attempting to apply his insights to our own is also a helpful reminder of a basic hermeneutical principle. Nevertheless, the new perspective has been too hasty to consign the Reformers' understanding of Paul to the curiosity shop of outdated interpretations. Judaism generally may not have lacked an understanding of God's grace, but some Jews (and, according to Rom. 11:11–24, some Gentiles) put confidence in ethnic privilege and human attainment. By doing this they implied that people were not so bad that they could not contribute something to their own justification.[26]

Against this notion Paul insists that one's own righteousness is tainted with evil and is therefore not capable of God's acceptance on the final day.

---

*The Law and Its Fulfillment.* For an attempt to steer a middle course between Sanders' view and more traditional notions about first-century Judaism, see Frank Thielman, *Paul and the Law: A Contextual Approach* (Downers Grove, Ill.: InterVarsity Press, 1994).

24. See Sanders, *Paul and Palestinian Judaism*, 474–511, and *Paul, the Law and the Jewish People* (Philadelphia: Fortress, 1983).

25. James D. G. Dunn, *Jesus, Paul, and the Law: Studies in Mark and Galatians* (Louisville: Westminster/John Knox, 1990), 108–264, and *Romans 1–8* (Dallas: Word, 1988) lxiii–lxxii.

26. Some have argued against Sanders that first-century Judaism generally did attach saving significance to doing the works of the law. See Seifrid, *Justification by Faith;* Schreiner, *The Law and Its Fulfillment.*

Salvation must come "from God," and it has come from God through the work of Christ Jesus. For an exposition of this idea, we cannot do better than turn to Luther. His comment on Galatians 2:16 from his 1535 lectures on Galatians articulates the theological truth behind Philippians 3:1–11 precisely:

> For Paul . . ."flesh" means the highest righteousness, wisdom, worship, religion, understanding, and will of which the world is capable. Therefore the monk is not justified by his order, nor the priest by the Mass and the canonical hours, nor the philosopher by wisdom, nor the theologian by theology, nor the Turk by the Koran, nor the Jew by Moses. In other words, no matter how wise and righteous men may be according to reason and the divine Law, yet with all their works, merits, Masses, righteousnesses, and acts of worship they are not justified.[27]

Luther's point is that, as good as many of the institutions and ideals he lists may be, substituting them for the gospel means trusting the flesh for salvation, and that can only end in disaster on the final day. That is also Paul's basic point in Philippians 3:1–11.

This passage is perhaps the most difficult in Philippians to convey safely out of Paul's cultural context and into our own. The terminology he uses to make his central point is strange to modern ears and apt to be misunderstood. The theological principles he expresses are compressed into a few sentences that we must carefully unpack to avoid the historical mistakes of the past and the interpretive excesses of the present. The passage is, however, worth all the effort we put into it, for it is the gospel in a nutshell: Humanity is incurably sinful, God requires sinlessness, and God in his grace has remedied this situation through the work of Jesus Christ.

MANY CONTEMPORARY WESTERN European and North American Christians find it difficult to draw theological boundaries.[28] There are many reasons for this but two reasons seem to be especially important. (1) Many Christians have been deeply scarred emotionally by people within the church who claimed to be on a crusade for truth but

---

27. *Luther's Works*, vol. 26, *Lectures on Galatians, 1535*, ed. Jaroslav Pelikan (Saint Louis: Concordia, 1963), 140.

28. See the comments of Thomas C. Oden, *Requiem: A Lament in Three Movements* (Nashville, Tenn.: Abingdon, 1995), 46–48, 152–61.

who instead were on a crusade for themselves and, under the guise of guarding the gospel from distortion, swayed the opinion of other people to capture positions of power and to banish all who did not agree with them. Like Diotrephes of old, they loved to be first and used the charge of heresy against Christian brothers and sisters to attain their goal (2 John 9–10). (2) The Christian claim that the Bible and the church are the repositories of truth about human nature, God, the human plight, and salvation is decidedly unpopular today. Many social theorists, political scientists, and theologians believe that the claims of Christians to know the truth about these matters produced untold suffering in the past and pose a threat to the peace and stability of a free society in the present. They would agree with the eighteenth-century philosopher Jean-Jacques Rousseau that "it is impossible to live in peace with those whom we believe to be damned."[29] At the popular level this translates into the notion that Christians who claim to know the truth are somehow comparable to extreme Islamic groups, so that both can be labeled "fundamentalists." Few today are willing to accept this label since it has been stretched to connote ignorance, rigidity, paranoia, and violence.

The result of all this is that Christians today are often unwilling to identify heresy as heresy. Christian denominations rarely discipline ministers on theological grounds, pastors sometimes feed their congregations a diet of self-help sermons that avoid potentially divisive doctrinal issues, and many church members would be hard-pressed to explain the meaning of the Apostles' Creed. Taking much of a stand on theological matters is simply too risky; it is subject to abuse by power-hungry people and is identified with intolerance and ignorance in the wider culture.

Who can deny that there is an element of truth to this position? The image from the period of the Inquisition of Dominican and Franciscan monks patrolling the Italian countryside in search of heresy and, with the help of the secular state, delivering the obstinate to prison, torture, and death is bone-chilling. The picture from more recent times of white youth ministers in rural America being released from their jobs for inviting African-American children to church is equally nauseating.

Drawing theological boundaries, then, can indeed be risky since the task can easily be derailed by false motives or unethical methods. Refusing to draw boundaries, however, is even more risky. Had the church taken this course in centuries past, nothing would be left of the gospel. In the second and third

---

29. Jean-Jacques Rousseau, "The Social Contract," *Social Contract: Essays by Locke, Hume, and Rousseau* (Oxford: Oxford University Press, 1962), 306. See the helpful discussion of this issue in Richard J. Mouw and Sander Griffon, *Pluralisms and Horizons: An Essay in Christian Public Philosophy* (Grand Rapids: Eerdmans, 1993).

centuries, for example, the orthodox church was nearly overwhelmed by the teaching of Marcion. Marcionite church buildings dotted the landscape of both city and country throughout the Middle East, Egypt, and Italy during the second century. Much of the teaching in these churches was unobjectionable, for the Marcionites preached vigorous sermons from Paul's letters and expressed intense devotion to Jesus. The format of their services seems to have closely followed the order of worship in orthodox churches.[30] Moreover, the Marcionites were a highly disciplined group who rejected indulgence in the flesh and endured martyrdom as valiantly as any orthodox Christian.[31]

Leaders of the church in Rome, where Marcion first began to advocate his position, might have been tempted at first to stay quiet about his ideas. After all, Marcion was content to work within the established church structures and, according to one tradition about him, even offered the church at Rome a considerable sum of money. Nevertheless, leaders of the Roman church excommunicated him in A.D. 144 and mounted a vigorous campaign over the next century and a half to refute his teachings.

We may be grateful that they did. The essence of Marcion's religion was the existence of two gods—the god of the Old Testament who created the "evil" world and the god who appeared in the form of Jesus Christ to rescue those who believed in him from their cruel creator. To support this idea, Marcion accepted as authoritative Scripture only heavily edited editions of Luke's Gospel and ten of the thirteen Pauline letters. Had the church not stood against the Marcionite threat, the gospel would have been distorted into an unrecognizable shape and "the faith that was once for all entrusted to the saints" (Jude 3) would have ended in shipwreck.

This is simply one example among many. Athanasius stood against an Arian emperor for the eternal equality of God the Son and God the Father. Luther stood against prelates of the church for justification by faith alone apart from works of the law. The Confessing Church in the Germany of the Third Reich stood against the so-called German Christians for its right to be independent of the control of a wicked Führer. More recently, some mainline Protestants have taken a courageous stand against the attempt by radical feminists within their denominations to redefine the image of God in unbiblical ways.[32] All of these events illustrate how important it is for the

---

30. The worship services of orthodox and Marcionite churches were so similar that Cyril, Bishop of Jerusalem, had to warn Christian pilgrims to Jerusalem to be careful not to worship in a Marcionite church by mistake.

31. On the history of the Marcionite church see Adolf von Harnack, *Marcion: The Gospel of the Alien God* (Durham, N.C.: Labyrinth, 1990; orig. ed. 1924), 99–121.

32. See Oden, *Requiem*, 27–32, 140–51.

church in every age to draw theological boundaries. Paul's willingness to follow the same path in Philippians 3:1–11 provides biblical warrant for this solemn duty of the church.

But how can the church fulfill this duty and at the same time prevent the abuses of boundary-drawing that have sometimes plagued the church and hindered its witness? At least two principles should guide legitimate accusations of deviation from the truth of the gospel. First, the supposed false teaching should be a clear deviation from a principle that rests at the heart of the gospel or is clearly taught throughout Scripture. Paul did not pronounce an anathema on the Judaizers over some fine point of eschatology, a particular mode of baptism, or whether to use musical instruments in worship. Their false teaching went to the heart of how one entered the people of God—whether or not one would be saved or condemned on the final day. Similarly, Paul did not excommunicate an unrepentant member of the Corinthian church for some small deviation from the ethical standards demanded by the gospel but for sexual immorality so heinous that even pagans considered it distasteful (1 Cor. 5:1–5). Christians must choose their battles carefully, relying at every turn for guidance on biblical accounts of similar struggles.

Second, those who draw theological boundaries, particularly if they are in power, must constantly examine their own motives. They must ask themselves, "Will I profit by this boundary emotionally or in some other way, and if so, am I drawing the boundary to my own advantage?" Since we are prone to deceive ourselves in answering questions like this, it is also important at every step to seek the advice of mature and trustworthy Christians on the issues at stake and the proper way to handle them. Thus Confessing Christians in Germany in 1934 had the confidence that comes from knowing that the costly steps they took against the "German Christians" were based on a consensus of Christian leaders in Lutheran, Reformed, and United churches.[33] They did not act alone. Sometimes, of course, it is necessary to stand alone, like Paul at Antioch and Luther at Worms. Even in these situations, however, it is possible and necessary to seek consensus with the teaching of the church in ages past. If no significant figure in church history has battled the issue that vexes us or spoken on its importance, it would be prudent to proceed cautiously.

Having protected ourselves from using the charge of heresy for selfish ends, however, it is important for every believer, and particularly for ministers and

---

33. See "The Theological Declaration of Barmen," *The Constitution of the Presbyterian Church (U.S.A.), Part 1, Book of Confessions* (New York/Atlanta: The Office of the General Assembly, 1983), §§ 8.01–8.28.

other teachers in the church, to know where the theological boundaries of the faith lie and to hold to them without compromise. For this purpose, a familiarity with various ecumenical summaries of the faith is useful. Every believer should be acquainted with the Apostles' and Nicene Creeds and be able to explain their contents.[34] Familiarity with the common elements in other, more specific confessions, such as the Augsburg Confession, the Heidelberg Catechism, and the Westminster Standards, is also helpful. These great historic statements of the church's faith certainly do not agree on everything, and sometimes, because of their own historical and cultural contexts, make statements that no longer address the modern church; but what they have in common can safely be regarded as central to Christian belief, and threats from within the church to this common substance should be resisted.

The doctrine to which Paul holds fast in Philippians 3:1–11 is that salvation comes at God's initiative and through faith in Jesus, and this teaching is no less under attack today than it was in the time of Paul and Luther. Inroads into this doctrine are often made in two ways, one direct and the other more subtle. First, some groups who identify themselves as Christian and who, like the Marcionites of old, differ little from the Christian church in outward appearance and form of worship nevertheless hold beliefs that effectively deny that faith in Christ alone is sufficient for salvation. As with the Judaizers, the additional element is often something good in itself, and proof texts from Scripture can easily be cited in support of the group's position. But at the end of the day, after all the arguments have concluded, the group cannot reconcile its claims with Paul's steadfast refusal to admit within the circle of gospel truth anything that denies the complete sufficiency of faith in Christ for salvation.

For example, the principal leader of the nineteenth-century "restoration" movement in America, Alexander Campbell, taught that "to the believing penitent" baptism by immersion was "the *means* of receiving a formal, distinct and specific absolution, or release from guilt." As a result, "none but those who have first believed the testimony of God and have repented of their sins, and that have been intelligently immersed into his death have the full and explicit testimony of God, assuring them of pardon."[35] Some congregations of the

---

34. For a lucid explanation of the Apostles' Creed in contemporary terms, see C. E. B. Cranfield, *The Apostles' Creed: A Faith to Live By* (Grand Rapids: Eerdmans, 1993).

35. Alexander Campbell, *An Alexander Campbell Reader*, ed. Lester G. McAllister (St. Louis, Mo.: CBP Press, 1988), 82. The quotation is from the chapter on baptism in Campbell's *The Christian System, in Reference to the Union of Christians and a Restoration of Primitive Christianity, as Pled in the Current Reformation* (1839).

Churches of Christ and the Christian Churches, which are related to Campbell's movement, have continued to insist that baptism by immersion is necessary for salvation. They frequently point to such texts as Titus 3:5; 1 Peter 3:21; and 1 John 3:5, which connect baptism with salvation or regeneration in support of this teaching.

Baptism is, of course, a good and necessary Christian sacrament, but its value lies in its ability to demonstrate visibly to believers what actually happens when Christ's blood and the Holy Spirit cleanse them from sins. Why, then, does Scripture so explicitly connect baptism with salvation in such passages as 1 Peter 3:21? The Heidelberg Catechism puts it well:

> God has good reason for these words. He wants to teach us that the blood and Spirit of Christ wash away our sins just as water washes away dirt from our bodies. But more important, he wants to assure us, by this divine pledge and sign, that the washing away of our sins spiritually is as real as physical washing with water.[36]

Baptism, as sacramentally helpful as it is, cannot participate in the work of salvation. Faith alone justifies. Philippians 3:1—11 stands like a sentinel over this great doctrine, and no religious notion that cannot safely pass beneath its gaze should be admitted into the church.

It would be a serious mistake, however, to think that this particular deviation from the gospel only appears within groups whose official policies and doctrines espouse it. The belief that God will save people in the end on the basis of works is common to many people who identify themselves as Baptists and Presbyterians, Methodists and Episcopalians. These people may understand that Jesus is important and that his death had something to do with sin, but they continue to believe that heaven is a reward for the upright. These people frequently seem untroubled by this notion.

Anyone who believes that salvation comes through the good works people do, however, should be deeply depressed, for the biblical perspective on this understanding of salvation is that if it is true, then no one can be saved. "Do not bring your servant into judgment, for no one living is righteous before you," pleads the psalmist (Ps. 143:2), and Paul argues that "no one will be declared righteous in [God's] sight by observing the law; rather, through the law we become conscious of sin" (Rom. 3:20). Those who believe that salvation comes by works, then, should join the lament of Ezra in one of the apocryphal books bearing his name. Ezra also believed that salvation came

---

36. Lord's Day 27, A. 73. The translation belongs to the edition of the Heidelberg Catechism adopted by the 1988 Synod of the Christian Reformed Church. See this denomination's *Psalter Hymnal* (Grand Rapids: CRC Publications, 1987), 892.

by works, but unlike so many moderns, he understood the grave implications of this conviction:

> Everyone alive is burdened and defiled with wickedness, sinful through and through. Would it not have been better for us if there had been no judgment awaiting us after death? (2 Esdras 7:65–69 REB).

Those who claim that salvation comes through Christ *and* through some other mechanical rite or series of good works, however, often fail to appreciate how desperately sinful humanity is and that humanity is absolutely dependent on God for salvation. Philippians 3:1–11 provides us with an opportunity to explain the biblical perspective on the nature of the human plight. Despite Paul's impeccable credentials and faithful observance of the law, his righteousness was still insufficient to merit acquittal on the final day. If Paul, who excelled many others in his zeal for the law, could not claim salvation on the basis of his human privileges and achievements, surely advocates of salvation by works cannot do so either.

A second, and more subtle, way in which inroads are often made into the doctrine of justification by faith alone is that believers do not allow the principle to inform their practice. If it is true that Jesus came not to call the "righteous" but sinners to repentance, that God reckons the ungodly to be righteous apart from works, and that all of this is from God rather than from any privilege or attainment we can cite on our behalf, then believers should not limit their fellowship with one another on the basis of any external characteristic. The Judaizers did not want to associate with believing Gentiles (Gal. 2:12; cf. Acts 11:2–3), although both claimed to be Christians, because the Gentiles were not circumcised. The anger rising to the surface both in Philippians 3:1–11 and throughout Galatians is present not only because the doctrine of justification by faith apart from works of the law was threatened by the Judaizers' teaching but because an important ethical principle derived from that doctrine was at issue also: Christians cannot limit their fellowship with one another for external reasons. Those who have been embraced by God must embrace one another.

Sadly and ironically, the Protestant church, although founded as a protest against violations of the doctrine of justification by faith alone in the Roman Catholic Church of the sixteenth century, remains largely divided by race and social class. Tom Sine writes that "11 A.M. Sunday Morning is still the most segregated hour in American Life."[37] Most American Protestants can verify his statement by looking around them next Sunday. The homogeneity of

---

37. Tom Sine, as quoted in Russell Chandler, *Racing Toward 2001: The Forces Shaping America's Religious Future* (Grand Rapids: Zondervan, 1992), 31.

Christian worship and fellowship not only extends to distinctions based on race, but to socioeconomic and age brackets as well. Some of this can be attributed to simple racism and classism, to a selfish unwillingness, often fueled by ignorance and fear, to share our lives with those who are different from us. Most of it, however, seems to come from contentment with the status quo or from a fear that change in our homogeneous units will adversely affect the growth of our churches.[38] Whatever the cause, Christians should actively pursue ways to overcome the external barriers that divide them. Unless we do, we can hardly announce with integrity to those who do not believe that Jesus Christ "is the atoning sacrifice for our sins, and not only for ours but also for the sins of the whole world" (1 John 2:2).

Philippians 3:1–11 not only challenges Christians to live what they believe, but it also urges unbelievers to examine their own convictions. According to surveys, 88 percent of Americans say that they have never doubted the existence of God, 81 percent believe in a day of judgment in which they will "be called before God . . . to answer for . . . sins," 71 percent believe in life after death, but only 69 percent say that they belong to a church.[39] Most of us understand these statistics firsthand. We know people who believe in God, an afterlife, and even a day of judgment, but are not Christians. If engaged in conversation, they clearly think that although they do not believe the gospel and embrace the church, somehow God will accept them and, whatever the next life holds, it will not be bad.

This passage challenges all such comfortable ambiguities. Paul plainly says that even those who have thought about God and his requirements but who, nevertheless, have rejected the gospel will be found on the final day with nothing to present to God but their own righteousness. Any righteousness that is not the righteousness God himself provides, however, will be unable to withstand the time of judgment. It is eternally important, in other words, that people outside the church understand that salvation does not come simply from having some religious convictions. It must come through believing the gospel of Jesus Christ as it is contained in the Scriptures and as it has been preached in the faithful church throughout the ages.

---

38. Thus the "homogeneous unit principle" has become a standard doctrine of church growth strategists. See Donald A. McGavaran, *Understanding Church Growth*, rev. ed. (Grand Rapids: Eerdmans, 1980), 306–7; Donald A. McGavaran and Winfield C. Arn, *Ten Steps for Church Growth* (New York: Harper & Row, 1977), 74–79. The principle works, of course, but that is beside the point. It is hard to imagine that Paul, who parted company with Barnabas, Peter, and "the other Jews" in the church at Antioch in part over this issue (Gal. 2:11–13), would consider it theologically valid.

39. See George Gallup Jr. and Jim Castelli, *The People's Religion: American Faith in the 90's* (New York/London: Macmillan/Collier, 1989), 58–59, 132.

On the other side of this coin, this passage challenges people within the church to make sure that their understanding of the gospel is correct according to the standard of the Bible. Questions of eternal importance are at issue when the church bears witness to the world. Theological education, then, should be a serious enterprise and the calling to be a minister of the gospel a high and serious challenge. Too often, the opposite is the case. Stanley Hauerwas has commented on this by observing the difference between divinity schools and medical schools and between the level of tolerance the public has for physicians and the level of tolerance they have for ministers. Divinity schools sometimes bend their requirements, he observes, to accommodate the desires of individual students. If a medical student, on the other hand, refused to take gross anatomy, the medical school would tell that student to "simply ship out." Similarly, the public understands when doctors make them wait for hours or are unpleasant, but the minister is expected to be on time and polite whatever the circumstances. Hauerwas muses about the reasons for this state of affairs:

> I think they derive from the fact that no one believes an incompetently trained priest might threaten their salvation, since no one really believes that anything is at stake in salvation; but people do think that an incompetently trained doctor might hurt them.[40]

Philippians 3:1–11 shows us what is at stake in salvation. Without faith in Christ we cannot be acquitted on the final day. Getting this right is important, both for the spiritual health of the church and for the eternal well-being of those to whom the church proclaims it.

Paul's claim in 3:3 that believers place no confidence in the flesh but instead worship in the Spirit and have hearts that are spiritually circumcised provides a final primary point of connection between this passage and the modern church. Both churches and individual believers can easily fall into a "fleshly" frame of mind although they are formally committed to the gospel as Paul expresses it in this passage. The leadership of churches can allow a building program, a church growth strategy, or some other aspect of the church's life which, by its very nature, must be implemented and accomplished in much the same way that the world would accomplish the task, to slip from the direction of the Spirit and become an end in itself. When this happens, although we may be willing to go to the stake for the doctrine of justification by faith alone, we are behaving in a way that is incompatible with that belief. To become distracted from the church's primary task of Spirit-

---

40. Stanley Hauerwas, "Communitarians and Medical Ethicists, or 'Why I Am None of the Above,'" *Christian Scholars Review* 23 (1994): 293–94.

empowered obedience to God and to allow the world or a particular program to set the church's agenda instead is to cease placing confidence in Christ and to begin placing confidence in the flesh.

The leadership of churches can also adopt programs and strategies that, although intended is to aid the propagation of the gospel, are fundamentally flawed with the world's perspective. Thus Christians should be wary of applying the marketing strategies of the business world to the church. Those who use these strategies often have the laudable goal of communicating the gospel as clearly as possible to the greatest number of people and are frequently motivated by the bad experiences that some people have had in some small, uncomfortable, and boring church of the past. But the price of marketing the gospel with programs developed in a fallen and unbelieving world is too high for the church to adopt them wholesale.

An example from the world of church marketing will suffice to illustrate the problem. One church marketing strategist begins his handbook on marketing the church by referring to a standard marketing textbook. The textbook describes four basic marketing principles: "product," "place," "promotion," and "price." The product is described as something that meets the needs of the consumer. The place is the location at which the product is delivered to the consumer. Promotion involves telling potential consumers about the product and offering them a compelling reason for having it. The price of the product is determined by carefully balancing the amount that will bring the producer a return on his or her investment with the amount the consumer is willing to pay.[41]

The author of this handbook carefully explains that he does not intend the church, in following this strategy, to change its "product" or view "price" in terms of money. But the question continues to nag, Can the "business" of the church be shaped into the mold developed by a consumer-oriented society for selling its goods and services? The goal of secular marketing strategies is to enable businesses to design products people will buy and then to persuade people to buy them. If people do not already see a need for the product and if they cannot be persuaded to see such a need, good marketing principles dictate that the product-line be radically changed or its price reduced, or that it be dropped altogether in favor of something more marketable. The success of the strategy, in other words, is measured in terms of the response of people.

Preaching Christ and him crucified, however, is a marketing strategist's nightmare. Those who followed Christ early in his ministry responded to the

---

41. George Barna, *Marketing the Church* (Colorado Springs, Colo.: NavPress, 1988), 41–44.

message of the cross with the statement, "This is a hard teaching. Who can accept it?" and when Jesus insisted on its centrality, John tells us that "many of his disciples turned back and no longer followed him" (John 6:53–66). Even one of Jesus' closest disciples, Peter, rebuked Jesus when he "began to teach them that the Son of Man must suffer many things and be rejected by the elders, chief priests and teachers of the law" (Mark 8:31–32; cf. Matt. 16:21–22). Nor did the idea of a crucified Lord gain in popularity after the resurrection. Paul claims that "the message of the cross" preached by the early Christians was considered by many to be "foolishness" (1 Cor. 1:18), "a stumbling block to Jews and foolishness to Gentiles" (1:23).

Why the strong reaction? Two reasons emerge from the New Testament. (1) As we have already seen in our discussion of Philippians 2:5–11, the cross was an offense in the ancient Greco-Roman world. It was a cruel death reserved for the worst criminals of the lowest social classes and a symbol of social ostracism and powerlessness. (2) Not content with the stumbling block of Christ crucified, both Jesus and his followers insisted on speaking of the crucifixion of Jesus' followers with him. "If anyone would come after me," said Jesus, "he must deny himself and take up his cross daily and follow me" (Luke 9:23; cf. Matt. 16:24; Mark 8:34). Paul followed this path when he gave up his fleshly privileges and attainments in order to know "the fellowship of sharing in [Christ's] sufferings, becoming like him in his death" (Phil. 3:10).

The New Testament testifies that this utterly unattractive message succeeded at all only because the Spirit of God worked in the hearts of people to accept it (1 Cor. 1:26–31; 2 Cor 2:14–3:6). The strategies that we use to communicate the gospel effectively to others, therefore, must not soften or change this message in order to fill plush church buildings with more people or to meet the financial requirements of an ever-growing budget (Gal. 2:19).[42] That would mean taking our confidence away from Christ and putting it in the flesh. It would mean turning away from the purity of the gospel to human devices and imagining, like the Judaizers and the pre-Christian Paul, that we know how to conduct God's business better than God himself.

---

42. For a measured critique of using secular marketing strategies to prompt church growth, see Douglas D. Webster, *Selling Jesus: What's Wrong With Marketing the Church* (Downers Grove, Ill.: InterVarsity Press, 1992).

# Philippians 3:12–4:1

NOT THAT I have already obtained all this, or have already been made perfect, but I press on to take hold of that for which Christ Jesus took hold of me. [13]Brothers, I do not consider myself yet to have taken hold of it. But one thing I do: Forgetting what is behind and straining toward what is ahead, [14]I press on toward the goal to win the prize for which God has called me heavenward in Christ Jesus.

[15]All of us who are mature should take such a view of things. And if on some point you think differently, that too God will make clear to you. [16]Only let us live up to what we have already attained.

[17]Join with others in following my example, brothers, and take note of those who live according to the pattern we gave you. [18]For, as I have often told you before and now say again even with tears, many live as enemies of the cross of Christ. [19]Their destiny is destruction, their god is their stomach, and their glory is in their shame. Their mind is on earthly things. [20]But our citizenship is in heaven. And we eagerly await a Savior from there, the Lord Jesus Christ, [21]who, by the power that enables him to bring everything under his control, will transform our lowly bodies so that they will be like his glorious body.

[4:1]Therefore, my brothers, you whom I love and long for, my joy and crown, that is how you should stand firm in the Lord, dear friends!

Original Meaning

IN 3:12–4:1 PAUL turns away from the possibility that the Judaizers will make inroads into the Philippian congregation to two other possible problems. (1) He is worried that his teaching about losing all things in order to gain Christ will be misunderstood to mean that he has already arrived at spiritual perfection. (2) This concern leads him to warn the Philippians against becoming enemies of Christ's cross by making gods of their stomachs, glorying in that of which they should be ashamed, and setting their minds on earthly things. He concludes the entire section of warnings (3:1–21) with an admonition to stand firm in the Lord (4:1).

193

As the introduction to the commentary argues, in this passage Paul warns the Philippians against an error that plagued the Corinthian Christians. The Corinthian letters reveal a congregation fascinated with knowledge, the Spirit, outward signs of power, and spiritual perfection (1 Cor. 4:6–13; 8:1–13; 14:12). Some of the Corinthians believed that spiritual maturity should be defined in terms of these elements alone and, flourishing the slogan "Everything is permissible for me" (6:12; 10:23), neglected such basic ethical requirements as loving one another, remaining sexually pure, and avoiding idolatry (5:1–13; 6:12–20; 8:1–13; 10:1–22). The Corinthians may have appealed to Paul's claim that the Mosaic law was obsolete as proof that their position was compatible with his gospel.[1]

This distortion of the gospel had probably not become a serious problem at Philippi, but if Paul was writing from Ephesus sometime after the composition of 1 Corinthians, then Philippians 3:12–4:1 may be an attempt to prevent the growth of these ideas on Philippian soil. Thus, Paul is probably not concerned about false teachers in Philippi in this passage. Instead, having just said that he now considers his former righteousness in keeping the law to be rubbish (3:6–8), he hopes to forestall any indigenous misinterpretation of this teaching in the direction of the Corinthian error.

**Paul Forestalls a Misunderstanding (3:12–16).** According to 3:8–11, Paul had suffered the loss of all things in order to gain Christ, to be found in him, to know him in both his suffering and in his resurrection power, and to attain the resurrection of the dead. Did this mean that he had reached spiritual perfection? Paul was aware that at least in Corinth some would have drawn that conclusion from his words (1 Cor. 4:8; 15:12). He did not intend to allow such notions to take root in Philippi, however, and so in Philippians 3:12–16 he affirms the incompleteness of his own journey toward the final day stating that, paradoxically, only those who understand their lack of perfection (*teteleiomai*) have reached spiritual maturity (*teleios*).

In verses 12–14 Paul reveals the intensity of his concern that the Philippians not misunderstand verses 8–11 as a claim to spiritual perfection in two ways. (1) He repeatedly states that he is imperfect—he has not "obtained," he has not "been perfected," and he has not "taken hold" of his ultimate goal. (2) Although the NIV supplies the phrase "all this" after the verb "obtained" in verse 12, the Greek text leaves the object of the verb unexpressed. Liter-

---

1. Paul believed that the Mosaic law was no longer binding on believers. The Corinthians may have stretched this to mean that no ethical norms were binding on the believer. See Gordon D. Fee, *The First Epistle of Paul to the Corinthians* (Grand Rapids: Eerdmans, 1987), 251–52. For evidence that such distortions of Paul's teaching were not uncommon, see Rom. 3:8; 6:1; 6:15; James 2:14–26.

ally, Paul's Greek reads, "Not that I have already obtained, or have already been made perfect." The effect of this is to focus the reader's attention fully on the notion that Paul knows he is not perfect. In English we obtain the same effect when we say, "John thinks that he has arrived." The word "arrived" has no qualifier to tell us at what John thinks he has arrived. Thus all the emphasis is placed on the verb and the attitude of haughtiness it conveys. Although if asked what he had not obtained, Paul might have responded, as the NIV assumes, by pointing to the goals listed in verses 8–11, he has not made the object specific in order to stress the incompleteness of his spiritual journey.[2]

Paul also speaks positively in verses 12–14 of what he is doing in light of the incompleteness of his spiritual journey. His language comes from the world of war and athletics and emphasizes the strenuous nature of his efforts to fulfill his vocation. In verse 12 he says that he presses on to take hold of the goals listed in verses 8–11, choosing a pair of words that could, in military contexts, refer to the pursuit of one army by another.[3] Together the two terms connote a single-minded attempt to reach a particular goal.

According to the NIV, Paul's goal is to reach "that for which Christ Jesus took hold of me." But the Greek phrase behind "that for which" (*eph' ho*) usually expresses cause in Paul's letters, and it probably carries a causal force here. So the goal Paul pursues probably remains all that he has described in verses 8–11, and the second part of verse 12 should be rendered, "because Christ Jesus took hold of me."[4] That is to say, Paul vigorously pursues the

---

2. If "all this" is the correct complement to the verb, then it would include knowing Christ and his resurrection power (vv. 8a, 10), Christ himself (v. 8b), being found in Christ (v. 9a), fellowship with Christ's suffering (v. 10b), and attaining the resurrection of the dead (v. 11). Other contenders for the proper direct object are (1) the resurrection (v. 11), (2) the prize (v. 14), (3) the righteousness that comes from God (v. 9), and (4) Paul's goal of gaining Christ (v. 8). Some believe that Paul left the object unexpressed in order to deny any place to personal achievement in the Christian life. See the thorough discussion of these options in O'Brien, *Philippians*, 420–22.

3. See Walter Bauer, *A Greek-English Lexicon of the New Testament and Other Early Christian Literature*, 2d ed., trans., adapt., and rev. William F. Arndt, F. Wilbur Gingrich, Frederick W. Danker (Chicago: University of Chicago Press, 1979), 201. The ancient historian Herodotus (ca. 490–425 B.C.) describes a Persian regiment's pursuit of their Greek opponents this way: "The Persian horse, meaning to continue their old harassing tactics, had found the enemy gone from the position they had occupied during the last few days, and had ridden in *pursuit*. Now, *having overtaken* the retreating columns, they renewed their attacks with vigour" (9.58; see Herodotus, *The Histories* [Hammondsworth, Middlesex, Eng.: Penguin Books, 1972], 600). The italicized words correspond to Paul's expression "press on to take hold" in v. 12.

4. See Bauer, *Greek-English Lexicon*, 287; F. Blass and A. Debrunner, *A Greek Grammar of the New Testament and Other Early Christian Literature*, trans. and ed. Robert W. Funk (Chicago: University of Chicago Press, 1961), 123 (§235 [2]); O'Brien, *Philippians*, 425.

knowledge of Christ, his sufferings, his resurrection power, and union with him at the final day because on the road to Damascus, Christ took hold of him (Acts 9:1–19; 22:3–16; 26:9–18). Had that event not taken place, Paul might still be busy "persecuting (*dioko*) the church" (Phil. 3:6) instead of pressing on (*dioko*) toward these goals (vv. 12, 14).

Even more expressive of the difficulty of Paul's exertion to reach these goals is the athletic imagery in verses 12–14. Like a runner who knows that a backward glance at ground already covered will only slow his progress toward the finish, Paul says that he forgets what is behind and stretches out toward what is ahead, so that he might complete the race and win the prize.[5] Some interpreters have taken Paul's claim that he forgets what is behind as a reference to his pre-Christian past (cf. vv. 5–6), but two considerations point away from this interpretation. (1) The point under discussion here is Paul's progress as a believer, not his progress beyond his days of persecuting the church. (2) When Paul uses athletic imagery elsewhere, the subject is his apostolic labors (cf. 2:16; 1 Cor. 9:24–26). These labors are his focus here too. Paul's point, then, is that he refuses to rest on his past successes but presses on toward that day when he will present the Philippians and his other congregations blameless to Christ (1:10; 2:14–18; 1 Cor. 1:8; 1 Thess. 3:13; 5:23).

What is this prize? The term "call" in Paul's letters, both as a noun and as a verb, possesses a rich theological significance. Just as God called Israel to be his people in the Old Testament (Isa. 48:12; 51:2), so, in Paul's letters, God calls people from many ethnic and social backgrounds (1 Cor. 1:26; Eph. 3:1; 4:1) into fellowship with Jesus Christ (1 Cor. 1:9) and into his kingdom (1 Thess. 2:12), and he does this by his grace (Gal. 1:6). This call is not, moreover, to something that will be fully realized in the present but to the future for which the believer now hopes (Eph. 1:18; 4:4). Thus, the heavenly call toward which Paul stretches with all his might is God's call to be part of the people, made up of both Jews and Gentiles, who will stand justified before him on the final day because of their identification with Christ (vv. 8–11).

Paul's next statement (v. 15), at least in the Greek text, comes as a surprise. Literally, he says, "Those of us, then, who are perfect, let us think this." Having just denied that he has been "made perfect" (*tetleiomai*, v. 12), Paul now numbers himself among the "perfect" (*teleioi*). Why? The answer comes through a close examination of Paul's use of the term *teleios* in his other correspondence. When Paul applies this word to believers, it has the connotation not of perfection in the ultimate sense but of the maturity necessary to distinguish the wisdom of God from the wisdom of the world (1 Cor. 2:6; cf. Col. 1:28) and

---

5. See Victor C. Pfitzner, *Paul and the Agon Motif: Traditional Athletic Imagery in the Pauline Literature* (Leiden: Brill, 1967), 140–41.

to use spiritual gifts appropriately (1 Cor. 14:20; Eph. 4:11–13).

Paul's use of the term in 1 Corinthians 14:20 provides an example. "Brothers," Paul says, "do not be children in your thinking. In evil be infants, but in your thinking be perfect" (pers. trans.). Paul's contrast between those who think like "infants" and those whose thinking is "perfect" shows that his primary concern is not with ultimate perfection but with spiritual maturity.[6] In Philippians 3:15, then, maturity is a matter of refusing to focus on the spiritual attainments of the past and of realizing how much effort must be expended on the course that lies ahead.

Paul recognizes that everything he has just said will not be acceptable to some believers, perhaps even to some in Philippi. Is it possible that some in Philippi were already showing signs of the perfectionism that had made such deep inroads into the church at Corinth? Might the disunity at Philippi, like the disunity in Corinth, be related to the germination of this way of thinking? There is no need to imagine an itinerant group of troublemakers stirring up controversy at Corinth and then spreading their net in Philippi too. The Hellenistic world was full of notions of religious perfection and salvation, and it would have been as easy to mix these notions with the gospel at Philippi as it was at Corinth. If this had happened, the mixture was not as serious as it had been at Corinth (1:3–11). Thus Paul offers the mild corrective in 3:15b: If some among the Philippian believers hold another position, God will reveal to them the truth.

Paul has only one request of them in the meantime (v. 16): The believers in Philippi should not turn back from the progress they have already made in living lives worthy of the gospel. The verb the NIV translates "live up to" is a rare word in Paul (*stoicheo*), used only three other times in his letters. In these other occurrences, the word refers to living the life of faith (Rom. 4:12), a life characterized by the Spirit's fruit of "love, joy, peace, patience, kindness, goodness, faithfulness, gentleness and self-control" (Gal. 5:22–25), and a life that God himself has re-created (Gal. 6:15–16). God has begun a good work in the Philippians, and many of these qualities are evident among them (1:6, 9–11), but Paul does not want the slight deviations from the truth that may be present among them to destroy the progress they have already made. That would mean that his apostolic labor on their behalf had been in vain and that he would stand before Christ on the final day, at least with respect to the Philippians, empty-handed (2:16).

**Paul Warns Against Error (3:17–4:1).** To forestall that possibility, Paul now addresses the problem of more serious theological error directly. The

---

6. The NIV's rendering of 1 Cor. 14:20 captures this nuance well: "Brothers, stop thinking like children. In regard to evil be infants, but in your thinking be adults [*teleioi*]."

error itself is not new, for Paul has warned the Philippians of it often (v. 18a), but here he feels compelled to increase the intensity of his warning (v. 18b). We can only speculate about why Paul felt this urgency, but the reason may lie in his experience with the Corinthian church.

If Paul wrote Philippians from an otherwise unknown imprisonment in Ephesus, then the Corinthian situation must have been fresh on his mind.[7] The Corinthians had grown weary of the suffering apostle whose life had adopted the weak character of the crucified Savior whom he preached (1 Cor. 1:18–25; 2:1–5; 4:8–13; 2 Cor. 4:7–12; 13:4). Knowledge and power were their watchwords, and possession of both meant the possession of a spiritual maturity that freed them from Paul's injunctions against participation in cultic meals in idol temples (1 Cor. 8:1–10:22). It also allowed the wealthy among them to indulge their physical appetites at the Lord's Supper and remain oblivious to the needs and feelings of the poorer members of the community (11:17–34).[8] Moreover, since spiritual illumination and power alone were important, physical indulgence in shameful sexual conduct was not only tolerated in their midst but celebrated as a sign of spiritual freedom (5:1–13; 6:12–20; 2 Cor. 12:21).

These may be the problems Paul has in mind when he warns the Philippians against "enemies of the cross of Christ" (v. 18) whose "god is their stomach" and whose "glory is in their shame" (v. 19). Such thinking can only result in the eternal destruction of those who hold to it (cf. 1:28), Paul says, and is the product of a mind focused on earthly things rather than on the things of God (v. 19). "Earthly things" are not the practical affairs of everyday life, but things that characterize worldly life in opposition to God—"sexual immorality, impurity, lust, evil desires … greed … anger, rage, malice, slander, and filthy language" (Col. 3:1–11).[9] Only impurity and evil desires among this list are not specifically social sins; the rest of the list certainly works like a destroying acid on the unity of the church. If this type of thinking has already started to gain ground in Philippi, perhaps it accounts, in part, for the complaining and arguing that Paul addresses throughout the letter (esp. in 2:14; 4:2).

Paul recommends two antidotes for these problems: He asks the Philippians to unite in their efforts to follow the example he and other mature

---

7. Both 1 and 2 Corinthians were written around the time of Paul's Ephesian ministry, 1 Corinthians while Paul was still in Ephesus (1 Cor 16:8) and 2 Corinthians shortly after he left (2 Cor. 2:13; 7:5–7).

8. See also 1 Cor. 6:13 and 1 Cor. 15:32. On the probability that the Corinthian church was torn by strife among the social classes, see Gerd Theissen, *The Social Setting of Pauline Christianity: Essays on Corinth* (Philadelphia: Fortress, 1982).

9. Cf. O'Brien, *Philippians*, 458.

Christians have provided for them (v. 17), and he admonishes them to remember that they are citizens of a heavenly commonwealth (v. 20).

Paul has frequently reminded the Philippians of his example in subtle ways throughout the letter. He has claimed that his suffering and the Philippians' suffering are parallel (1:29–30), hinting that the Philippians should learn from his perspective on suffering (1:12–26). He has demonstrated what it means to put the interests of others ahead of his own (2:4) by his willingness to send Epaphroditus back with his commendation (2:25, 29–30). His own willingness to reject a past marked by confidence in his own righteousness rather than by confidence in God's righteousness exemplified how the Philippians should respond to any Judaizers who might arrive on their shores (3:1–11). And he has just urged the Philippians to think as he thinks about the need to continue striving for the final goal of full identity with Christ (3:15). All of these inferences that the Philippians should imitate him now become explicit in verse 17.

To us it may at first seem brash that Paul would urge the Philippians to imitate him. Is this compatible with what he has just said about not having "arrived" spiritually? Paul's words are not an egocentric claim that everyone should act precisely as he acts, however, for the pattern is larger than Paul himself. As Paul says in verse 17, others also can serve as examples of how to follow the pattern (cf. 1 Cor. 4:17), and as he says elsewhere, his example is worthy of emulation only insofar as it in turn follows the example of Christ (1 Cor. 11:1; cf. 1 Thess. 1:6).[10]

In addition to following Paul's example, the Philippians should remember that their "citizenship is in heaven" (3:20). The term the NIV translates "citizenship" (*politeuma*) appears only here in the New Testament, and like the verb "conduct yourselves" (*politeuesthe*) in 1:27, has political overtones.[11] Paul probably chose it carefully. Philippi at the time during which Paul wrote this letter was a Roman colony. This meant that it was ruled by Roman law rather than native custom and that its citizens were Roman citizens, something of which at least some of them were proud (Acts 16:21). Paul probably plays on this civic pride here and encourages the Philippians to think of themselves as members of a commonwealth located in heaven. As citizens of the heavenly realm, he explains in verses 20b–21, they understand that the fallen

---

10. The Greek word that stands behind the NIV's "example" is *typos*. Philosophical writers of Paul's time frequently used this word to refer to the "impression" that learning leaves on the mind, as a seal leaves an impression on wax. See Robert A. J. Gagnon, "Heart of Wax and a Teaching That Stamps: ΤΥΠΟΣ ΔΙΔΑΧΗΣ (Rom. 6:17b) Once More," *Journal of Biblical Literature* 112 (1993): 667–87.

11. The term is probably best rendered "commonwealth" rather than "citizenship" (see Bauer, *Greek-English Lexicon*, 686).

---

earthly realm is not the sum of their existence. The goal of their existence will instead be reached on the day when the Lord Jesus Christ returns (v. 20b).

When that happens, Paul says, Christ will transform fallen existence into glorious existence, and Paul's beloved friends in Philippi, already his joy and crown, will become his crown in the fullest sense (3:21–4:1). This statement reminds the Philippians of three truths. (1) The reference to Christ's coming reminds them of the day when both they and Paul will stand before Christ to give an account of themselves. Paul hopes that on that day the Philippians will stand before their Savior pure and blameless (1:10), as the fruit of his apostolic labor (2:14–16). They are his joy and his crown even now (4:1) because he is confident (1:6) they will adorn his brow at the final day, just as the crown of leaves adorned the brow of a victorious athlete in Paul's time (cf. 1 Thess. 2:19).[12] Only if they stand firm (Phil. 4:1) by avoiding the excesses of the enemies of the cross of Christ, however, will this be possible.

(2) The way in which Paul describes Christ's coming in verse 21 reminds the Philippians that as long as they are in their fallen, "lowly" bodies, they have not arrived at their ultimate goal (cf. vv. 12–14). Fully apprehending Christ's resurrection power and fully attaining the resurrection of the dead lie in the future, and the believer must patiently, albeit eagerly, await Christ's appearance and full conformity to his resurrection body.

(3) Verse 21 echoes the description of Christ's humiliation and exaltation in 2:6–11 and reminds the Philippians of the result for them of that event. Just as Christ humbled himself (*etapeinosen heauton*), became obedient unto death on the cross (2:8), and was exalted as a result (2:9–11), so at that final day he will, from his exalted position where all things are subject to him (v. 21b; cf. 2:10–11), draw the lowly bodies (*to soma tes tapeinoseos hemon*) of believers up into his glorious existence. He identified with their humility so that they might in turn be identified with his resurrected body.[13]

In 3:12–4:1, then, Paul hopes to prevent a misunderstanding of 3:1–11 and to forestall problems similar to the ones he has encountered in Corinth. The times have changed, the Mosaic law is no longer in force, and believers are now united with Christ; but this does not mean that they have

---

12. See Bauer, *Greek-English Lexicon*, 767; Walter Grundmann, "στέφανος, στεφανόω," *Theological Dictionary of the New Testament*, ed. Gerhard Kittel and Gerhard Friedrich, 10 vols. (Grand Rapids: Eerdmans, 1964–76), 7:620, 629–30; Pfitzner, *Paul and the Agon Motif*, 105–6.

13. Morna D. Hooker, "Philippians 2:6–11," in E. Earle Ellis and Erich Grässer, eds., *Jesus und Paulus: Festschrift für Werner Georg Kümmel zum 70. Geburtstag* (Göttingen: Vandenhoeck & Ruprecht, 1978), 155–56; idem., "Interchange in Christ," *Journal of Theological Studies* 22 (1971): 349–61 (here 355–57). For an exhaustive list of verbal similarities between the two passages, see Andrew T. Lincoln, *Paradise Now and Not Yet: Studies in the Role of the Heavenly Dimension in Paul's Thought With Special Reference to His Eschatology* (Cambridge: Cambridge University Press, 1981), 88.

"arrived" spiritually. Still less does it mean that spirituality is divorced from behavior. The gospel reveals a pattern of conduct that believers must follow as they await the final chapter in God's redemption of his fallen creation.

**Bridging Contexts**

AS WE TRAVEL with this passage out of the first century and into our own time, we must remember that it is a warning both against the notion that it is possible, prior to the day of Christ, to "arrive" spiritually and against some disastrous side effects of not allowing this truth to sink deeply into our spiritual consciousness. The passage also offers an antidote to these problems by claiming that believers should have a correct understanding both of God's requirements that his people be set apart from the rest of the world by their conduct and of God's intention to end the present suffering and sin in the world by the future appearing of the Lord Jesus Christ. Both the problems and their solutions have much to say to the contemporary church if we are careful to find true correlations between Paul's situation and ours and to avoid some common interpretive pitfalls.

**True Parallels Between the Ancient and Modern Contexts.** In Paul's time the problem lay in the commonly accepted notion that the world of human existence was a changeable, unpredictable, and corruptible place that everyone would do well to escape or manipulate. Astrology and magic offered ways of "controlling" the forces that were thought to govern the world, and various new religions from the eastern part of the empire offered redemption from the world itself.

In places like Corinth and Philippi, it is easy to see how recent converts might be tempted to combine elements of these popular religious convictions with the gospel message they had lately embraced. Manifestations of the Spirit's power in miraculous healings and ecstatic utterances could become signs that the believer had already been transferred out of the realm of the corruptible world and into the pure, spiritual realm of the heavenly world. Since the body belonged to the corruptible realm, moreover, its conduct was irrelevant—some might feel that denying legitimate bodily pleasures such as sexual intercourse within marriage was consistent with their new status as spiritual people (1 Cor. 7:1–7), while others might insist that bodily appetites could be indulged without restriction (1 Cor. 6:12–13).[14]

---

14. For the general religious spirit of the first-century Mediterranean world, see Helmut Koester, *Introduction to the New Testament*, vol. 1, *History, Culture, and Religion of the Hellenistic Age* (Philadelphia/Berlin: Fortress/Walter de Gruyter, 1982), 355–89; for the mixture of these notions with the gospel in Corinth, see Gordon D. Fee, *The First Epistle to the Corinthians* (Grand Rapids: Eerdmans, 1987), 10–15.

In some parts of the modern church a similar merger of astrology, magic, and Eastern mysticism in the form of the "New Age" movement continues to pose a threat. Like their ancient counterparts, the religions that make up the New Age movement give greater importance to the mind than to matter and greater weight to the imagination than to rational thinking. The result, as in ancient times, is often moral relativism. "There are no victims in this life or any other," says New Age publisher Jack Underhill. "No mistakes. No wrong paths. No winners. No losers. Accept that and then take responsibility for making your life what you want it to be."[15] Evil is an illusion, and salvation comes from within. As in ancient times, the threat to certain parts of the church is real. New Age spokespersons have occasionally received a warm reception among certain Roman Catholic groups and in the mainline Protestant denominations.[16]

More theologically conservative parts of the church have their own version of this ancient error, however. Some extreme groups whose theological heritage stems from the American holiness movement of the late nineteenth century have fallen prey to an imbalanced understanding of what God has accomplished and will accomplish for his people in the death and resurrection of Jesus Christ. Within these groups, too great an emphasis on the presence of the eschatological age within the church sometimes results in the claim that mature Christians should not experience sickness, should have all their material desires met, or should have wholly overcome sin.[17] Physical wealth and physical health can belong to any who follow the inexorable "laws of prosperity," say the advocates of this other gospel. As in ancient times, although for different reasons, the biblical emphasis on ethical behavior sometimes becomes lost in all of the excitement over the Spirit's supposedly miraculous manifestations of power; and as in the modern New Age movement, a sober understanding of human evil seems to dissolve into a self-actuated vision of utopia in the present.

---

15. As quoted in Russell Chandler's *Understanding the New Age*, rev. ed. (Grand Rapids: Zondervan, 1993), 28.

16. See ibid., 189–99. For an example of the encroachment of New Age thinking into the church, see *New Age Spirituality: An Assessment*, ed. Duncan S. Ferguson (Louisville, Ky.: Westminster/John Knox, 1993). At the time of the book's publication, Ferguson directed the Committee on Higher Education of the Presbyterian Church (U.S.A.). The book's "assessment" of the New Age movement is largely positive.

17. Kenneth Copeland, a leading advocate of the notion that victorious Christian living involves freedom from sickness and poverty, proclaims, "The world's shortages have no effect on someone who has already gone to heaven. Therefore, they should have no effect on us here who have made Jesus the Lord of our lives." See his book, *The Laws of Prosperity* (Fort Worth, Tex.: KCP Publications, 1974), 8.

These are only examples of the theological deviations to which this passage supplies an antidote. The passage is equally applicable to any theological error that places a less than biblical value on the present physical world and a less than biblical emphasis on the fallenness of humanity. Paul's antidote consists of two elements.

First, Paul urges the Philippians to imitate him and others like him who follow the pattern of behavior he has laid down. Today, of course, we do not have the memory of Paul's physical presence to guide us; thus, we must infer the shape of that behavioral pattern from his letters. Several passages give clear hints about its content. In 1 Corinthians 4:16–17 the imitation of Paul is a matter of following his "way of life in Christ Jesus." This phrase should in turn be defined by the statement a few paragraphs later in this letter, that the Corinthians should imitate Paul just as he imitates Christ. Following Paul's example, therefore, means following Christ's example. As we have already seen in our study of Philippians 2:5–11, that is primarily a matter of humble service to others, of putting their interests above our own (cf. 2:4; 2 Cor. 8:9). As Jesus himself said,

> You know that those who are regarded as rulers of the Gentiles lord it over them, and their high officials exercise authority over them. Not so with you. Instead, whoever wants to become great among you must be your servant, and whoever wants to be first must be slave of all. For even the Son of Man did not come to be served, but to serve, and to give his life as a ransom for many (Mark 10:42–45; cf. Matt. 20:25–28; Luke 22:24–27).

Like Paul, Jesus says that his life of humble service provides an example for his disciples to follow. They should be slaves of all *because* he came to serve.

The opening of the new era in which the Sinaitic covenant is no longer valid (3:5–9), then, does not mean that believers are thrown into a world of fuzzy ethical guidelines where virtually anything can be legitimized with the claim that mistakes and wrong paths are only a figment of a warped consciousness or with the assertion that "the Spirit has led me thus." We are, instead, to follow Christ, and here we have an advantage over the Philippians. They had Paul's adequate, but limited, knowledge of the story of Jesus, but we have four Gospels rich with accounts of his teaching and ministry, each from a different, Spirit-inspired perspective. They had Paul's teaching and example to interpret the ethical ramifications of Jesus' life and instruction, but we have thirteen Pauline letters, an account of the early church, other apostolic letters, and an apocalypse to reveal the ethical implications of the gospel.

This new covenant contains clear ethical guidance just as its ancient counterpart did, and although Paul can only expect the Philippians to follow the "pattern" he left with them, the modern church should understand Paul's advice to cover all that is now available that reveals and explains such a pattern. The difference between the old covenant and the new is not that the old covenant was dominated by works and the new by grace. Both covenants are gracious and both demand works, not for salvation, but as the outworking of the sanctity that should characterize the people of God.

Second, Paul pointed the Philippians forward to the final day when Christ would transform the bodies of believers to make them like his glorious body. Since that day is still awaited, it is important not to rest on past accomplishments but to strain forward in anticipation of winning the prize at the race's end. Paul wanted the Philippians to know that although he was confident of God's willingness and ability to bring "to completion" the "good work" God had started in them (1:6), there was no time for them to relax the effort to become "blameless and pure" (2:15; cf. 1:10) and no time for him to rest in his struggle to help the Philippians in the effort (2:16).

In the modern church we too should seriously consider the witness of Scripture that the visible church is a mixed company. Matthew's Gospel affirms this perhaps more clearly than any other portion of Scripture. There Jesus teaches that some people who call him Lord and even claim to prophesy and do miraculous works in his name do not belong among his followers because they have not borne the fruit that is the sign of genuine membership in his people (Matt. 7:15–23; cf. 25:11).[18] He also implies that the visible church consists of both wheat and weeds and that an infallible distinction between the two will only be possible on the final day of harvest (Matt. 13:24–30, 36–43; cf. 25:10–13).[19] All of this serves as an admonition to Christians of every age to make their calling and election sure (2 Peter 1:10) and to maintain a healthy respect for that harvest day when God will come and purge all offenses from his field. It stands as a warning against every teaching that assures the believer so completely of salvation that it engenders complacency and every teaching that so focuses on the signs and wonders of the new age that it encourages spiritual pride and moral laxity.

**A Major Interpretive Mistake to Avoid.** None of this should be taken to mean, however, that Paul now assigns some role to human effort in salvation.

---

18. The "Sir! Sir!" in the NIV's rendering of the tardy virgin's urgent plea in Matt. 25:11 is literally "Lord! Lord!" (*kyrie kyrie*).

19. Cf. David Hill, *The Gospel According to Matthew* (Grand Rapids/London: Eerdmans/Marshall, Morgan & Scott, 1972), 230–33, 235–37. Not all are agreed, however, that this parable implies the existence of "weeds" within the visible church. See, for example, Craig L. Blomberg, *Matthew* (Nashville, Tenn.: Broadman, 1992), 222.

The righteousness in which he will stand before God on the final day is still not his own but God's, and it still comes by faith (v. 9). Two elements of the passage demonstrate this. (1) Although Paul speaks of his own strenuous efforts to take hold of all that he has described in verses 8–11, he also explains that he does this because Christ has first taken hold of him. In other words, had Christ not first intervened and dramatically reoriented Paul's life on the Damascus Road, his efforts would be in his own strength and mis-guided. Instead of salvation at the end of the race, he would find only con-demnation, for his own efforts could never bring him to a successful finish (cf. v. 9; Rom. 9:30–33). Thus the effort Paul describes in Philippians 3:12– 14 is not expended in *working for* his salvation but in *working out* his salvation— in living out the implications of Christ's intervention in his life (cf. 2:12–13; cf. Eph. 2:8–10).

(2) Paul asserts that his effort to attain all that he has mentioned in verses 8–11 is a "prize for which God has called me heavenward in Christ Jesus" (v. 14). His efforts are a response to God's call, and God's call is always effective. God's call brought the universe into being from nothing, it is equally effective in accomplishing salvation (cf. 2 Cor. 4:6; Rom. 4:17), and it cannot be revoked (Rom. 11:29).[20] Thus Paul can be confident that what God has started he will finish (Phil. 1:6), and that at the end of the day he can take no credit for achieving the goal toward which he runs with all his might.

In this passage, then, Paul is essentially applying to himself the principle he expresses even more clearly in Ephesians. After describing the immense privileges that belong to the Ephesians because they, although Gentiles, have been included among God's people (Eph. 2:11–22), he says "I urge you to live a life worthy of the calling you have received" (4:1; cf. 1 Thess. 2:12; 4:7). Those who have been called must stretch every muscle in the effort to live out their calling, but they must also remember that "the one who calls [them] is faithful and he will do it" (1 Thess. 5:24).

We must be careful in interpreting this passage, then, not to lose sight of the point Paul has made in Philippians 3:1–11. The righteousness in which we stand on the final day, although we will have been busy working out its implications from the moment of our initial encounter with the gospel, is not our righteousness but God's. It came from him to us as a gift. It was not won by our strenuous efforts but appropriated by faith.

**Four Minor Interpretive Mistakes to Avoid.** In addition to avoiding this major interpretive mistake, it is important when applying this passage to

---

20. See J. Eckert, "καλέω," *Exegetical Dictionary of the New Testament*, ed. Horst Balz and Ger-hard Schneider, 3 vols. (Grand Rapids: Eerdmans, 1990–93), 2:240–44.

escape four less serious pitfalls. First, it is easy to misinterpret Paul's claim that as he stretches forward toward his final goal, he forgets what lies behind him. This statement is frequently taken to mean that Paul does not continue to feel the weight of his pre-Christian sins, particularly the persecution of the church that he has mentioned in verse 6. Thus, one popular exposition of Philippians interprets the statement through the lens of Paul's claim in 1 Timothy 2:12–17, that he was once a blasphemer, persecutor, and violent man but that God had mercy on him. The author of this usually helpful work then implies that when Paul remembers these events, he also remembers God's mercy to him and so encounters the future with greater confidence.[21]

But that is not Paul's point. The contrast Paul draws in verses 12–14 is between the mistaken notion that he has already "arrived" spiritually and the reality that he has yet to reach the goal and win the prize. Within this context, the past things he forgets in order to strain forward are spiritual successes that might lend specious support to the fiction that he had already been perfected. This passage is not about overcoming remorse for preconversion sins, but about humility and realism in assessing spiritual maturity. The mature believer, Paul says, will not rest on past obedience but will labor to maintain purity and blamelessness until the day of Christ.

Second, it is also tempting to interpret Philippians 3:12–14 as a description of moral progress, as if Paul is saying that he constantly strives to do better and better. During Paul's time Stoic philosophers divided people into two categories, "wise" and "foolish," and actions into two categories, "virtuous" and "sinful." Between the "wise" and the "foolish" person stood the person who attempted to progress toward wisdom, and between the "virtuous" and "sinful" action lay actions that might be neither in themselves but were "fitting" in a given situation. The goal of the person who wanted to progress toward complete wisdom was to do what was "virtuous" whenever possible and to do what was "fitting" with the certainty that can only flow from a wise disposition.[22]

In our own time, analogous notions of moral progress are well understood and highly valued. The "self-help" section of the local book store offers ample evidence that people are searching for ways to improve their financial discipline, parenting skills, and ability to relate well to others. The idea behind such literature, of course, is not bad, and Christians have properly provided self-help literature on a variety of topics from a biblical perspective, but this is not Paul's concern in this passage.

---

21. Wiersbe, *Be Joyful*, 109.

22. A. A. Long and D. N. Sedley, *The Hellenistic Philosophers*, 2 vols. (Cambridge: Cambridge University Press, 1987), 1:359–68.

Here Paul speaks from an eschatological perspective as foreign to notions of moral progress in our own time as to the Stoic notions of his own.[23] He works hard to be faithful to the call of God, not in order to become a wise man who can always decide what is best in a given situation but so that when he stands before God on the day of Christ, he will not have run the race in vain (2:16; cf. Gal. 2:2). His present striving, then, is oriented toward the final day in a way that seems strange to our culture. It is important, in spite of this strangeness, not to "update" and therefore cloud Paul's meaning with the notion that he is simply trying to become a better person. He is evaluating his life in light of the judgment seat of Christ, before whom he, and all believers with him, will one day stand (2 Cor. 5:10; cf. Rom. 14:10).

Third, it would be a mistake to miss the way in which Paul, as elsewhere in the letter, provides a personal example for the Philippians to imitate (v. 15). The disunity within the Philippian church (2:1–18; 4:2–3) may have resulted from disputes over theological matters; in verse 15 Paul provides a model of the humility he has admonished the Philippians themselves to exhibit in their disagreements with one another. On one hand Paul does not compromise his convictions on not having yet attained perfection, maintaining that those who are mature will agree with his perspective (v. 15a). On the other hand he shows his unwillingness to break fellowship with or lash out against those who think differently on this matter (v. 15b). Instead he trusts that God will make the truth clear to them in his own time.[24]

The passage demonstrates the simple but often neglected principle that we should not expect every believer to be fully mature. As long as the church is composed of fallible people, it will include some who try the patience of mature believers. When that happens, Paul's example shows us that we should trust such people to God's care and not allow our disagreements with them to disrupt the church's unity.

Fourth, because this passage mentions the transformation of the believer's body into a body like that of the risen Lord, it raises an issue that has sometimes produced controversy among evangelical Christians: What was the nature of Christ's resurrection body, and what will be the nature of the believer's resurrection body? The New Testament evidence on the nature of

---

23. Pfitzner, *Paul and the Agon Motif*, 151–52.

24. Cf. Beare, *Philippians*, 131. This approach does not, of course, prevent him from speaking in straightforward language about "enemies of the cross of Christ" (vv. 18–19). The difference is that the enemies of Christ's cross, like the "dogs" of v. 2, claim to be believers but are not, and they are, in addition, leading others astray.

the resurrection body is not entirely clear, and this ambiguity has engendered a debate over whether Jesus' resurrected body was a fleshly body or had been transformed into a new, non-fleshly body.[25]

In light of Jesus' own affirmation that he had flesh and bones (Luke 24:39), and because the passages that appear to require Jesus to be immaterial speak only of the disciples' perception of Jesus (Luke 24:31b, 36; John 20:19, 26), it seems best to affirm that Jesus' resurrection was the fully physical resurrection of the body that had died.[26] As Philippians 3:21 says, and as many other passages of Scripture affirm, it was a body that had taken on new properties (Luke 24:31a, 37; John 20:15b, 17; cf. 1 Cor. 15:42—44), but it was nevertheless a physical body of flesh and bones that could consume and digest food (Luke 24:39—43).[27] If this is so, then the resurrection was a powerful affirmation of the goodness of God's physical creation prior to the corrupting effects of sin and of God's ability to reverse those corrupting influences through the work of Christ. As Athanasius put it long ago, Jesus saw the ravaging effects of sin on the human race and, "moved with compassion for our limitation," he took

> to Himself a body, a human body even as our own. . . . Thus, taking a body like our own, because all our bodies were liable to the corruption of death, he surrendered His body to death in place of all, and offered it to the Father. This He did out of sheer love for us, so that in His death all might die, and the law of death thereby be abolished because, when He had fulfilled in His body that for which it was appointed, it was thereafter voided of its power for men. This He did that He might turn again to incorruption men who had turned back

---

25. The ambiguity of the New Testament evidence is apparent in Jesus' claim to his disciples after his resurrection on one hand that he had "flesh and bones" (Luke 24:39) and his apparent ability, on the other, to pass through locked doors (Luke 24:36; John 20:19, 26). For the details of the debate, see Murray J. Harris, *Raised Immortal: Resurrection and Immortality in the New Testament* (Grand Rapids: Eerdmans, 1983), 53–57; idem, *From Grave to Glory: Resurrection in the New Testament* (Grand Rapids: Zondervan, 1990); N. L. Geisler, *The Battle for the Resurrection* (Nashville, Tenn.: Thomas Nelson, 1989). A useful review of the controversy appears in a series of three articles in the *Journal of the Evangelical Theological Society* 33 (1990): 369–82. .

26. Francis J. Beckwith, "Identity and Resurrection: A Review Article," *Journal of the Evangelical Theological Society* 33 (1990), 369–73 (here 372).

27. Paul's statement that "flesh and blood cannot inherit the kingdom of God" (1 Cor. 15:50) probably uses the phrase "flesh and blood" to signify mortality since the phrase stands in synonymous parallelism with the statement "nor does the perishable inherit the imperishable." It would not then refer to literal flesh and blood but only to the kind of body subject to decay. See the helpful discussion of Fee, *First Corinthians*, 798–99.

to corruption, and make them alive through death by the appropriation of His body and by the grace of His resurrection.[28]

**Interpreting 3:12–4:1: A Summary.** In bringing this passage into the modern church, we must apply Paul's primary point that a mature spiritual outlook is impossible if the tension between what God has already done and what he will do in Christ is destroyed. An extreme form of this error produces not believers but "enemies of the cross of Christ," who do not take seriously enough the need to strive toward the final goal to which God has called his people. As we apply this perspective, however, we should avoid the other error of thinking that Paul has now reintroduced human achievement into the process of salvation. That process, though it will result in strenuous effort in the life of all true believers, is nevertheless God's from start to finish. We should also avoid several smaller interpretive mistakes that can prevent the passage from having its full impact and dull the sharpness of its primary message: Believers must not rest on past successes but must earnestly strive to take hold of the one who has already apprehended them, to love him who first loved us (1 John 4:19).

IN 1741 JOHN Wesley preached a sermon on "Christian Perfection" from Philippians 3 that has become a landmark within Protestant Christianity of the great divide between Reformed and Wesleyan groups on the doctrine of sanctification. In his sermon Wesley tried to define carefully his teaching that the believer can attain sinlessness. He noticed that Paul refers to perfection twice in this chapter, once in verse 12, where he maintains that he is not already perfect, and once in verse 15, where he implies that he is. From this Wesley deduced that the Christian must be imperfect in some sense in this life and perfect in another.[29] The senses in which the believer continues to be imperfect, he said, are in "ignorance, or mistake, or infirmities, or temptations," but the believer can and should attain freedom from outward sins and from sins of the heart, including "evil thoughts" and "evil tempers."[30] The sermon concluded with a paraphrase of Philippians 3:13–14 and the admonition that believers should cry

---

28. Athanasius, *On the Incarnation* (Crestwood, N.Y.: St. Vladimir's Orthodox Theological Seminary, 1989), 34.

29. John Wesley, "Christian Perfection," *John Wesley's Fifty-Three Sermons*, ed. Edward H. Sugden (Nashville, Tenn.: Abingdon, 1983), 508–9.

30. Ibid., 512, 523, 525.

to God "day and night" until they experience deliverance "from the bondage of corruption, into the glorious liberty of the sons of God" (cf. Rom. 8:21).[31]

The Reformed response to this emphasis has focused on the depth and complexity of sin's inroads into humanity and the present incompleteness of God's eradication of sin. If the apostle John has said that it is self-deception to claim that we have no sin (1 John 1:8), if Jesus instructed us to pray for forgiveness for our sins (Matt. 6:12), and if Paul assumes that the believer is the battlefield on which the fallen flesh wars against God's indwelling Spirit (Gal. 5:16–17), then surely the Bible does not envision Christian perfection until Christ's second coming.[32] The Wesleyan view can be realistic, then, only if the definitions of both sin and perfection are weakened to allow for the obvious foibles toward which humanity is prone.

The Wesleyan and Reformed traditions were both thoughtfully constructed on the basis of biblical evidence. Wesley claimed that he came to his conclusions after a careful study of the Bible, "the only standard of truth and the only model of pure religion."[33] The Reformed response was built on John Calvin's understanding of sin and the depths of Adam's fall, itself forged on biblical teaching. Wesley stressed the biblical evidence that God had overcome sin in Christ and that the Bible called upon all believers to live in undivided devotion to their Savior. The Reformed tradition refused to relinquish the notion, based on Galatians 5:17, that as important and necessary as sanctification is, "there abideth still some remnants of corruption in every part" of the believer and that this condition would remain until the final day.[34]

Both traditions have produced groups that have accentuated the distinctive emphases of their primary spokesman. Wesley himself emphasized the importance of a second work of God's grace by which the believer's sanctification is perfected, but maintained that even this experience does not exempt the believer from spiritual growth. Some of Wesley's followers in the American Holiness movement, however, place such weight on this crisis experience that they pay insufficient attention to the spiritual growth Wesley believed sanctification requires.[35] The result is occasionally a rigorous demand for absolute rejection of minutely defined worldly ways and occa-

---

31. Ibid., 526.

32. Anthony A. Hoekema, "The Reformed Perspective," *Five Views on Sanctification*, 59–90 (here, 83–84).

33. John Wesley, *A Plain Account of Christian Perfection* (London: Epworth Press, 1952), 6.

34. *The Westminster Confession of Faith*, 13.2.

35. See Melvin E. Dieter, "The Wesleyan Perspective," *Five Views on Sanctification*, 41; R. G. Tuttle, "Wesley, John," *Evangelical Dictionary of Theology*, ed. Walter A. Elwell (Grand Rapids: Baker, 1984), 1164.

sionally a freewheeling claim that those who have experienced instanta-neous sanctification are free from the bothersome rules of any moral code.[36] The Reformed tradition, on the other hand, has produced churches and groups so uninterested in the Spirit's power that they have retreated into a sterile and outwardly lifeless scholasticism. Doctrinal precision occasionally becomes so important to them that they forget that the believer's life is to be characterized, as Wesley said, by a heartfelt and visible love for both God and people.[37]

Philippians 3:12–21 has much to contribute to the debate between fol-lowers of these two noble Christian traditions. Its first contribution is to the rules of the debate. Both Wesleyans and Calvinists believe that they hold what Paul calls the mature view of sanctification (v. 15), and both believe that the departure of the other from this mature view is a serious matter. Paul would instruct both to continue the debate because the subject is important and misunderstanding of it can have serious effects. But Paul would also com-mend his own example to the participants in the debate. Each should rec-ognize the other as a brother or sister in the Lord, acrimony should find no place in the discussion, and if no consensus is possible, then Paul recommends simply leaving to God the task of revealing the truth to the other.

Second, the passage also makes a contribution to the substance of the debate. It demonstrates that the extreme positions on both sides of the debate are wrong. Holiness groups should not lay such emphasis on a past experience of God's second work of grace that they forget to work out their salvation with fear and trembling in the present, and Reformed groups should not so emphasize the manifestation of God's grace in justification that they neglect the manifestation of his grace in sanctification. To adherents of both positions, Paul would advise not looking back to the past but forward to the future and to strain every spiritual muscle in the effort to be faithful to God's gracious call to salvation.

In part because each one was steeped in Paul's letters and theology, both Calvin and Wesley embraced this notion. After saying that it is possible to be a Christian without attaining "evangelical perfection" and that all are far removed from that state, Calvin qualified his position this way:

---

36. For the first, see the useful article, "Holiness Movement, American" by R. V. Pier-ard in *Evangelical Dictionary of Theology*, 516–18 (here 517); for the second see the descrip-tion of the closing years of Robert Pearsall Smith's ministry in Benjamin Breckinridge Warfield, *Perfectionism*, 2 vols. (New York: Oxford, 1931–32), 2:505–8.

37. B. B. Warfield's attack on the "higher life" movement in *Perfectionism*, 2:463–58, for example, occasionally lapses into unnecessarily harsh characterizations of the movement's principal advocates.

What then? Let that target be set before our eyes at which we are earnestly to aim. Let that goal be appointed toward which we should strive and struggle. For it is not lawful for you to divide things with God in such a manner that you undertake part of those things which are enjoined upon you by his Word but omit part, according to your own judgment.

... Only let us look toward our mark with sincere simplicity and aspire to our goal; not fondly flattering ourselves, nor excusing our own evil deeds, but with continuous effort striving toward this end: that we may surpass ourselves in goodness until we attain to goodness itself.[38]

Wesley, in attempting to explain his teaching on Christian perfection, said that on his way back to England from America in 1738, he expressed his understanding of perfection in the following verse:

> O grant that nothing in my soul
> > May dwell, but Thy pure love alone!
> O may Thy love possess me whole,
> > My joy, my treasure, and my crown;
> Strange fires far from my heart remove;
> My every act, word, thought, be love!

His point, like Calvin's, was that the believer's heart should be undivided in its devotion to God. Wesley appropriately commented, "I never heard that anyone objected to this. And indeed who can object?"[39] Wesley and Calvin were of different minds about how close the believer could come to the ideal of undivided devotion to God in this life, but the emphasis of both lay on the ideal itself and on the necessity of striving for it, not on whether or not one could reach it. Paul's emphasis on not attaining perfection until the final day appears to favor Calvin's understanding of sanctification. But Wesley as much as Calvin, and largely because of this passage, emphasized the necessity of striving for complete godliness.[40] That should be the emphasis of every believer, and it is an emphasis that can draw Christians of both the Wesleyan and the Reformed traditions closer to the kind of unity Paul wished for the Philippians.

If the believer's effort to remain faithful to God's heavenly call is the point of this passage, however, it is difficult to see how it squares with the influential teaching usually associated with the Keswick convention. This

---

38. John Calvin, *Institutes of the Christian Religion*, ed. John T. McNeill, 2 vols. (Philadelphia: Westminster, 1960), 1:688–89 (3.6.5).

39. Wesley, *A Plain Account of Christian Perfection*, 9.

40. Wesley, "Christian Perfection," 526.

school of thought teaches that believers can be divided into two groups, subnormal and normal, and that the normal Christian has somehow "let go" of personal efforts to attain godliness and "let God" do the work of sanctification. Normal Christians are usually said to be in the minority, and the average Christian experience is supposedly of the subnormal type. Advocates of this view believe that a faith crisis is often necessary for an average, subnormal believer to surrender fully to God and move into the realm of normal Christian experience. The Keswick conventions, which have been held annually in Keswick, England, since 1875 and have given birth to parallel meetings in the United States and Canada, have provided the opportunity for this faith crisis.[41]

Although much good has come from the Keswick movement and although its advocates are often godly, charitable people who provide worthy examples for all believers to follow, their division of believers into defeated and victorious and their emphasis on passively surrendering to God seem out of harmony with passages such as Philippians 3:12—14 and 1 Corinthians 9:24—27. Paul was unwilling to claim victory in the Christian life even for himself. Thus, although he was certain that when God had started a good work, he would complete it (1 Cor. 1:8—9; Phil. 1:6), he was unwilling to claim for himself in the present a victory that still lay in the future. The spiritual dangers of his apostolic labor were too vivid, the labor too strenuous to claim victory yet (1 Cor. 9:27). Instead, like an athlete, the apostle went into strict training and stretched toward his final goal so that on the final day his running and labor would not be in vain.

The evidence does not indicate, moreover, that Paul would have been happy with the division of Christians into classes of subnormal and normal. He knows a distinction between believers who are mature and those who are not (Phil. 3:15), but the mature believers appear to realize how far they have to go before they finally lay hold of victory, while the immature apparently claimed victory too early. The more biblical view is that if people are Christians at all, they understand the effects of Christ's death and resurrection to be not only salvation from God's wrath (Rom. 1:18—3:26; 5:9) but also rescue from the dominion of sin (6:1—23; 8:1—17).

Some, because of their biological makeup and family history, struggle to keep in step with the Spirit who indwells them; others, because of their biological and environmental advantages, find it easier to keep the righteous requirements of the law under the Spirit's power. A believer converted out of a desperate situation may always look like a subnormal Christian to those who

---

41. See the summary of the "Keswick" understanding of sanctification by J. Robertson McQuilkin, "The Keswick Perspective," *Five Views on Sanctification*, 151—90.

divide believers into such groups, but in God's eyes that person may be as faithful as the believer who has absorbed many of the Christian virtues during his or her upbringing and therefore finds it easy follow to the example of Christ.

As C. S. Lewis has said, when we stand before God on the final day, all external advantages and disadvantages will dissolve, and our true selves, the part of us that chooses good or ill, obedience or disobedience, will remain. Then we will see ourselves as we really are, and this moment of revelation will contain surprises.[42]

---

42. C. S. Lewis, *Mere Christianity* (New York: Macmillan, 1943), 86.

# Philippians 4:2–9

I PLEAD WITH Euodia and I plead with Syntyche to agree
with each other in the Lord. ³Yes, and I ask you, loyal
yokefellow, help these women who have contended at my
side in the cause of the gospel, along with Clement and the
rest of my fellow workers, whose names are in the book of life.

⁴Rejoice in the Lord always. I will say it again: Rejoice! ⁵Let
your gentleness be evident to all. The Lord is near. ⁶Do not
be anxious about anything, but in everything, by prayer and
petition, with thanksgiving, present your requests to God.
⁷And the peace of God, which transcends all understanding,
will guard your hearts and your minds in Christ Jesus.

⁸Finally, brothers, whatever is true, whatever is noble,
whatever is right, whatever is pure, whatever is lovely, whatever is admirable—if anything is excellent or praiseworthy—
think about such things. ⁹Whatever you have learned or
received or heard from me, or seen in me—put it into practice. And the God of peace will be with you.

**Original Meaning**
IN THIS NEW section Paul continues his discussion
of how the Philippians should "conduct" themselves "in a manner worthy of the gospel of
Christ" (1:27). Once again he is concerned, as he
has been throughout the letter (1:1, 18a, 27; 2:1–4, 14, 29; 3:15), with the
unity of the Philippians. The section is, nevertheless, clearly separate from
the previous section. It contains no particles linking it to chapter 3, and
beginning with verse 4 the apostle uses brief, unconnected statements
instead of sustained argumentation. This procedure is not atypical of the conclusions of Paul's letters, as the short, pithy exhortations in 1 Thessalonians
5:12–25 and Colossians 3:18–4:6 demonstrate. In addition, for the first
time in this letter Paul calls the names of several of his Philippian readers. It
is almost as if, knowing that he is coming to the end of the letter, he is concerned to place as much emphasis as possible on his concluding admonitions
and to make sure that those in Philippi who need to hear them most will pay
close attention.

This part of the letter can be divided into two paragraphs, one that
exhorts two women to be united with one another (vv. 2–3) and the other

that advises the Philippians how to live amid the persecution they are experiencing (vv. 4–9).

**A Plea to Two Coworkers (vv. 2–3).** In verse 2 Paul singles out two of his Philippian readers by name and asks them to adopt a common mind "in the Lord." Although the point is disputed among commentators, the disagreement between these two women may have been at the bottom of the disunity that has concerned Paul throughout the letter. Two indicators point in this direction. (1) The unusual tactic of calling the women by name in a letter to be read to the entire congregation (cf. 1 Thess. 5:27; Col. 4:16) shows that Paul considered their disagreement to be unusually significant. (2) The phrase that the NIV translates "agree with each other" represents a Greek phrase (*to auto phronein*) nearly identical to the one Paul used in his general exhortation in 2:2 to be "like-minded" (*to auto phronete*). The clear verbal echo of this general exhortation probably indicates that Euodia and Syntyche, more than any of the others, needed to put the interests of each other first and, "in the Lord," to drop their quarrel.

As we have seen often in this letter, the manner in which Paul exhorts his readers is as significant as the content. Three elements of the way in which he exhorts Euodia and Syntyche are particularly significant. (1) He addresses each woman equally. The repetition of the word "plead" is not grammatically necessary and produces a slightly ponderous sentence, but the use of the term before each name communicates a desire to be evenhanded—not to take sides but to exhort each participant in the dispute with equal firmness.[1] In a letter that would have been read to the entire congregation, Paul probably considered such evenhandedness of paramount importance.

(2) Paul asks for help from an unidentified third party, a man whose name we do not know and whom Paul calls simply "loyal yokefellow." If Paul wrote Philippians shortly after 1 Corinthians, perhaps he had fresh in his mind the dispute between two believers in Corinth that led to an embarrassing lawsuit before the unbelieving civil authorities (1 Cor. 6:1–11). Paul had angrily asked the Corinthians in his letter to them, "Is it possible that there is nobody among you wise enough to judge a dispute between believers?" (6:5). The Philippians were certainly on better terms with the apostle than the Corinthians, and there is no indication that the dispute between Euodia and Syntyche was of the type that could be taken before civil authorities. But as with the Corinthians, Paul finds value in calling in a third party to adjudicate the disagreement. The unity and sanctity of the church is too important to consider the dispute a private matter to be settled by the women alone.

---

1. Cf. Beare, *Philippians*, 144; Bruce, *Philippians*, 114.

(3) Paul mixes his exhortation to these two women with commendation. This is a common feature of Paul's hortatory style, both when admonishing whole congregations (1 Cor. 1:4–7; 1 Thess. 1:2–10) and when admonishing individuals. In Philemon, for example, Paul mingles his request that Philemon forgive his slave Onesimus and return him to Paul with praise for Philemon's "faith in the Lord Jesus and ... love for all the saints" (Philem. 5, 7). Thus when Paul exhorts Euodia and Syntyche, he speaks warmly of "these women who have contended at my side in the cause of the gospel" (Phil. 4:3). He also places them in company with Clement, one of Paul's coworkers whose identity is otherwise unknown, but who must have been a highly respected member of the Philippian congregation.[2] In addition, he says that their names, along with those of his other coworkers, "are in the book of life" (v. 3), a traditional title of honor frequently used in Jewish literature for the people of God who have suffered persecution but have nevertheless remained faithful (Dan. 12:1; Rev. 3:5; cf. Isa. 4:3; Luke 10:20).[3]

Paul's actual exhortation to Euodia and Syntyche is simple: He asks them to overcome their dispute with one another. The language he uses helps us see Paul's primary concern in issuing this exhortation. Since his language echoes 2:2, Paul likely wants Euodia and Syntyche to put into practice toward one another the qualities mentioned in 2:1–4. They should be in Spirit-produced fellowship with one another, and this relationship should be characterized by "tenderness and compassion," a mutual love, and a unity of purpose. It should, in addition, lead them to put the interests of the other ahead of their own interests.

Paul is under no illusions, however, that Euodia and Syntyche will end their dispute with one another on some purely human grounds. Thus he adds to his admonition the qualification that their agreement should be "in the Lord." The phrase "in the Lord" has played a prominent role in the letter as a qualifier of surprising human conduct whose source is the Lord. It seems strange that Paul's imprisonment would create courage in his fellow believers to proclaim the gospel, but that is what happens "in the Lord" (1:14). Similarly, Paul's

---

2. Cf. Hawthorne, *Philippians*, 181. It might at first seem plausible to identify the Clement mentioned here with the Clement of Rome who wrote to the Corinthians in A.D. 96. That Clement, however, is associated with Rome rather than with Philippi, and since he died after A.D. 110, would have lived to an unusually ripe age if the identification were correct. See Lightfoot, *Philippians*, 168–69.

3. See O'Brien, *Philippians*, 482–83; Robert H. Mounce, *The Book of Revelation* (Grand Rapids: Eerdmans, 1977), 113–14. Since ancient Greek and Roman cities normally kept registers of their citizens, it is likely that Philippi had such a register as well (Hawthorne, *Philippians*, 181). This phrase may have been another reminder to the Philippian community of their heavenly citizenship (3:20; cf. 1:27).

travel plans are more tentative than they would otherwise be because he makes them "in the Lord" (2:19, 24). The Philippians must overcome any resentment against Epaphroditus' early return and welcome him "in the Lord" (2:29), and they can be joyful "in the Lord" despite persecution (3:1; 4:4). In the same way Paul says in this passage that Euodia and Syntyche, although they might normally let their disagreements disrupt their fellowship, must seek unity because they are "in the Lord." Those who live within the sphere of Christ's Lordship are equipped to overcome circumstances that would dishearten unbelievers and disrupt their friendships, and Paul wants Euodia and Syntyche to put this principle into practice in their relationship with one another.

**A Brief Set of Exhortations (vv. 4–9).** The second part of this passage, like the first, is unattached to the sentences preceding it by any connecting word. At least through verse 8, the passage itself makes only minimal use of connecting words ("but" in v. 6, "and" in v. 7, and "finally" in v. 8 are the exceptions). This lack of connecting words was a stylistic device called "asyndeton" by the grammarians of Paul's time. It was used for emphasis and was especially effective at the end of a discourse.[4] Indeed, the device continues to be used in similar ways in modern times. "We shall pay any price," said John F. Kennedy in a famous speech, "bear any burden, meet any hardship, support any friend, oppose any foe to assure the survival and the success of liberty."[5] Paul uses the device to similar effect here. As he begins to close the admonitory part of his letter, he trims his language to a minimum in order to communicate his meaning with as much precision, emphasis, and persuasion as possible.

Verses 4–7 contain four admonitions ("rejoice," "let your gentleness be evident," "do not be anxious," and "present your requests to God"), which at first seem to have little to do with one another. A closer look at the meaning of the terms standing behind these admonitions, however, reveals a common background for them all. The term "gentleness" (*epieikes*) was often used of an attitude of kindness where the normal or expected response was retaliation. Thus in the apocryphal book of Wisdom, a group of evil people who believe that life is short and that nothing lies beyond the grave decide to "crown" themselves "with rosebuds before they wither" and "everywhere … leave signs of enjoyment" (Wisd. 2:8–9, NRSV). But since the righteous man does not approve of their irresponsible merriment, they decide to persecute him. "Let us test him with insult and torture," they say, "so that we may find out how

---

4. *Ad Herennium*, 4.30; Quintilian, *Institutio Oratoria*, 9.3.50; Aristotle, *Rhetoric*, 3.19.6.

5. For this and other modern examples, see Edward P. J. Corbett, *Classical Rhetoric for the Modern Student*, 2d ed. (New York: Oxford, 1971), 470.

gentle he is (*ten epieikeian autou*), and make trial of his forbearance" (2:19, NRSV). This is probably the connotation of the term in 2 Corinthians 10:1, where Paul appeals to "the meekness and gentleness (*epieikeias*) of Christ" as the reason for his own gentleness with the recalcitrant Corinthians. Paul, like Christ, refused to answer his detractors in kind.

The words "be anxious" (*merimnao*, 4:6) can refer to being unduly concerned about anything, but it is often used in contexts where persecution is the issue. Thus both Matthew and Luke use this word in their record of Jesus' admonition to his disciples not to be concerned about what they will say before the local councils, governors, and kings who hunt them down because of their commitment to the gospel (Matt. 10:19; Luke 12:11). The term "guard" (*phroureo*) likewise is a figure drawn from the arena of conflict and is frequently used to refer to the action of a military garrison stationed inside a city (Judith 3:6; cf. 2 Cor. 11:32).

All of this points to the context of persecution as the background for Paul's admonitions. The Philippians were suffering under opposition from their pagan neighbors, just as Paul and Silas had suffered when among them (Acts 16:19–24; Phil. 1:28–30). Thus, just as Paul had started the admonitory section of the letter with a command for the Philippians, despite their persecution, to conduct themselves in a manner worthy of the gospel (1:27–30), so he returns to this theme at the end of the section, asking the Philippians to maintain an attitude of joy "in the Lord" at all times (v. 4; cf. 3:1), urging them to adopt toward their persecutors Christ's approach of gentle nonretaliation (v. 5; cf. Rom. 12:17–21; 15:3; 1 Peter 2:23; 3:8–9; cf. Isa. 53:7–9), and admonishing them not to be anxious about anything (v. 6; cf. 1 Peter 5:7). Instead, they should remember that the Lord is near (v. 5; cf. 3:20–21) and replace their anxiety with thankful prayer about their suffering (v. 6).[6]

The "and" at the beginning of verse 7 is more important than it looks. It does not simply attach another statement to verses 4–6 but gives the result of the thankful prayer that Paul has described in verse 6.[7] If the Philippians follow Paul's advice, he says, then "the peace of God, which transcends all understanding" will stand like a garrison over their hearts and minds. But what is the "peace of God"? Is it an overwhelming sense of inner contentment? Is

---

6. Thus, the phrase "the Lord is near" probably does not have both temporal and spatial connotations (as O'Brien, *Philippians*, 488–89, argues). Paul is instead reminding the persecuted Philippians that recompense for wrongs belongs not to them but to the Lord, who could return at any time (cf. Rom. 12:19; 1 Peter 2:23; 3:9).

7. Cf. O'Brien, *Philippians*, 495. For this use of the Greek term *kai*, see Walter Bauer, *A Greek-English Lexicon of the New Testament and Other Early Christian Literature*, 2d ed., trans., adapt. and rev. William F. Arndt, F. Wilbur Gingrich, Frederick W. Danker (Chicago: University of Chicago Press, 1979), 392 (I.f.).

it the serenity that characterizes God himself, who is never anxious? Is it the peace (cf. Rom. 5:1) that results from God's justifying work in Christ Jesus?[8] Since the peace mentioned here stands in contrast to the anxiety mentioned in verse 6, it is probably an inner sense of contentment supplied by God. It transcends all understanding because the anticipated response to the persecution the Philippians are experiencing is anxiety, but just as throughout this letter Paul expects Christian behavior to break the bonds of normal behavior, so here God supplies an attitude in the face of adversity that does not fit the normal categories (cf. 2 Cor. 1:3–11).[9]

Paul's next paragraph begins with the same loose connective phrase he had used at 3:1. The NIV translates it "finally," and indeed a close approximation of the phrase appears near the end of 1 Thessalonians (4:1) and 2 Corinthians (13:11). But, as in 3:1 (which is far from the letter's conclusion), the phrase here probably means something like "as far as the rest is concerned," "beyond that," or "in addition."[10] It expresses no logical connection between verses 8–9 and verses 4–7, but simply shows that Paul is now moving to a different set of admonitions. This new set of instructions is bound closely together by the style in which he expresses them and by the balance of their content. In verse 8, Paul tells the Philippians how they should *think* and, as in verses 4–7, leaves out connecting words for emphasis ("asyndeton"). In verse 9 Paul tells the Philippians how to *act* and, using precisely the opposite stylistic device ("polysyndeton"), repeats the connective word "or" (*kai*) over and over. The effect, again, is emphasis.

The list of virtues that Paul asks the Philippians to "think about" is not a distinctively Christian list and could have been embraced by many right-thinking people in ancient times.[11] Paul seems to place special emphasis on the breadth of these qualities by repeatedly using the indefinite adjective "whatever" (*hosa*). He tells the Philippians to look for the true, noble, right, pure, lovely, admirable, excellent, and praiseworthy everywhere around them and to ponder the things in which these qualities are exemplified. Perhaps Paul knows that since the Philippians are being persecuted by the soci-

---

8. For the various options see Caird, *Paul's Letters From Prison*, 151; Bruce, *Philippians*, 119; O'Brien, *Philippians*, 496.

9. Silva, *Philippians*, 226.

10. See Bauer, *Greek-English Lexicon*, 480.

11. Lists of virtues are not uncommon in ancient literature. The Stoic philosopher Cleanthes (331–232 B.C.), for example, defines "the good" as that which is "well-ordered, just, holy, pious, self-controlled, useful, honourable, due, austere, candid, always secure, friendly, precious, . . . consistent, fair-famed, unpretentious, caring, gentle, keen, patient, faultless, permanent." See A. A. Long and D. N. Sedley, *The Hellenistic Philosophers*, 2 vols. (Cambridge: Cambridge University Press, 1987), 1:373.

ety around them, they will be tempted to reject everything outside the church as indelibly tainted with evil. If so, then this list, with its admonition to look for the virtue (*arete*; NIV "excellent") in the wider world, reminds the Philippians that, although society sometimes seems hostile and evil, it is still part of God's world and contains much good that the believer can affirm.

---

verse 8
whatever is *true*
whatever *noble*
whatever *right*
whatever *pure*
whatever *lovely*
whatever *admirable*
if anything is *excellent*
or [if anything is] *praiseworthy*
**think about these things**

verse 9
Whatever you have *learned*
or [you have] *received*
or [you have] *heard* from me
or [you have] *seen* in me
**put [these things] into practice**

THE RHETORIC OF 4:8–9

---

Whatever Paul's intention in giving this list, he goes on to say that the Philippians must practice the distinctively Christian ethic they find exemplified in his teaching and conduct (v. 9). The four verbs Paul uses here all show that he is reminding his readers both of his personal conduct while with them and of the Christian tradition he passed on to them. The term "learned" (from *manthano*) refers to learning from someone else's example (cf., e.g., 1 Cor. 4:6).[12] The term "received" (from *paralambano*), on the other hand, refers to the reception of a particular body of teaching (cf. 1 Cor. 11:23; 15:3; Gal. 1:9, 12; Col. 2:6; 1 Thess. 2:13; 3:6), sometimes teaching specifically about how Christians should live (cf. 1 Thess. 4:1).[13] The Philippians would have received this teaching by hearing Paul, and they would have learned from his example by seeing how he conducted himself. Thus, they are not simply to ponder the best of the moral standards valued in the culture around them,

---

12. Bauer, *Greek-English Lexicon*, 490.
13. Ibid., 619.

but they are to follow the distinctively Christian pattern of behavior they learned from Paul's words and deeds.

THIS PASSAGE PROVIDES a good illustration of two classical interpretive problems. The first section (vv. 2–3) is so obviously dependent on the historical context of the letter for its meaning that it is tempting to resort to flights of fancy about the identity of Euodia, Syntyche, Clement, and the mysterious "loyal yokefellow" in order to make the passage more suitable for application to the modern church. The second section (vv. 4–9), on the other hand, contains such general advice that it is easy to miss the connection it has to the situation in Philippi—a connection that is crucial for discovering the primary meaning of these verses. As we apply these two sections to the modern church, we should find their theological underpinnings, discover how Paul applies those theological principles to the Philippians, and then apply those principles in the same way to the modern situation.

**Theology and Application in 4:2–3.** Paul's plea to Euodia and Syntyche is built on two theological principles. (1) The unity he has urged on the Philippians as a group throughout the letter and in general ways (1:1, 27; 2:1–16, 29) must be implemented in practical ways in specific disputes. Paul has no interest in putting his admonition on merely an abstract level, simply issuing a general command that he then leaves the Philippians to work out on their own. Here he shows that the heady concept of Christian unity must be worked out on the ground, one quarrel at a time. So Paul singles out Euodia and Syntyche, identifies them as two people who have contributed to the disunity within the church, and urges them to "agree in the Lord." Because they understand the implications of living in the sphere marked out by the Lordship of the Christ described in 2:6–11, they must seek reconciliation with one another. In 4:2, Paul pours all the theological richness of 2:6–11 into a single dispute between two people. For him there can be no dichotomy between reflection on the Incarnation and the behavior that the Incarnation requires of individual Christians.

Similarly in the modern church, no dichotomy can exist between what we believe and what we practice. If we believe that God is the "Creator of heaven and earth," we cannot exploit his creation in ways that dishonor him. If we believe in "the forgiveness of sins" through the death of Jesus Christ, then we cannot refuse to forgive the sins of others. If we believe in "the resurrection of the body and the life everlasting," then we cannot grieve over death as if we had no hope. But especially in light of this passage, if we believe in "the holy catholic church" and in the "communion of saints," then when relationships within the church are broken, we must work for their reconciliation. It should be unthinkable to confess our faith in the words of the Apostles' Creed but to refuse to associate with our brothers and sisters across the church aisle.[14]

(2) Paul provides an example to his readers of how to work for the unity with which he has been so concerned throughout the letter and with which he is especially concerned here. Such disputes are not the private concern of those quarreling, but of the entire church. It is appropriate, then, for the church to seek to arbitrate such disputes through the mediation of a believer who is gifted with the ability to help people overcome their differences. In addition, Paul's example demonstrates that when the church must address such problems, it must do so with gentleness and evenhandedness, affirming the gifts of the people involved and guarding against bias in favor of one party.

Verses 2–3, then, reveal the principle that the way we think about God must be worked out in the way we conduct our day-to-day lives. This passage shows especially the importance of applying what we believe about the need for Christian unity to disputes within our churches. The way in which the apostle himself makes this application in the Philippian church also provides a model for us. The church should be willing to mediate between antagonists in its midst, but must do so in the gentle and impartial way that he demonstrates here.

**Theology and Application in 4:4–9.** The short, pithy, and rhetorically sophisticated admonitions of verses 4–9 flow from four theological sources: The Lord is near, God is sovereign and merciful, the world belongs to God, and those who live in the world can only be fully obedient to God by following his revelation of himself in the gospel. The first two principles are bound closely together and dominate verses 5–7; the second two are also tightly linked and stand beneath verses 8–9.

In two memorable phrases, Paul calls on the Philippians to rejoice in the Lord at all times and to let their gentleness be evident to all. Although these admonitions were particularly important within the Philippians' situation of persecution, where suffering could dampen joy and prompt a vengeful response, the way in which Paul phrases them shows that he did not intend to limit their application to this setting. Believers are to rejoice "always" and

---

14. In his wise book, *The Apostles' Creed: A Faith to Live By* (Grand Rapids: Eerdmans, 1993), 7, C. E. B. Cranfield says, "We will certainly not have understood [the creed] if we fail to see its relevance to the life of the modern world and to all the problems which that world presents."

to be gentle to "all." Even when persecution is not present in the modern context, then, these admonitions provide a guide to the attitude and conduct that the gospel requires of believers. We should "rejoice" in both good and bad times and should have a reputation for gentleness rather than for vengeful retaliation.

Although nothing in the grammar connects these two admonitions to Paul's statement that "the Lord is near," that phrase nevertheless forms the logical basis for adopting the attitude and conduct that Paul advises. These words do not mean that the apostle mistakenly thought Christ was going to appear immediately. If he had thought this, it is hard to understand why he would reckon with the possibility of his own death in 1:18b–26, or why he would lay complex travel plans for Timothy, himself, and Epaphroditus in 2:19–30. Paul probably means, then, that the Lord is near in the sense that he is nearer now than when the Philippians first believed (cf. Rom. 13:11). The New Testament generally, and Paul's letters especially, speak of the appearance of Christ as an incentive for obedience (see, e.g., Rom. 13:11–14; Phil. 1:10; 2:16; 1 Thess. 5:4–11). That is the way Paul speaks of it here, and we should not allow modern ridicule of apocalyptic thinking to lead us away from this legitimate and important incentive to ethical behavior.

Perhaps because he wants to forestall any notion that the believer must await the Lord's return to have a vision of his sovereignty and to have access to his merciful provision for his people, Paul follows his reminder that the Lord is near with an admonition to pray. The believer should pray, Paul says, about every circumstance and should couple requests with thanksgiving. In the peace that passes all understanding which such prayers will produce, believers will experience God's presence immediately, making the time of Christ's appearing irrelevant to their spiritual well-being.[15]

Paul's list of virtues in verse 8 assumes that the world contains many good qualities that merit the believer's consideration and affirmation.[16] It also assumes that the pagan world has some notion of good and bad, right and wrong, duty and irresponsibility, beauty and ugliness, honor and shame. Elsewhere Paul speaks of Gentiles who have the requirements of God's law written on their hearts and says that occasionally they actually do these things (Rom. 2:14–15). He can also speak of the pagan authorities in government as God's agents for adjudicating right and wrong in society at large (13:1–7). Paul assumes, in other words, that absolute moral standards exist, that people other than Jews and Christians have affirmed them, and that the

15. Cf. Caird, *Paul's Letters From Prison*, 150–51.
16. Cf. Witherington, *Friendship and Finances in Philippi*, 52, 117.

believer can benefit from pondering examples of them wherever they occur, even in the pagan world.

Within the present climate of moral relativity, the modern church would do well to reaffirm this theological principle. Christian standards of morality and beauty are not simply expressions of subjective feelings but truths graciously revealed from God for the welfare of his people and of all creation.[17] People other than Christians frequently recognize their validity, and when they do, Christians should support them, learn from them, and take comfort that what they acknowledge to be right on the basis of God's Word the rest of the world often acknowledges to be right on the basis of their own understanding of how the world and society function best.

Christians would be remiss, however, if they allowed the unbelieving world to guide their ethical decisions. Elsewhere Paul acknowledges that because of the insidious effects of sin, unbelievers are often misguided about right and wrong—indeed, so misguided that they sometimes worship the creature rather than the Creator and seek human intimacy in precisely the wrong places (Rom. 1:21–27). Moreover, even when they retain a clear understanding of right and wrong, they are often incapable of doing it (Rom. 1:28–32; cf. Phil. 2:15). Thus, in verse 9 Paul reminds the Philippians of the importance of the specifically Christian witness to correct moral conduct. It is not simply contained in the Old Testament, although as Paul's rather subtle use of Israel as a negative example in 2:14–16 shows, the Philippians must have been familiar with the Old Testament and, if the moral content of Paul's other letters provides any insight into how he taught the Philippians, he must have reaffirmed much of the morality contained in it. Nevertheless, Paul's own example and teaching, shaped by his knowledge of Christ (1 Cor. 4:17; 11:1), provided the Philippians with a sure moral compass within a "crooked and depraved generation" (Phil. 2:15).

The modern church, likewise, should applaud and learn from unbelieving expressions of truth and beauty. Mature Christians should feel no compulsion to read only literature written by other Christians, to view only movies and plays that fellow believers have produced, or to listen only to Christian music. Paul urges believers to discover and learn from the true, noble, right, pure, lovely, admirable, excellent, and praiseworthy *wherever it occurs*. Not only will believers who do this shape their lives into the form that God desires, but they will uphold the truth within a relativistic age that claims

---

17. A classic argument for the validity of this theological principle and a succinct statement of its significance for the education of children appears in C. S. Lewis, *The Abolition of Man or Reflections on Education With Special Reference to the Teaching of English in the Upper Forms of Schools* (New York: Macmillan, 1947).

truth cannot be known. Christians should nevertheless not forget that the touchstone of what is true and good is the Word of God and that every moral expression within the wider unbelieving world should be measured against the standard of the gospel as preserved in Scripture.[18]

Our task of bridging the ancient and the modern contexts is not complete, however, after simply identifying the general theological principles underlying this passage. Although the application of these general principles to the modern context is certainly legitimate, the passage is most clearly applicable to situations in the modern church that parallel the ancient Philippian situation of persecution. The temptation is as strong in modern contexts of persecution as it was in ancient times to lash out in retaliation at those who injure us and to wring our hands in anxiety about what will become of us, our families, and our property. The temptation is also strong to develop a dualistic view of the world—to think that everything outside the persecuted church is evil, including fellow Christians who for some reason are not experiencing persecution. If this is our context, Philippians 4:2–9 urges us to be gentle rather than vindictive, prayerful rather than anxious, and appreciative of the good within our culture rather than intellectually cloistered behind the fortified walls of a narrow ideology.

**Two Interpretive Pitfalls to Avoid.** Before leaving the mechanics of how to apply this passage, we must issue a warning against two interpretive pitfalls, both associated with the same element in the passage. This passage identifies two women as important participants in the life of the Philippian church, as fellow contenders with Paul in the cause of the gospel, and as fellow workers with Paul. These are impressive credentials. Paul's only other use of the verb "contend together with" (*synathleo;* NIV "contended at my side") appears in 1:27, where he tells the entire congregation that they should be "contending as one man for the faith of the gospel." Since Paul is speaking of steadfastness in the face of persecution in 1:27, there is no reason to think that he refers to anything else in 4:2. Euodia and Syntyche, then, have bravely withstood persecution alongside Paul, perhaps during the time when he originally preached the gospel in Philippi.[19]

More impressive still, these women were Paul's "fellow workers," a word the apostle reserves for a circle of associates who have been especially helpful to him in fulfilling his calling to preach the gospel among the Gentiles.

---

18. On the consequences to Christians of allowing the world to set the church's moral agenda, see Dorothy L. Sayers, "Christian Morality," in *Unpopular Opinions* (London: Victor Gollancz, 1946), 9–12.

19. Francis X. Malinowski, "The Brave Women of Philippi," *Biblical Theology Bulletin* 15 (1985): 60–64 (here 62).

This company included such notables as Priscilla and Aquila (Rom. 16:3; cf. 16:9), Timothy (Rom. 16:21; 1 Thess. 3:2), Titus (2 Cor. 8:23), Epaphroditus (Phil. 2:25), Philemon (Philem. 1), Mark (Philem. 24), and Luke (Philem. 24).[20] Since Paul takes the unusual step of admonishing Euodia and Syntyche by name, moreover, they probably held prominent positions within the Philippian congregation. Perhaps they were even among the "overseers and deacons" whom Paul has mentioned in the letter's opening (1:1).

All of this has sometimes led interpreters of this passage down two widely divergent, but equally deviant, paths. Some have apparently been so amazed that Paul would attribute to women such important roles in his own ministry and in the life of the church that they have tried to make them men, or at least to make Euodia a man and Syntyche his wife. Thus the seventeenth-century Dutch jurist and theologian Hugo Grotius took both names to be masculine, and the fourth-century church father Theodore of Mopsuestia records a popular interpretation of the passage in his day that spelled Euodia as Euodias (a masculine form) and made Syntyche "his" wife. This tradition was apparently accepted by the translators of the King James Version.[21] These efforts simply cannot succeed, since both names are feminine in the Greek text and Paul refers to the people who stand behind the names with feminine pronouns (*hautais* and *haitines*).[22]

Others, eager to find biblical precedent for the involvement of women in the ministry of the modern church, have assigned Euodia and Syntyche functions within the Philippian community that go beyond the evidence. Occasionally it is said that since Paul calls them fellow contenders and coworkers, they must have been preachers and teachers of the gospel.[23] At the end of the day, however, it must be admitted that Paul's reference to Euodia and Syntyche as his fellow contenders says nothing more of them than Paul says of the whole congregation in 1:27, and that the title "fellow workers," although indicative of importance and perhaps leadership, is not precise enough to allow us to say that Euodia and Syntyche were preachers or teachers. The term certainly does not exclude such a role, but neither does it demand it.

In interpreting this passage it is best neither to change the text to correspond with our preconceived notions about a passive role for women in the

---

20. In addition, Paul calls Urbanus (Rom. 16:9), Jesus (Col. 4:11), Aristarchus (Col. 4:10–11; Philem. 24), and the notorious Demas (Philem. 24; cf. 2 Tim. 4:10) his "fellow workers."

21. See Meyer, *The Epistles to the Philippians and Colossians, and to Philemon*, 160–61; Lightfoot, *Philippians*, 158.

22. Hawthorne, *Philippians*, 179.

23. See, for example, W. Derek Thomas, "The Place of Women in the Church at Philippi," *The Expository Times* 83 (1971–72): 117–20, esp. 119.

church nor to enhance the text to supply greater support for the opposite position. No enhancement of the text is necessary to show that these women were not passive participants in their community and that they made a valuable contribution to the advancement of the gospel.[24] Certainly women in the modern church should be encouraged to do no less than this, but the precise form their service should take cannot be decided on the basis of this passage. Paul's interests in 4:2–3 lay elsewhere.

**Applying 4:2–9: A Summary.** This passage, then, speaks to situations where lip service is given to the great theological principles of the faith, particularly to the importance of Christian unity, but the practical application of those principles is not visible. More specifically, the passage shows the value of arbitration and the importance of evenhandedness in mediating between rival parties within the church. The passage also applies to those situations, particularly when they are produced by persecution, in which Christians are tempted to return evil for evil, to become anxious about the future, and to become so suspicious of the prevailing pagan culture that they stand in danger of an embattled denial that the world contains anything of value. On the other hand, the passage stands as a reminder to any who are tempted to embrace the world's standards wholly that only a mind informed by the gospel tradition is fully equipped to discern where the world exemplifies what is good and where it has perverted the good in various ways.

As in 1:27–30 and 2:14–16, in this passage Paul has mingled concerns over the church's internal dissension with concerns over its encounter with an unbelieving and hostile world. The passage speaks most powerfully, therefore, to equivalent situations in modern times.

IT MAY COME as a surprise to many Western Christians that one of the deepest divisions in the church is racial. Since the term "segregationist" has finally developed the evil connotations in most communities that it should have had from the beginning, it is no longer socially acceptable to believe that people of northern European descent should not mix with people from African and Latin countries. Most white Christians today nod in the direction of racial equality and the need for unity, if they think about the issue at all, and many think that the problem no longer exists.

African-American believers usually disagree. They point not only to frustration with the silence of white believers on the plight of African-American

---

24. See Malinowski, "The Brave Women of Philippi," 60–64, esp. p. 62.

people generally, but to anger over a persistent undercurrent of racism in their relationships with white Christians that appears to go unaddressed from the pulpit.[25] An African-American family that belongs to a white church is not invited to go on a church outing to the beach because "we just felt that—well, you know that there aren't very many black people at Myrtle Beach . . . and we just thought you would be uncomfortable."[26] An African-American pastor occasionally receives calls from white pastors in the area recommending to him families who might want to attend his church. Without fail, these referrals turn out to be efforts to send African-American families who have visited white churches to a predominantly African-American church instead.[27] In addition, many African-American church leaders perceive white evangelicals to be so consumed with a conservative political agenda that they are not even aware of the plight of the African-American community and, when aware of it, are often unsympathetic.

How can the problem be addressed? Perhaps following Paul's example of interposing a mediator between two rival groups would be a wise course. Paul himself acted as such a mediator in this letter by admonishing Euodia and Syntyche, evenhandedly and with ample encouragement, to agree with one another in the Lord. He also asked someone within the community to stand in the gap between these two women in his absence and to help them to be reconciled. Several such "loyal yokefellows," who have understood the problem and who believe that the church has both the mandate and the ability to do what society seems unable to do, are emerging within today's church. Christians should heed the call of these prophetic voices and should support them in their efforts.[28] What better way could there be for the modern church to fulfill in its own time Paul's hope that the Philippians would shine like stars in the midst of a crooked and perverse generation (2:15)?

---

25. Statistics demonstrate that the plight of African-Americans is worse now than it was during the years of the civil-rights struggle. In this country alone, the infant mortality rate among African-Americans from 1960 to 1990 grew from slightly less than twice that of whites to slightly more. In 1960 only 19.9% of African-American children lived only with their mothers, but in 1990 that figure had risen to 51.2%. In 1960 only 2.1% of African-American children were born to unwed mothers, but in 1990 that figure stood at 35.3%. See Andrew Hacker, *Two Nations: Black and White, Separate, Hostile, Unequal* (New York: Charles Scribner's Sons, 1992), 231.

26. Kay Coles James, "Separate Vacations," *Christianity Today* (October 4, 1993), 18.

27. Robert Suggs, "The Issue Is Sin," *Christianity Today* (October 4, 1993), 19.

28. See, for example, the moving stories of Raleigh Washington, Glenn Kehrein, and Chicago's "Rock Church" in *Breaking Down Walls: A Model for Reconciliation in an Age of Racial Strife* (Chicago: Moody Press, 1993), and the story of Mission Mississippi in Joe Maxwell, "Racial Healing in the Land of Lynching," *Christianity Today* (January 10, 1994), 24–26. In both of these success stories of racial reconciliation, visionary mediators played a prominent role.

The history of the church has shown that when Christians do act as a moral compass for society, they often act as a lightning rod as well. The Christians to whom Peter wrote were being slandered for their good behavior (1 Peter 2:16) and abused because they did not enter into the "same flood of dissipation" that their pagan neighbors found so entertaining (4:4). In the second and third centuries, Christians were regularly derided for their willingness to accept into their ranks members of the lowest social classes and were viewed as serious threats to the widely accepted (if oppressive) social order.[29] Believers in Germany who during Hitler's Third Reich opposed the treatment of the Jews and the mentally retarded were viewed as enemies of the state.[30] Today, Christians who work for racial equality are sometimes ostracized, and those who attempt to bring their Christian convictions into public policy debates are lampooned and told to leave.

It is easy in such circumstances to punch back—if not literally, at least verbally and in demeanor. Whether fairly or not, Christians sometimes have the reputation of being irascible and touchy, of stalking from home to work to voting booth with a scowl on their faces. But Paul's advice is for Christians in these circumstances to rejoice in the Lord and to make gentleness an obvious characteristic of their lives. He advises further that believers should dispense with anxiety and instead place troubling issues and situations before God in a spirit of gratitude.[31] Whereas it is important to avoid a pietistic attitude that refuses to confront difficulties, it is also important to remember that the success of the gospel and the shape of our personal circumstances do not depend on our efforts but lie in the hands of an all-powerful and merciful God.

It is also important to remember that the world, although fallen, belongs to God. In the face of dramatic social changes that threaten the peaceful existence of evangelical piety in our culture, many evangelical Christians in recent decades have adopted a pessimistic attitude toward the world around them, retreating into an anti-intellectual stance. Instead of viewing the natural world as God's creation and an appropriate object of investigation, evangelical Christians have sometimes focused solely on the supernatural. The result has been both a wistful yearning for the supposedly better days

---

29. See, for example, the opinions of Celsus, the second-century opponent of Christianity as they are preserved in Origen's *Contra Celsum*, 68–76.

30. Victoria Barnett, *For the Soul of the People: Protestant Protest Against Hitler* (Oxford: Oxford University Press, 1992), 104–54.

31. Paul's admonition not to be anxious about "anything" is, of course, applicable to any situation that might worry believers, but the most immediate application of the text is to those situations in which they are experiencing hardship because of their commitment to the gospel.

of a bygone era and an excited hope that the latest news from the Middle East will betoken Christ's second coming and the end of the world as we know it. Thus, both Christian novels set in yesteryear and books outlining the latest revision of the end-time timetable continue to rank at the top of the religious bestseller lists.[32]

In this passage, however, Paul asserts the need for believers to cast their intellectual nets widely—to allow all that is true, noble, right, pure, lovely, admirable, excellent, and praiseworthy, wherever it is found, to shape their thinking. He then urges them to practice what they have learned from him of the Christian tradition. Christians today should not retreat from face-to-face encounters with the best unbelieving minds of the age, but should read them and hear them in the hope of learning truth, justice, and excellence from them and thereby becoming more obedient followers of Christ. At the same time, Christians should strive for minds so steeped in the Scriptures and Christian tradition that they are able to approach the values of the unbelieving world with a critical eye, an eye able to discern between what appears to be true but is, in subtle ways, false.

Christians have often in the course of their history had to endure social ostracism and outright persecution. But the proper response to these tragedies is not a retreat from the unbelieving world or a strictly reactionary response to it. It is instead a proactive attempt to embrace truth wherever it is found within the world and to integrate it with the truth found in Scripture.[33]

All of this is so important because the way we think determines how we act. Paul belies any attempt to separate thought from deed in verses 8–9 when he uses the term "think" in verse 8 and the expression "put into practice" in verse 9. Since the Philippians must think about his teaching and example in order to put them into practice, and since Paul will not believe that the Philippians have obeyed his command to think about the virtues he lists if they have not also acted on them, the two words have much the same meaning.[34] Our thinking and our actions, then, are closely bound together. Indulging evil thoughts and tolerating sloppy thinking can have terrible consequences. Thus, if instead of loving my enemy I indulge the temptation to resent him,

---

32. Elizabeth Cody Newenhuyse, "Our Novels, Our Selves," *Christianity Today* (April 25, 1994), 35–36; Mark A. Noll, *The Scandal of the Evangelical Mind* (Grand Rapids/Leicester, Eng.: Eerdmans/Inter-Varsity, 1994), 14.

33. For a provocative record of the failure of evangelicals to do this properly and some suggestions about how evangelicals can recover the rich heritage of Christian contribution to the life of the mind, see Noll, *The Scandal of the Evangelical Mind*.

34. O'Brien, *Philippians*, 511.

resentment turns to anger, anger to hatred, and the link between hatred and murder, as Jesus saw, is close (Matt. 5:21–22).[35]

The erudite biblical scholar Gerhard Kittel did not begin his career with the notion that he would promote the Jewish Holocaust, but by 1933, when Hitler seemed to be working miracles in his native land, he could give a public lecture in which he said,

> The Jewish question is absolutely not a question of individual Jews but a question of Jewry, the Jewish *Volk*. And, therefore, whoever wants to get to the root of the question may not first ask what shall become of the individual Jew, but what shall become of Jewry.[36]

What we think as Christians does matter, for it will inevitably influence what we, and those under our influence, do.

---

35. See the insightful comments on the insidious way in which evil thoughts can become evil actions in C. S. Lewis, *Mere Christianity* (New York: Macmillan, 1943),106.

36. Quoted in Robert P. Ericksen, *Theologians Under Hitler: Gerhard Kittel/Paul Althaus/Emanuel Hirsch* (New Haven, Conn.: Yale University Press, 1985), 55.

# Philippians 4:10–23

I REJOICE GREATLY in the Lord that at last you have renewed your concern for me. Indeed, you have been concerned, but you had no opportunity to show it. [11]I am not saying this because I am in need, for I have learned to be content whatever the circumstances. [12]I know what it is to be in need, and I know what it is to have plenty. I have learned the secret of being content in any and every situation, whether well fed or hungry, whether living in plenty or in want. [13]I can do everything through him who gives me strength.

[14]Yet it was good of you to share in my troubles. [15]Moreover, as you Philippians know, in the early days of your acquaintance with the gospel, when I set out from Macedonia, not one church shared with me in the matter of giving and receiving, except you only; [16]for even when I was in Thessalonica, you sent me aid again and again when I was in need. [17]Not that I am looking for a gift, but I am looking for what may be credited to your account. [18]I have received full payment and even more; I am amply supplied, now that I have received from Epaphroditus the gifts you sent. They are a fragrant offering, an acceptable sacrifice, pleasing to God. [19]And my God will meet all your needs according to his glorious riches in Christ Jesus.

[20]To our God and Father be glory for ever and ever. Amen.

[21]Greet all the saints in Christ Jesus. The brothers who are with me send greetings. [22]All the saints send you greetings, especially those who belong to Caesar's household.

[23]The grace of the Lord Jesus Christ be with your spirit. Amen.

## Original Meaning

PAUL ENDS HIS letter with a paragraph of thanks to the Philippians for their gifts to him through Epaphroditus (4:10–20), some final words of greeting (4:21–22), and a benediction (4:23). The first section is the longest and most theologically significant, although both the final greetings and the benediction are much more than routine pleasantries.

**Thanks, Sort of (4:10–20).** In 4:10–20 Paul returns to the themes and style of the letter's opening prayer (1:3–11). The similarities between the two sections include the note of joy that begins each section (1:4/4:10), the concern of each section with the Philippians' practical display of fellowship with Paul in the work of the gospel (1:5, 7/4:10, 14, 18), the importance to each section of the Philippians' progress in the faith (1:6, 9–11/4:17b), and the conclusion of each section with an ascription of glory to God (1:11/4:20). In 4:10–20, then, Paul provides a fitting conclusion to the body of the letter by visiting again the central themes of the letter's opening.

The section is basically an expression of thanks to the Philippians for a monetary gift they sent to him through their messenger Epaphroditus. The note of appreciation appears in three places: in verse 10, where Paul speaks of his great joy because of the Philippians' expression of concern for him; in verse 14, where he tells them that "it was good" of them to help him in his affliction; and in verse 18, where he uses both financial and cultic metaphors to describe the immense value of their gift to him. Paul's expression of thanks is qualified, however, by two efforts to distance himself from the Philippians' gift. In verses 11–13 he claims that ultimately he did not need their gift, and in verse 17 he says that he did not seek it.

Why this concern? Paul's use of a series of financial terms in verses 17b–18a shows that the gift at least included, and was perhaps entirely composed of, money. Yet Paul was always circumspect about money matters. Charlatan philosophers were a frequent sight on the street corners of cities like Philippi in ancient times. They dressed like philosophers, and many were able to gather a following that was willing not only to hear and submit to them but to give them financial support. According to the second-century satirist Lucian, "they collect tribute, going from house to house, or, as they themselves express it, they 'shear the sheep': and they expect many to give, either out of respect for their cloth or for fear of their abusive language."[1]

Like itinerant philosophers both sincere and otherwise, Paul sometimes preached in the open and sometimes used the workshop as a platform for evangelistic efforts.[2] Because of this resemblance, Paul was aware that misunderstanding could arise if he depended on the churches he established for his financial support. Although he recognized the principle that those pri-

---

1. Lucian, *Fugitivi*, 14. The words belong to "Philosophy" and describe the tactics, from Lucian's perspective, of Cynic philosophers. The translation is from the Loeb Classical Library edition of Lucian's works.

2. On the similarities between Paul's evangelistic strategy and the strategies of ancient philosophers for gaining a following, see Abraham J. Malherbe, *Paul and the Thessalonians: The Philosophical Tradition of Pastoral Care* (Philadelphia: Fortress, 1987).

marily responsible for the spiritual nurture of a Christian community could ask for the community's financial support (1 Cor. 9:3–14; 2 Thess. 3:9; 1 Tim. 5:17–18), he usually refused such support to avoid even a hint of an unfair scandal over his proclamation of the gospel. "We did not use this right," he explains to the Corinthians. "On the contrary, we put up with anything rather than hinder the gospel of Christ" (1 Cor. 9:12b; cf. 1 Thess. 2:1–12).[3]

In addition, Paul took precautions with his collection for the needy believers in Jerusalem to be sure that everyone understood his intentions and to make certain that no cause for scandal could develop. Thus, when Paul asked the Corinthians to contribute to the collection, he told them that after the funds had been gathered, emissaries from the Corinthian church itself would carry them to Jerusalem and that he would only accompany the group if it seemed advisable (1 Cor. 16:4). Other churches in which Paul had raised funds for this special project contributed their own representatives to the embassy (Acts 20:4; 2 Cor. 8:18–19). Paul apparently insisted on it, "for we are taking pains to do what is right," he explains, "not only in the eyes of the Lord but also in the eyes of men" (2 Cor. 8:21).

In Philippians 4:10–20, therefore, Paul faces the difficult task of showing the Philippians his genuine appreciation for their financial support, both past and present, but of also showing that his work is neither dependent on nor motivated by this support. He does this through combining expressions of gratitude with qualifications designed to prevent misunderstanding.

Paul begins in verse 10 with an exuberant expression of joy that the Philippians have again shown their concern for him. The Philippians had generously supplemented the income Paul earned in the workshop during his attempts to establish other churches both in Macedonia (4:15–16) and Achaia (2 Cor. 11:7–9).[4] Perhaps because of their poverty (2 Cor. 8:1–2),

---

3. In ancient times a financial gift, particularly to a philosopher, sometimes implied that the giver was the philosopher's patron. In addition to avoiding the misunderstandings mentioned above, Paul's cautious words of thanks had the advantage of distancing Paul from this type of patron-client relationship with the Philippians. See Witherington, *Friendship and Finances in Philippi*, 123–24, 127.

4. This statement assumes that the "brothers who came from Macedonia" in 2 Cor 11:9 included Philippians, although the mention of "churches" who supported Paul in 2 Cor 11:8 may mean that other churches in Macedonia, such as the Thessalonian and Berean churches, sent Paul support also. Verlyn D. Verbrugge (*Paul's Style of Church Leadership Illustrated by His Instructions to the Corinthians on the Collection* [San Francisco: Mellen Research Univ. Press, 1992], 118–27) suggests that Paul did not allow churches to contribute to his support while he was with them but encouraged them to support his work in other communities. This may explain why Paul received support from Philippi when in Thessalonica (4:16) but refused to burden the Thessalonians with support of his work among them (1 Thess. 2:6b, 9; 2 Thess. 3:8–9).

however, they had not been able to help Paul in this way recently. Thus Paul rejoices "greatly" that the opportunity to show their concern for him has returned.

Despite this, Paul wants the Philippians to know that his joy does not depend on the alleviation of his physical discomfort; thus, although he is in prison, Paul says that he is not in need (vv. 11–13). He has learned to be content in every circumstance. The term "content" (*autarkes*, v. 11) was used by Stoic philosophers of Paul's time to mean "self-sufficient," and in their view this characteristic was the most valuable attribute of the wise person.[5] Indeed, like the wise Stoic, Paul does not consider physical deprivation an unmitigated disaster nor physical comfort the sign of success. But unlike the Stoic, Paul does not find the resources for this attitude in himself. They reside instead in the Lord, through whom he can face all things (v. 13).[6]

So Paul remains unperturbed either by his own imprisonment and possible death or by fellow believers who seek to intensify his suffering. As long as Christ is being preached, Paul is joyful (1:18), and he does not want the Philippians to think that the physical comfort their gifts have made possible has increased his ability to cope with the difficulties at hand.

The apostle is also concerned that the Philippians not read his comments as ingratitude. Thus, he follows this qualification with a second expression of appreciation to the Philippians for their generosity both present and past (vv. 14–16). Unlike the believers around him who have stirred up "trouble" (*thlipsis*) for him in his imprisonment (1:17), the Philippians have shared in Paul's "troubles" (*thlipsis*, 4:14). They have done this through a practical display of their mutual friendship: Not only has Paul given to them spiritually, but they have given to him financially.[7]

---

5. For example, the Roman emperor and Stoic philosopher Marcus Aurelius (born A.D. 121) describes his adoptive father as the ideal Stoic man, and one of his traits is that he is "self-sufficient in all things" (*to autarkes en panti*)—see his *Meditations*, 1.16.11; J. N. Sevenster, *Paul and Seneca* (Leiden: Brill, 1961), 114. The Roman statesman Seneca (born about 4 B.C.) likewise claimed that whereas the wise man might want friends, he had no need of them because ultimately he was self-sufficient—see his *Epistulae*, ix; Lightfoot, *Philippians*, 305.

6. Phil. 4:13, then, does not mean that Christ enables Paul to *do* anything, but to *endure* any problem he encounters as he seeks to be faithful to his apostolic calling. Col. 1:28–29 provides a close parallel: "We proclaim him, admonishing and teaching everyone with all wisdom, so that we may present everyone perfect in Christ. To this end I labor, struggling with all his energy, which so powerfully works in me."

7. The phrase "giving and receiving" uses common financial terms for "payments" and "receipts," and the NEB actually translated them this way. But, as Peter Marshall, *Enmity in Corinth: Social Conventions in Paul's Relations With the Corinthians* (Tübingen: J. C. B. Mohr [Paul Siebeck], 1987), 157–64, points out, the terms were also commonly used to describe the mutual obligations of friendship.

Paul is still not satisfied that he has forestalled misunderstanding about his attitude toward this financial help, however. So in verse 17 he explains that he does not "wish for" a gift.[8] His hope instead is that the Philippians' account might grow ever greater. The NIV's "what may be credited to your account" is more literally "continuously increasing profit for your account," and the imagery is of a bank account that receives compounded interest.[9] The phrase "what may be credited" (*karpos*), moreover, renders the same Greek word Paul used in 1:11 to refer to the Philippians' "fruit" of righteousness on the final day. The notion of a future day when the Philippians would give an account of themselves before Christ, therefore, is probably not far from Paul's mind. If so, this verse means that Paul was not interested in the gifts that the Philippians had sent for his own advantage, but for the Philippians' spiritual advantage. Their generosity was a concrete demonstration that God was completing the good work that he had started in them when they believed the gospel (1:6).

In verse 18 the emphasis shifts again to gratitude. Paul at first continues the financial imagery and, perhaps with a touch of friendly humor, composes a "receipt" for the Philippians' gifts to him. Behind the NIV's "I have received full payment" stands a technical term from the business world of Paul's day (*apecho*), which was often used to refer to the receipt of full payment for goods delivered or services rendered.[10] Paul says that he has not only received full payment from his friends at Philippi, but that they have paid him more than enough.

Paul then drops the financial metaphor and begins to speak in language that the Old Testament uses to describe the sacrifices of God's people (see, e.g., Ex. 29:18, 25, 41; Lev. 1:3–4; 17:4; 19:5; 22:19–20). In Israel's history these sacrifices were often corrupted by the people's idolatrous practices or social injustices. But Isaiah looks forward to a time when God's people will once again offer "acceptable" sacrifices to the Lord (Isa. 56:7; 60:7). Perhaps Paul understands the generous commitment the Philippians have shown to the gospel to be a partial fulfillment of these prophecies within the new Israel.[11] In any case, the adjectives "fragrant," "acceptable," and "pleasing"

---

8. This is the translation of *epizeto* (NIV "am looking for") in Walter Bauer, *A Greek-English Lexicon of the New Testament and Other Early Christian Literature*, 2d ed., trans., adapt., and rev. William F. Arndt, F. Wilbur Gingrich, Frederick W. Danker (Chicago: University of Chicago Press, 1979), 292.

9. See Bauer *Greek-English Lexicon*, 405; O'Brien, *Philippians*, 539.

10. Bauer, *Greek-English Lexicon*, 84.

11. For a more detailed treatment of this theme in Philippians see Frank Thielman, *Paul and the Law: A Contextual Approach* (Downers Grove, Ill.: InterVarsity Press, 1994), 156–58, 286, n. 49.

will leave no doubt in the Philippians' minds that Paul is grateful to them for their gifts.

In response to these gifts, Paul says, God will meet all of the Philippians' needs (v. 19). As with God's exaltation of Christ to the highest place in 2:9–11, this response is not recompense but God's gracious and freely given blessing. Interpreters have engaged in a vigorous debate over precisely what this blessing is. Does it cover only material needs? Only spiritual needs? Both? Certainly. it may cover some physical needs (v. 16), but if Paul's own understanding of "need" (vv. 11–13) is the key to understanding the term here, then surely Paul is promising that God will supply the Philippians with the greatest need of all—the ability to face all circumstances through the one who gives them strength (v. 13).

Paul ends his expression of gratitude to the Philippians for their partnership with a doxology that echoes the note of praise at the end of the letter's opening prayer (v. 20; cf. 1:11). Here, as there, this is more than a perfunctory expression of piety. It focuses the reader's attention on the primary goal both of Paul's apostolic vocation and of the Philippians' participation in it: God's glory.

**Greetings and Grace (4:21–23).** Paul closes his letter with what at first looks like an uninteresting greeting formula and a routine benediction, but in light of the letter's twin themes of internal unity in the face of dissension and outward steadfastness in the face of persecution, these seemingly humdrum features of the letter take on new meaning.

The final greetings in Philippians (vv. 21–22) are apparently formulated with care to encourage the unity of the church. Thus the way Paul phrases his personal greetings to the church is unique among his letters in its stress on each member of the congregation without distinction.[12] The NIV's rendering does not capture this nuance since the words "all" and "saints" are actually singular in Greek. Translated more literally, the sentence says, "Greet every saint in Christ Jesus," or as one commentator puts it, "Give my greetings to each member of God's people in Christ Jesus."[13] Just as Paul stressed the unity of the congregation at the letter's beginning when he addressed them as "all the saints in Christ Jesus at Philippi," so here at the letter's conclusion he again stresses the equal worth before God of each member of the congregation. Each has been set apart to belong to God's chosen people.

---

12. Paul certainly sends general, nameless greetings elsewhere (2 Cor. 13:11–14; Eph. 6:23; 1 Thess. 5:26; Titus 3:15), but in no other letter does he extend greetings to "every saint" as he does here.

13. O'Brien, *Philippians*, 551 (cf. his discussion of this verse, p. 553).

The greetings from Paul's associates are likewise general and all-encompassing in nature. They come not only from the brothers with Paul—probably a reference to close coworkers, such as Timothy—but from all the saints in the area. Paul's only effort to make distinctions in the greeting comes in the last phrase of verse 22, where he singles out the members of Caesar's household for special attention. If the Philippians were caught in the tension between their own civic pride as members of a Roman colony and the offense they presented to their city's unbelieving citizenry (cf. 1:27; 3:20), then perhaps Paul hopes to encourage them with the news that even some of the Roman emperor's staff have turned to the gospel.[14]

Paul concludes the letter (v. 23) in much the same way as he began it (1:2), with a reference to "the grace of the Lord Jesus Christ." The same grace that transformed Paul from a persecutor of the church into its apostle (1:7; 3:6) will sustain the Philippians as they seek to "stand firm in one Spirit, contending as one man for the faith of the gospel" (1:27). This benediction, then, serves as much more than a rote formula tacked onto the end of the letter. It leaves ringing in the Philippians' ears the message that the gospel, because it reveals God's grace (*charis*), is good news and reason enough to rejoice (*chairein*) in the Lord.

Bridging Contexts

FROM PAUL'S PERSPECTIVE, the primary purpose of this passage is to show the Philippians that, while he appreciates their gifts, the chief value of their generosity does not lie in the help which it gives to him. Instead, as verses 17–18 say, it lies in increasing the spiritual capital of the Philippians and in rendering to God a fragrant, acceptable, and pleasing sacrifice. If we read verses 17–18 in light of Paul's opening prayer in 1:3–11, moreover, we can be more specific about the way in which the Philippians' spiritual capital has increased: Their aid to Paul demonstrates their partnership with him in the work of the gospel and shows that they are progressing in sanctification as they move toward the day of Christ.

An important subsidiary point is that God will meet the Philippians' needs, just as he has met Paul's. Although Paul is surrounded by hostility both

---

14. The phrase "Caesar's household" refers to slaves and freed slaves who served the emperor either as part of his entourage of personal attendants in Rome or as part of the more widely dispersed group of servants who supervised his financial affairs. Both groups were proud of the status that their work in the emperor's service accorded them, and they often added to their names an abbreviation showing that they were slaves or freedmen of the emperor. See P. R. C. Weaver, *Familia Caesaris: A Social Study of the Emperor's Freedmen and Slaves* (Cambridge: Cambridge University Press, 1972), 1–8.

from the unbelievers who have imprisoned him and from the believers whose selfish ambition has driven them to make life miserable for the apostle, and although Paul is facing a possible death sentence, God has nevertheless met his needs, not least by using these circumstances to guide him safely into salvation (1:19).[15] The One who is powerful enough to subject all things to himself (3:21) therefore has enabled Paul to face even the most grim of circumstances (4:13). In the same way, the Philippians are poverty-stricken (2 Cor. 8:1–2), persecuted (1:28–30), and divided (2:14; 4:2), but God will nevertheless meet their needs out of his limitless resources (4:19). Not simply despite these hardships, but through the Philippians' obedient handling of them, God is working in them to guide them safely to salvation (cf. 2:12–13). This is the ultimate need of God's people, and this is the primary sense in which to understand the promise of 4:19.

These concerns can move into the modern context easily. They tell us first that our financial support of the church's mission is at least as important for our own spiritual development as for any good that it might do those to whom we give. As Paul has said in various ways throughout this letter, and as the rest of the New Testament and church history confirms, God's purposes will march forward despite every human hindrance, including the disobedience of his people. The accomplishment of God's purposes does not depend on human help. When we give our lives sacrificially to his purposes, however, we benefit spiritually because we confirm that God is at work in us for the ultimate purpose of salvation. We show that we are "saints" (1:1; 4:21–22) and that we are progressing toward that day when we will stand before Christ "pure and blameless ... filled with the fruit of righteousness that comes through" him (1:10–11).

Paul's subsidiary point is as true of Christians today as it was of him and the Philippians: God is fully able (4:13) and fully willing (4:19) to meet whatever needs surround the believer. Unfortunately, this principle is widely misunderstood today to refer primarily to physical needs. The literature of the infamous "prosperity gospel" movement is spangled with references to Philippians 4:19, which, it claims, promises not simply to meet the needs of believers but to supply them with luxury, in accord with God's "riches in glory by Christ."[16]

More mainstream popular expositions of Philippians are not innocent of a similar error, however. Thus one expositor illustrates verse 19 by referring

---

15. The word "deliverance" in the NIV's rendering of 1:19 is literally "salvation" (*soteria*). See the discussion of Paul's use of this term in 1:19 in the "Original Meaning" section of the commentary on 1:18b–26.

16. Kenneth Copeland, *The Laws of Prosperity* (Fort Worth, Tex.: Kenneth Copeland Publications, 1974), 24.

to his experience of charging traveling expenses to his employer. In the same way, he says, when he shares with others, "God is coming right behind picking up the tab. He's committed to meeting my needs." Another explains verse 19 by means of Hudson Taylor's famous dictum, "When God's work is done in God's way for God's glory, it will not lack for God's supply." The reference is to the way God supplied the physical needs of this great missionary when he prayed about them.[17]

Certainly, verse 19 allows for the possibility that God will supply the physical needs of his people, but this is not the primary concern of the verse. We sometimes forget that many faithful Christians have suffered deeply for the sake of the gospel and have prayed as earnestly as Hudson Taylor that God might alleviate their suffering, but it has nevertheless continued. We dare not claim that the faith of these Christians was somehow flawed, that their lives were less committed than they should have been, or that their suffering must not have been as intense as we imagine. If we take Jesus and Paul as examples, it becomes apparent that sometimes obedience to the will of God requires physical deprivation to the point of death.

The promise of verse 19 must instead be linked with verse 13, and both verses must be read in light of verses 11–12: God supplies the needs of his people by giving them the resources to cope with hardship. Hardship tempts us to think that God is unmoved by our plight or is against us, and so we despair. Thus, when we experience difficult times, we need the moderating presence of God, who shows us by the cross of Christ that he is for us, not against us, and that he was so filled with love for us that he sent his Son to die on our behalf. If this powerful truth dominates our lives, then we can face even the ultimate human hardship with the equanimity of Paul (1:18b–26), and we can rest assured that God is conducting us toward salvation even in the midst of our hardship.

We should not forget, however, that we need God's presence and help as much when we experience affluence as when we experience poverty. When life is comfortable, we are tempted to forget the grace of God and rely on ourselves.[18] We forget easily that many have worked as diligently and capably as we but have not had our success. God has given it to us, not because we deserve it, but as a concrete reminder that he is a gracious God. In the midst of affluence as much as in times of deprivation, we need God's help to survive spiritually.

As we bring Philippians 4:10–23 out of Paul's time and into our own, then, we need to focus on the spiritual implications of poverty and wealth,

---

17. Briscoe, *Philippians*, 165–66; Wiersbe, *Be Joyful*, 140.
18. See Deut. 8:10–18.

of suffering and comfort. Western societies are obsessed with these issues, and for the churches within them, these verses carry a powerful message.

MODERN CHRISTIANS TEND to view money in two ways. Sometimes they view it as a blessing to which Christians are entitled. Thus advocates of the "prosperity gospel" believe that since the curse of the law involved poverty (Deut. 28:18) and Christ has redeemed us from the curse of the law (Gal. 3:13–14), the believer should no longer be subject to poverty.[19] Did Jesus not preach good news to the poor (Luke 4:18; 7:22)? Does Jesus not say to give and it will be given to you (Luke 6:38), and does Paul not confirm the same principle (2 Cor. 9:6)? If these promises are true, say advocates of this position, then Christians who give away some of their income should prosper financially.[20] In fact if they follow the inexorable "laws of prosperity," Scripture promises that they will be rewarded with one hundred times what they have given away (cf. Mark 10:29–30). "The success formulas in the Word of God," says Kenneth Copeland, "produce results when used as directed."[21]

More often Christians view wealth simply as something neutral, which can be used for either good or evil purposes.[22] The Christian's responsibility is to use wealth for good purposes, to be like the two servants in the parable of the talents, who used their money wisely and pleased their master (Matt. 25:14–30; cf. Luke 19:12–27), or to be like the shrewd manager, who used "worldly wealth" to gain friends for himself (Luke 16:1–9). Wealth is a powerful tool for good, and Christians should, to paraphrase John Wesley, make all they can, save all they can, and give all they can.[23]

Neither of these positions, however, adequately faces the persistently cautious approach to wealth in Scripture.[24] The Old Testament warns that

---

19. Copeland, *The Laws of Prosperity*, 41–43; idem, *Prosperity: The Choice Is Yours* (Fort Worth, Tex.: Kenneth Copeland Publications, 1992), 23–25.

20. Copeland, *Laws of Prosperity*, 26; Kenneth E. Hagin, *Obedience in Finances* (Tulsa, Okla.: RHEMA Bible Church, 1983), 2, 6.

21. Copeland, *Laws of Prosperity*, 16.

22. This view appears as early as Clement of Alexandria (born about 150) in his treatise *Quis Dives Salvetur?* 14–15.

23. Cited by D. K. Adie, "Wealth, Christian View of," *Evangelical Dictionary of Theology*, ed. Walter A. Elwell (Grand Rapids: Baker, 1984), 1161. Adie's article argues for this commonly accepted view of wealth.

24. In what follows I am particularly indebted to the understanding of wealth in Jacques Ellul, *Money and Power* (Downer's Grove, Ill.: InterVarsity Press, 1984).

wealth tempts those who possess it to believe that they are self-sufficient, that they have no need of God, and that they are in fact themselves gods. "Give me only my daily bread," says Proverbs, "otherwise, I may have too much and disown you and say, 'Who is the Lord?'" (Prov. 30:8–9). Similarly, God promises destruction for the King of Tyre since his wealth has caused him to swell with pride and to claim that he is as wise as a god (Ezek. 28:5–6). The Lord also reminds Israel that when he fed them in the wilderness, they became proud and forgot him (Hos. 13:6).

The teaching of Jesus on wealth can hardly be clearer. He pronounces a woe on the rich and a blessing on the poor, and claims that the wealthy can only enter the kingdom of God with great difficulty (Matt. 19:23–24; Mark 10:23–25; Luke 6:20, 24; 18:24–25). It is true, of course, that some people who are both wealthy and righteous appear in the pages of Scripture— Abraham in the Old Testament and the wealthy women who supported Jesus in the New are two examples—but the list is remarkably short.[25]

Why is the Bible so wary of wealth? Jesus explains in Luke 16:1–15, where he tells the puzzling tale of a man who has mismanaged his employer's funds and is called to account for his actions. Knowing that he will be released from his position for his actions, he "cooks the books" for his employer's creditors so that they will be able to pay less than they actually owe. At least these partners in crime, he reasons, will look after him when he is unemployed. Strangely, the employer finds out about the swindle and *commends* the dishonest steward for his shrewdness.

The story is difficult at a number of levels, but according to Jesus' subsequent commentary, it illustrates that, far from being neutral, wealth is "unrighteous" (not "worldly," as the NIV has it).[26] Apparently because it is not only unrighteous but powerful enough to sway people into unrighteous deeds, Jesus speaks of it in personified terms as a power. Money can take the place of God in one's life. "No servant can serve two masters," he says, "either he will hate the one and love the other, or he will be devoted to the one and despise the other. You cannot serve both God and Money" (Luke 16:13; cf. Matt. 6:24).

Jesus recognizes in these statements that for the unbelieving world, money takes on divine status. It is the god of this age, a god for which many people are willing to sacrifice their happiness, their children, their health, indeed their own lives. The "workaholic" father, seldom home and never in church because he is too busy "providing" for a family, was once a well-known

---

25. Abraham's wealth can be inferred from the account of his life in Gen. 12:1–25:11. Luke 8:3 speaks of women who supported Jesus and his disciples financially.

26. The Greek word is *adikos* (see Bauer, *Greek-English Lexicon*, 18).

fixture in our society. He has now given way to the "workaholic" couple, who hardly know their children because they are too busy paying off expensive mortgages and car loans. This kind of zeal for income borders on the irrational, and we are hardly remiss in thinking of it as "religious."

The believer who possesses wealth should be wary of money's ability to gain the upper hand. Like the governing structures of the society in which we live, we must make use of it, but we should always do so with our eyes open, aware that it can subtly tempt us to do homage to it rather than to God. It can lead us into dishonesty just as it did the unjust steward (Luke 16:10–12), or it can lead us to think that God has rewarded us with wealth because we are hardworking and clever.

This second deception is the more destructive because it leads us to think that God's grace is for sale and that we have earned it. It appears alike in the smug philosophy that "God helps those who help themselves" and in the claim of one radio preacher who writes:

> There are certain rules governing prosperity revealed in God's Word. Faith causes them to function. They will work when they are put to work and they will stop working when the force of faith is stopped.[27]

Both claims take the initiative in blessing his people away from God and put it in human hands, for both imply that God can be manipulated. According to one view, our hard work forces God's hand; according to the other, the mantra-like invocation of biblical words wrenched from their contexts and laden with special materialistic meaning sets in motion a divine law as impersonal as the law of gravity.[28]

How can Christians, who must use "unrighteous wealth" in order to survive, guard themselves from its deceptive tendency to take the place of God? In Philippians 4:10–20 Paul and the Philippians supply the antidote. Both are detached from the money they own—Paul by refusing to find contentment in the Philippians' gift, and the Philippians by being willing to give it. Paul's contentment rests in the advancement of the gospel, and so he is joyful despite the physical deprivations of prison and the emotional struggles of opposition from fellow believers. The Philippians' monetary gift will help to alleviate his physical distress, and the presence of another friendly face in the form of Epaphroditus is undoubtedly an emotional comfort, but Paul can do without both; and if the gospel's purposes will be advanced by sending Epaphroditus back, Paul is willing to do so.

---

27. Copeland, *Laws of Prosperity*, 16; idem, *Prosperity: The Choice Is Yours*, 34.

28. The literature of the "prosperity gospel" movement is bespeckled with comparisons between the laws of prosperity and natural laws such as the law of gravity. See, for example, Copeland, *Laws of Prosperity*, 15.

The Philippians, on the other hand, by their very act of giving have refused to let their wealth control them and have instead taken control of it. They have therefore taken away its power and refused to allow it sacred status. Jacques Ellul puts it well: "There is one act par excellence which profanes money by going directly against the law of money, an act for which money is not made. This act is *giving*."[29] Paul rejoiced in the Philippians' gift (4:10), then, not because he required it but because it was a useful step in their own sanctification. By giving their money, they demonstrated where their loyalties lay and strengthened their commitment to the God who would supply all that they ultimately needed through his riches in glory in Christ Jesus.

And so it is with us. As Richard Foster has said, anyone with enough money to buy a book is wealthy relative to the rest of the world.[30] Christians who live in the West, particularly Christians who live in North America, are especially wealthy. Yet we often accrue our wealth unreflectively, never imagining that we have invited into our homes and lives a powerful force for evil. We need to remind ourselves that wealth can deceive us into dishonest dealings with others and, even worse, into thinking that we are wealthy because we are good.

The most powerful antidote to these deceptions is to give generously from our wealth to those who have need, especially, as Paul would say, to those who are of the household of faith (Gal. 6:10). In this way we provide equality among God's people (2 Cor. 8:13–15) and begin to view ourselves as the channel of God's blessing to others, rather than as the recipients of payment we have earned. This will in turn serve as a powerful reminder of a principle that runs like a thread throughout Philippians, and indeed through all of Paul's writings. It is perhaps best expressed in Romans 11:35–36:

> Who has ever given to God, that God should repay him? For from him and through him and to him are all things. To him be the glory forever!

---

29. Ellul, *Money and Power*, 110.

30. Richard Foster, *Money, Sex, and Power: The Challenge of the Disciplined Life* (New York: Harper & Row, 1985), 33.

# Scripture Index